39.95
80E

Speak
No
Evil

PRAEGER SERIES IN POLITICAL COMMUNICATION

Robert E. Denton, Jr., General Editor

Speak
No
Evil

The Promotional Heritage of Nuclear Risk Communication

Louis Gwin

Praeger Series in Political Communication

PRAEGER

New York
Westport, Connecticut
London

Library of Congress Cataloging-in-Publication Data

Gwin, Louis.
    Speak no evil : the promotional heritage of nuclear risk
communication / Louis Gwin.
        p.   cm.— (Praeger series in political communication)
    Includes bibliographical references (p.   ).
    ISBN 0-275-93445-4 (alk. paper)
    1. Nuclear power plants—Environmental aspects—Information
services—Government policy—United States.   2. Nuclear power
plants—Accidents—Information services—Government policy—United
States.   I. Title. II. Series.
HD9698.U52G85   1990
363.17′99—dc20   90-32299

Library of Congress Catalog Card Number: 90-32299
ISBN: 0-275-93445-4

First published in 1990

Praeger Publishers, One Madison Avenue, New York, NY 10010
An imprint of Greenwood Publishing Group, Inc.

Printed in the United States of America

∞

The paper used in this book complies with the
Permanent Paper Standard issued by the National
Information Standards Organization (Z39.48-1984).

10 9 8 7 6 5 4 3 2 1

Contents

Tables

Series Foreword

Those of us from the discipline of communication studies have long believed that communication is prior to all other fields of inquiry. In several other forums I have argued that the essence of politics is "talk" or human interaction.[1] Such interaction may be formal or informal, verbal or nonverbal, public or private, but always persuasive, forcing us consciously or subconsciously to interpret, to evaluate, and to act. Communication is the vehicle for human action.

From this perspective, it is not surprising that Aristotle recognized the natural kinship of politics and communication in his writings of *Politics* and *Rhetoric*. In the former, he establishes that humans are "political beings" who "alone of the animals is furnished with the faculty of language."[2] And in the latter, he begins his systematic analysis of discourse by proclaiming that "rhetorical study, in its strict sense, is concerned with the modes of persuasion."[3] Thus it was recognized over fifteen hundred years ago that politics and communication go hand in hand because they are essential parts of human nature.

Back in 1981, Dan Nimmo and Keith Sanders proclaimed that political communication was an emerging field.[4] Although its origin, as noted, dates back centuries, a "self-consciously cross-disciplinary" focus began in the late 1950s. Thousands of books and articles later, colleges and universities offer a variety of graduate and undergraduate coursework in the area in such diverse departments as communication, mass communication, journalism, political science, and sociology.[5] In Nimmo and Sanders' early assessment, the "key areas of inquiry" included rhetorical analysis, propaganda analysis, attitude change studies, voting studies, government and the news media, functional and systems analyses, technological changes, media technologies, campaign techniques, and research techniques.[6] In a survey of the state of the field in 1983 by the same authors and Lynda Kaid, they found additional, more specific areas of concerns such as the presidency, political polls, public opinion, debates, and advertising, to name a few.[7] Since the first study, they also noted a shift away from the rather strict behavioral approach.

Then as now, the field of political communication continues to emerge. There is no precise definition, method, or disciplinary home of the area of inquiry. Its domain, quite simply, is the role, processes, and effects of communication within the context of politics.

In 1985 the editors of *Political Communication Yearbook: 1984* noted that "more things are happening in the study, teaching, and practice of political communication than can be captured within the space limitations of the relatively few publications available."[8] In addition, they argued that the backgrounds of "those involved in the field [are] so varied and plurist in outlook and approach, . . . it [is] a mistake to adhere slavishly to any set format in shaping the content."[9]

In agreement with this assessment of the area, Praeger established the series entitled "Praeger Studies in Political Communication." The series is open to all qualitative and quantitative methodologies as well as contemporary and historical studies. The key to characterizing the studies in the series is the focus on communication variables or activities within a political context or dimension.

Until the "incident" at Three Mile Island in 1979, the public and government of the United States had been rather inamored by the prospects of nuclear power as a safe and an environmentally sound source of energy. However, new rules and regulations were initiated after the accident including the establishment of emergency management programs. The programs required public education about nuclear power and emergency actions and procedures. This study is one of the first to examine the effectiveness of risk communication by the nuclear power industry.

This book is an important contribution to the field of political communication and, more specifically, public relations for several reasons. First, it provides an insightful and useful example of an investigation of non-governmental public communication. We need more studies that analyze the persuasive efforts of corporate advocacy and issue management of various agencies and industries. Second, this is a "ground breaking" work on the nature of risk communication, especially examining the linkage between information and behavior. The focus of this study is an area of public relations research at the leading edge of the field. Finally, and more importantly, this study reveals the inadequacies of the nuclear industry's efforts in preparing, not only the general public, but also those close to facilities for emergency situations. After a decade of experience, not only are nuclear industry programs ineffective in informing the public, but their activities actually minimize safety concerns and promote nuclear power as the energy of the future. As Professor Gwin concludes this most significant study, "while the future of nuclear power is uncertain, the nuclear industry must realize that it can no longer afford to perpetuate the promotional history of the nuclear ethic. For the safety of those who live near our nation's nuclear plants, can we afford to allow nuclear risk communication to do otherwise?"

I am, without shame or modesty, a fan of the series. The joy of serving as its editor is in participating in the dialogue of the field of political communication and in reading the contributors' works. I invite you to join me.

Robert E. Denton, Jr.

NOTES

1. See Robert E. Denton, Jr., *The Symbolic Dimensions of the American Presidency* (Prospect Heights, IL: Waveland Press, 1982); Robert E. Denton, Jr. and Gary Woodward, *Political Communication in America* (New York: Praeger, 1985); Robert E. Denton, Jr. and Dan Hahn, *Presidential Communication* (New York: Praeger, 1986); and Robert E. Denton, Jr., *The Primetime Presidency of Ronald Reagan* (New York: Praeger, 1988).

2. Aristotle, *The Politics of Aristotle*, trans. Ernest Barker (New York: Oxford University Press, 1970), 5.

3. Aristotle, *Rhetoric*, trans. Rhys Roberts (New York: Modern Library, 1954), 22.

4. Dan Nimmo and Keith Sanders, "Introduction: The Emergence of Political Communication as a Field," in *Handbook of Political Communication*, eds. Dan Nimmo and Keith Sanders (Beverly Hills: Sage Publications, 1981), 11–36.

5. Ibid., 15.

6. Ibid., 17–27.

7. Keith Sanders, Lynda Kaid, and Dan Nimmo, eds., *Political Communication Yearbook: 1984* (Carbondale: Southern Illinois University: 1985), 283–308.

8. Ibid., p. xiv.

9. Ibid.

Preface

Nearly three and one-half million people live within the shadow of the more than one hundred commercial nuclear power reactors that dot the American landscape. Like most Americans, these "nuclear neighbors" appear to have settled into an uneasy peace with nuclear power. Some have reservations about the safety of the plants while others are decidedly pro-nuclear, but most are apparently either unwilling or unable to relocate. These individuals live daily with the risk that a major release of radiation from a nearby plant may suddenly force them to leave homes, farms, and businesses—perhaps never to return again.

It has only been within the past decade that the U.S. government has made a serious effort to prepare the public for the consequences of a nuclear plant accident. Prior to the accident at Three Mile Island in 1979, the government's policy toward nuclear power was heavily tilted toward promotion of the nuclear energy option, hence ignoring or playing down the safety, environmental, and financial risks of continued nuclear development. Following World War II, the federal government forged a protective regulatory relationship with the nuclear industry—a relationship supported by atomic scientists who wanted to convert the destructive power of the atom into peaceful applications. Only after Three Mile Island did the regulatory environment change as the Nuclear Regulatory Commission, under pressure from both the executive and legislative branches, reassessed its previous assumptions that serious nuclear plant accidents were unlikely. New administrative rules were issued that initiated a massive emergency planning process involving the Federal Emergency Management Agency, the utilities that own and operate the plants, and state and local governmental agencies. Among the goals of that process was the establishment of an emergency management program specifically to prepare and thereby protect the public from the consequences of a major release of radiation from an operating nuclear reactor.

Today, government and utility personnel prepare and practice for accidents at all commercial nuclear power plants. Sirens and other warning devices are tested monthly to insure that people living near the plants will be promptly alerted when an accident occurs, and various communication strategies have been devised by plant operators to educate the public about nuclear power. News media representatives are also trained in the nuances of nuclear terminology and plant operations so they can accurately report accident conditions. Millions of dollars have been invested in training and equipment to ensure that everyone knows what to do when trouble strikes a nuclear power plant.

This book examines how the nation's nuclear power industry communicates information about nuclear power risk to the public living near the plants. Such an examination into one of the nation's most comprehensive and sustained efforts to communicate information about technological risk is long overdue, particularly as society devotes increasing resources to relying on risk communication as a substitute for more stringent regulatory measures necessary to protect public health and safety in a technological age. However, before those concerned with preparing the public for technological emergencies rush to embrace nuclear risk communication as a "success" to be emulated, they should recognize that atomic scientists, governmental officials, and the nuclear industry have taken a long, tortuous path to reach today's modern nuclear risk communication program.

Through an analysis of how nuclear power was introduced into America's cultural consciousness, this book demonstrates how that path is strewn with rhetoric and images that have minimized safety concerns and promoted nuclear power development—images that have become imbedded in modern nuclear risk communication. Furthermore, despite increased federal scrutiny of nuclear plant licensing, construction, and operation in an effort to *prevent* accidents, I have found that federal regulatory agencies make little effort to assess whether people understand information that is developed to help them survive accidents *after they happen*. Instead, the government relies on the utilities that own and operate the plants to communicate information to the public about nuclear power risks, asking an industry that has actively promoted the safety of commercial nuclear power for more than thirty years to produce materials that raise troubling questions about the ability of the industry to achieve that level of safety.

Although many nuclear utilities have made a serious effort to develop risk communication programs that accomplish the government's objectives for nuclear risk communication, this study questions whether these programs have convinced nuclear plant residents to follow emergency instructions in a nuclear plant emergency. Because emergency plans for protecting public health and safety in a nuclear plant accident are predicated on the assumption that people will follow instructions, a failure to do so has serious consequences for how well a community will cope with a dangerous nuclear plant accident. I believe that the roots of that failure can be traced back to the promotional history of nuclear risk communication—a history that promotes nuclear power development, de-emphasizes potential dangers from nuclear radiation, and reassures people that accidents are unlikely. I begin this analysis with a discussion of the issues surrounding risk communication before showing how the narrative of the promotional history of nuclear power developed and eventually contaminated modern nuclear risk communication messages—to the ultimate detriment of public safety.

Acknowledgments

The genesis of this book began a decade ago when I assumed responsibility for notifying the news media whenever one of the Tennessee Valley Authority's several nuclear reactors malfunctioned. I was struck at the time by how different groups within the federal agency perceived nuclear power risk, particularly the plant operating personnel who tended to dismiss most operating abnormalities as temporary problems that could be solved without the necessity of notifying the public. It was then that I first learned of the great gap that exists between expert and public perceptions of nuclear power risk, a gap that I had to learn to bridge if I was to meet my responsibilities for providing information that warned people about such risk.

I was fortunate throughout this period to have a supervisor who never wavered in providing me with the resources and the administrative support to make certain that the public was fully and promptly informed about problems both great and small at the agency's nuclear power plants. As TVA Director of Information, Craven Crowell taught me and my Information Office colleagues to both appreciate the role of an informed press in helping responsibly educate the public about risk and to always question the opinions of "experts" when decisions about what constitutes risk have to be made. His contribution to my thinking about this issue is immeasurable.

I am also deeply indebted for the support of B. K. Leiter, former dean of the College of Communication at the University of Tennessee in Knoxville. Teacher, mentor, and valued friend for more than twenty years, Kelly Leiter has never hesitated to respond to my requests for advice and assistance, always with good humor and wise counsel. I number myself among thousands of his former students who treasure their time with him both inside and outside the classroom.

I also wish to recognize the support that I have been given throughout my work on this project by the Virginia Polytechnic Institute & State University Department of Communication Studies, and particularly former department heads Sam Riley and Ken Rystrom, and current head Bob Denton. All provided moral and financial support while smoothing out the rough spots that surfaced when my work on this project occasionally conflicted with departmental responsibilities.

No project of this nature could ever be completed without the help of many individuals, but I particularly want to thank Gary Wamsley, Charles Goodsell, and John Rohr of the VPI&SU Center for Public Administration and Policy, and W. David Conn of the Department of Environmental Design and Planning. They responded to my efforts to deal with this material with sound suggestions, thoughtful criticisms, and considerable patience. Patricia Goldman and Cathy Roche of the Washington office of the U.S. Council for Energy Awareness were also responsive to many requests for assistance and information, as was Frank Ingram of the Nuclear Regulatory Commission and Bill McAda of the Federal Emergency Management Agency. I am also appreciative of a grant from the VPI&SU Graduate Student Assembly that helped fund a portion of this research.

Finally, it is difficult for me to find the right words to convey my feelings about the contribution that Minrose Gwin has made to this project. A distinguished scholar in her own right, Minrose never once hesitated to turn from her work to offer encouragement, support, and constructive criticism—all expressed with the faith that this research would make a meaningful contribution to our mutual concerns about the dangers people face while living in a technological age. Had she not so strongly believed in me and the worth of what I was doing, I doubt that this work would ever have been completed. To her and to our daughter Carol, who has coped beautifully with all of the traumas that come with growing up in a household of academics, this project is dedicated.

Chapter One

The Social Construction of Nuclear Risk Communication

Increasing numbers of chemical plant leaks, train derailments, oil refinery fires, nuclear plant accidents, toxic waste problems, and other technological crises provide grisly testimony to the seriousness of the task facing those who must communicate information about risk so that people can prepare for and survive a technological disaster. The nightmare of Bhopal, India, is but one example of the tragedy that can result when technology goes awry and an unsuspecting public does not know how to get out of the way.[1] And although the technological revolution has made life "easier" for most people, it has made life immensely more difficult for those who must manage the risks created by that technology.[2] As Baruch Fischhoff and his colleagues point out, our decision making is becoming "swamped" by the magnitude of the choices that must be made to effectively manage each new risk. "Coping with these problems demands a decision-making revolution commensurate with the technological revolution of the last 30 years."[3]

Historically, the government has met its responsibilities for protecting human life and property against risk by providing the public with information about the risk and ways either to avoid or to mitigate its effects. We put our faith in the assumption that human beings are rational creatures who can effectively manage risk if only given adequate information and freedom to act in the marketplace. But providing the public with information about the possibility that a technological disaster may occur must necessarily begin with an admission that such a disaster is possible—an acknowledgment that those who manage the technology are often reluctant to make because of the potential liabilities involved, the costs of adding safety equipment, the impact of such an admission on public relations, or simply a lack of knowledge about the risks associated with the technology. For these reasons, those who operate risky technologies have often been reluctant to inform the public about those risks. The growth of regulatory agencies is a testament to the failure of the free market approach to risk management, and as technological hazards have become a major factor in twentieth-century life, these agencies have become increasingly mired in complex issues surrounding questions of identifying risk, its consequences, and the regulators' responsibilities to the public.

One way that U.S. regulatory agencies have sought to meet these responsibilities has been to create numerous information programs about risk. The government's investment in such programs is considerable, no doubt exceeding several hundred million dollars annually. Indeed, some argue that provision of this information is the most important function of regulatory agencies.[4] National attention to the need for risk information has stimulated a virtual risk communication "industry" as public and private organizations devote increasing attention and resources to the development of improved ways to communicate this information to the public. For example, the Superfund Amendments and Reauthorization Act of 1986 (SARA) established sweeping requirements for the federal, state, and local governments and industry to provide information to the public on the presence of hazardous chemicals in their communities and releases of these chemicals into the environment.[5] As a result, thousands of companies have sought guidance from risk communication specialists on how best to inform the public about toxic chemicals. In the area of public health, an unprecedented risk communication effort was undertaken in 1988 when the U.S. Surgeon General's office mailed information to American households detailing the risks associated with AIDS.[6] In an effort to integrate risk communication research with public policy, several universities have established risk and environmental communication centers where researchers seek to discover the most effective techniques for communicating risk information. Dozens of federal studies are being supported by the Environmental Protection Agency, the National Science Foundation, and other agencies concerned with risk communication, and recent issues of several scholarly journals have been devoted solely to articles about risk communication.[7]

INFORMATION, AWARENESS, AND BEHAVIOR

The underlying logic of government risk communication programs has been to provide information to the public in advance of an emergency on the assumption that the information will (1) increase public awareness and (2) lead to the adoption of protective measures. That logic is reflected in a 1985 article on techniques for communicating hazard information by Ronald W. Perry, a pioneer in natural hazards research, and Joanne M. Nigg. They conclude that "the more attention that an emergency manager can give to providing information on hazards, risk, and protective measures in non-crisis situations, the more likely it is that such information communicated during an actual emergency will result in adaptive citizen actions."[8] This reasoning seems logical, but the bulk of scholarly research on risk communication has failed to demonstrate the validity of the assumption that education leads to changes in behavior. In their 1983 summary of education programs to increase public awareness of natural hazards, John H. Sims and Duane D. Baumann conclude that "contrary to conventional wisdom, the fact that an individual is aware of the risk of a natural hazard and the range of damage mitigation measures is no guarantee that he or she will act on that information." They found that whereas education programs often increased public awareness of a natural hazard, "the available evidence is weak on the relationship between awareness or knowledge and the consequent adoption of damage mitigation measures."[9]

Similar findings have resulted from the relatively few studies of educational campaigns for informing the public about technological hazards. A report on a Maine program to provide homeowners with information about health risks from indoor radon gas concludes that "the evidence does not support the naive assumption that merely giving people a quantity of fairly technical information on health risks will induce either accurate perceptions of the problem or cost-effective protective measures."[10] Similar conclusions were reached by Robert S. Adler and R. David Pittle when they examined three government education programs designed to inform consumers about risk—the National Highway Traffic Safety Administration program to increase automobile seat belt use, a Consumer Product Safety Commission program to help prevent injuries from burns, and a federally financed program to develop a heart disease education campaign in three California communities. Although the three programs had been carefully developed, well implemented, and adequately financed, the researchers concluded that none was an unqualified success and each left major questions unanswered about the effectiveness of health and safety education campaigns.[11]

Despite these generally pessimistic results, there is some evidence to indicate that pre-emergency communication does produce some limited behavioral change. Sims and Baumann report on a study in which informational brochures produced "mild success" in increasing flood hazard awareness and mitigation behavior,[12] and a 1978 study of a hurricane awareness program among Texas coastal residents indicates that brochures were successful in increasing both hurricane awareness and preevacuation planning.[13] These positive although limited findings lead Sims and Baumann to assert cautiously that "sometimes, under highly specified conditions, and if properly executed, with certain target publics, information *may* lead to awareness and awareness may lead to behavior."[14] They are cautious because a large body of social science research has shown that people have distorted perceptions of risk—perceptions that make effective risk communication a far more difficult matter than simply making information available.

Nobel prize-winner Herbert A. Simon pioneered an explanation of why human decision making is not always the product of adequate information and free choice by demonstrating that people and organizations make decisions on the basis of limited information, alternatives, and cognitive ability.[15] Simon's theory of "bounded rationality" argued that people often settle for "good enough" decisions within these limits by constructing simplified models of the world and then making decisions on the basis of these models. Simon's work has had tremendous impact on research into how people make decisions when confronted with risk and uncertainty. As Paul Slovic notes, risk communicators "must recognize and overcome a number of obstacles that have their roots in the limitations of scientific risk assessment and the idiosyncracies of the human mind."[16]

Chief among those obstacles is the tendency of risk analysts to make faulty assumptions about how the public perceives and responds to risk. Risk researchers have demonstrated that a considerable gap exists between public perception and "expert" assessment of the same risks, even in cases where the consequences of the risk are well known and the information about the risks has been widely circulated.[17] In one study, researchers asked four different groups of people (college students, members of the League of Women Voters, business and professional people, and "experts" in risk assessment) to rate thirty activities, substances and technologies according to the risk of death from each. The experts' judgment of risk differed markedly from those of the other groups. For example, the league representatives and the college students ranked nuclear power as the most risky activity on the list, whereas the experts ranked it twentieth.[18]

Lack of complete or accurate information may account for some of this discrepancy, but other factors influencing people's perceptions of risk include the extent to which the risk is faced voluntarily, the length of delay between cause and effect, the degree of control over the risk, and the potential for large and catastrophic effects.[19] Judgmental heuristics that help people simplify complex tasks also play a role in how people assess risks.[20] For example, a person's perception of risk can become distorted because of a bias in what is called the availability heuristic. People using this heuristic tend to judge an event as occurring frequently if instances of it are easy to recall. But because dramatic or sensational events are memorable, they are generally perceived as occurring more frequently than less sensational events. Thus people tend to overestimate the number of deaths from risks that are dramatic, such as murder, cancer, and natural disasters, and underestimate deaths from prevalent causes such as diabetes.

Individuals also overestimate the accuracy of their risk judgments made under this heuristic because a sense of certainty about such decisions helps reduce anxiety. They feel personally immune to certain risks, such as traffic accidents, because they believe those risks are under their control or because their experience with the risk has been benign. Finally, the overconfidence that people have in risk judgments based on the availability heuristic is no doubt bolstered by the tendency of the news media to focus on sensational events (frequent media reports of murders may indicate to an individual that murders occur more often than other causes of death). Experts are just as prone to overconfidence in their risk judgments as the public.[21]

RISK COMMUNICATION HAS MULTIPLE OBJECTIVES

These research findings strongly suggest that government risk communication programs, if they are to be effective, must overcome a variety of psychological problems influencing the ways in which human beings think about risk. "Government programs that seek to reduce health and safety risks with information programs instead of using more conventional enforced standards must be crafted very carefully to accommodate this complex process," note F. Reed Johnson and Ralph A. Luken.[22] However, some have suggested that many of these programs are doomed to failure from the beginning because they seek to achieve goals other than their stated purpose of informing the public about risk. Adler and Pittle point out in their analysis that government risk education programs have become a substitute for direct regulation because (1) regulators believe that direct regulation is ineffective in preventing injuries and illnesses; (2) information and education programs are easier and faster to implement than rule making; (3) such programs enhance the agency's image as "doing something" about risk; and (4) information and education programs, particularly in recent years, have given regulatory agencies a way to preserve freedom of individual choice in the marketplace while avoiding substantial intervention into industry production techniques. "While we do not challenge the value of all information and education programs," they write, "we suggest their popularity rests more on philosophical and ideological grounds than on solid empirical evidence supporting their ability to alter consumer behavior."[23]

The recognition that risk communication may seek to serve goals other than the public welfare has caused several scholars to expand their conception of risk communication beyond that of mere information exchange between technical experts and the public. Harry Otway and Kerry Thomas have looked critically at research traditions in risk research as having an "ideological commitment" to either an objective "science of facts" or a subjective "and ultimately socially constructed, view of the world."[24] They take a subjectivist view, arguing that "truths" do not exist independently of people:

It is *people*, and not independent facts, who constrain the way concepts are framed, questions posed, and research goals set. And it is people who design event and fault trees, choose options, choose attribute sets, fund data collection, interpret, and publish findings. Once the criterion of an absolute truth is abandoned, then surely no one can avoid the inference that *people see the world differently* and that these differences emerge from different experiences of differently constructed social worlds. And furthermore, that *people* want different outcomes (for themselves or on behalf of others) and have different resources (in kind and extent) to employ in the service of those wants.[25]

A subjectivist approach fully acknowledges that risk research is a political "tool in a discourse . . . whose hidden agenda is the legitimacy of decision-making institutions and the equitable distribution of hazards and benefits."[26] Alonzo Plough and Sheldon Krimsky adopt a subjectivist view of risk by arguing that conventional risk communication research "neglects cultural themes, motivations, and symbolic meanings which may be of equal or greater importance to the technical understanding of how and why a risk message gets transmitted."[27] By studying risk communication within a cultural context, Plough and Krimsky believe that certain symbolic meanings within the communication emerge: "A scientist speaking to a community about the health risks of a chemical dump may be carrying out a ritual that displays confidence and control. The technical information . . . is secondary to the real goal of the communicator: 'Have faith; we are in charge.' . . . For a company, risk communication is frequently not about risks but about safety and confidence."[28]

By communicating information that reinforces safety and confidence, risk communication may symbolically serve to make both regulatory agencies and regulated industries appear to conform to valued societal goals rather than play a functional role of effectively communicating the nature of risk. Philip Selznick was one of the first organizational theorists to recognize that the formal and social structure of organizations is shaped by the institutional environment in which the organization finds itself.[29] Expanding on Selznick's pioneering work, John W. Meyer and Brian Rowan argue that public organizations frequently incorporate myths from their external environments to gain legitimacy, resources, stability; and to enhance survival.[30] This concept of organizational myth comes out of a growing body of literature concerned with organizational culture. Culture, as Gareth Morgan notes, is an "ethos . . . sustained by social processes, images, symbols, and ritual." Rituals, myths, and ceremonies "continually reaffirm the organization's culture" in both the eyes of its employees and with outsiders. He points out that the belief systems of modern organizations are sustained by myths, rituals, and cultures that function "to demonstrate rationality and objectivity in action."[31]

According to Meyer and Rowan, the sources of these organizational myths are deeply institutionalized societal beliefs that are supported by public opinion, the educational system, the desire for social prestige, and the law. By adopting these highly institutionalized beliefs as myths, public organizations become isomorphic with their institutional environments and thereby increase their chances for success and survival. Organizational characteristics are modified to conform to environmental characteristics. Risk communication programs may serve a symbolic function within regulatory agencies because the existence of such programs provides evidence that the organization is concerned with societal norms of safety and confidence as it monitors risky technologies.

Meyer and Rowan also emphasize the role that language plays in the legitimatizing process, as organizations label their structures in accordance with institutionalized myths so that they appear to be oriented toward collectively defined and legitimate ends. Their example concerning environmental safety has relevance for risk communication: "environmental safety institutions make it important for organizations to create formal safety rules, safety departments, and safety programs. No Smoking rules and signs, regardless of their enforcement, are necessary to avoid charges of negligence and to avoid the extreme of illegitimation: the closing of buildings by the state."[32] Similarly, risk communication programs may serve to legitimize both regulatory agencies and regulated industries within society through highly visible activities that may or may not contribute to safety. For example, Perry and Nigg suggest that one of the principal functions of pre-emergency risk communication programs is to establish the credibility of emergency management agencies with the public through distribution of brochures, publication of hazard-information telephone numbers, creation of citizen advisory committees, and other attention-getting activities. "A major thrust of citizen contacts during normal times . . . should be to establish the technical expertise of the manager and his/her staff," they write. "Making the public aware that emergency managers have both technical training and access to special equipment to cope with environmental threats sets the manager apart as having a *professional* approach to handling community threats. By establishing expectations of professionalism for emergency management personnel during normal times, public recognition of the agency is enhanced and credibility is heightened."[33]

Communicating information that makes organizations appear isomorphic with societal goals of safety and confidence may be particularly important for organizations that Todd La Porte has labeled high reliability organizations (HROs) and for the public agencies that regulate HROs. La Porte and Paula M. Consolini have shown that HROs such as nuclear power plants and air traffic control operations differ from other kinds of organizations in that they cannot rely on trial and error learning to improve their operations, but must operate from the beginning in nearly error-free fashion:

Operators and watchful publics, in effect, assume that some organizations can avoid system failure. Organization representatives play to this hope assuring us that they will not fail. They claim sufficient technological knowledge to prevent it. As long as these organizations succeed at what they do, we assume they will continue to do so. We grow to take their benefits for granted. Reliability and safety are technically assured. We need not worry overly about the social and political dynamics in these organizations.[34]

However, as HROs continue to proliferate, there will be increased demands by the public to reduce their risks through improving their operational reliability. We may then discover, writes La Porte, that it is not possible to reach the level of operational perfection required by society:

If substantial errors do occur, it is likely that the institutions directly involved in the production and regulation of the responsible technologies will be blamed. If there were relatively frequent and significant errors, the legitimacy of those institutions would decline as would confidence in the efficacy of incremental legislative and regulatory-policy processes, which is perhaps the most troubling aspect of the social response to potentially hazardous technologies.[35]

Risk communication, therefore, may serve a symbolic role for HROs by communicating messages that reinforce societal values for HROs (e.g., safety and security), rather than a functional role of effectively communicating the nature of the risk posed by HRO technology. A cultural approach to the study of risk communication programs may help illuminate the symbolic underpinning of such programs and explain why many such efforts do not effectively communicate risk information to the public.

A CULTURAL APPROACH

Raphael Kasper suggests that many risk communication programs fail because policymakers typically place public perceptions on a lower footing than those of technical experts. This disparity arises from a technocratic arrogance that tends to view "objective" expert characterizations of risk "as somehow more real or more valid than the perceptions of the rest of the public."[36] Carrying Kasper's observation a step further, Plough and Krimsky believe that the disparity between technical and lay perceptions of risk reflects a political conflict between the values of scientific rationality and democracy, and that policymakers have tended to judge risk communication as either success or failure depending upon how closely popular attitudes conform to "expert" estimations of risk. They reject this approach as a "deviant model of risk communication":

Lay people bring many more factors into a risk event than do scientists. For technical experts, the event is denuded of elements that are irrelevant to the analytical model . . . many events that are deemed to have very low or insignificant risk by experts are viewed as serious problems by the laity. Burial of low level radioactive wastes and releasing a natural organism minus a few genes into the environment are among such cases. Where there has been discussion of rationality, it has focused on the scientific grounds of a decision. And yet there are clear instances of reasonable decisionmaking at the community level that are inconsistent with expert opinion. Once it is accepted that two inconsistent decisions can be rational and consistent *on their own grounds*, it is possible to reach beyond the deviant model of risk communication.[37]

Plough and Krimsky call for risk research that focuses on analysis of cultural factors that may influence public perceptions of risk, an approach also advocated by Mary Douglas and Aaron Wildavsky. "Between private, subjective perception and public, physical science there lies culture, a middle area of shared beliefs and values," they write. "The present division of the subject that ignores culture is arbitrary and self-defeating."[38] Kasper also acknowledges the value of the cultural approach when he observes that the manner in which a risk activity is originally presented to the public greatly affects public perception of that risk:

Consider what possible current conceptions of the automobile might be if the introduction of petroleum products to the public had been in the form of napalm rather than in the form of oil for light and heat. (Nuclear power, it should be recalled, was introduced to the public through the awesome destructive power of the atomic bomb and it is almost certainly true that current public perceptions of nuclear power are shaped largely by the first impression.) If people's visual image of petroleum were the hideous scenes of Vietnamese cloaked in flames (as their visual image of uranium is a mushroom shaped cloud) rather than the cozy warmth of a fire on a cold day, it might be more difficult to cruise down the highway with equanimity atop a twenty-gallon tank of gasoline.[39]

Similarly, Slovic cites research showing that the way information is "framed"—for example, asking people to choose between two options for cancer treatment with one choice framed in terms of survival rate and the other framed in terms of a death rate—can produce dramatic differences in the choices people make. He makes the significant point that "the fact that subtle differences in how risks are presented can have such marked effects suggests that those responsible for information programs have considerable ability to manipulate perceptions and behavior. This possibility raises ethical problems that must be addressed by any responsible risk-information program."[40] Risk communicators may not even be aware of such biases in their presentation of information. A study involving more than a dozen non-metropolitan communities experiencing ground water contamination from toxic chemicals found that the manner in which risk communicators chose to present information was often determined by many subtle cultural influences: "Each messenger operating in the community is an individual with his or her own personal attitudes and perspectives about risk. Messengers are also products of institutions, and as such they have internalized the assumptions and biases about risk that characterize the discipline in which they were trained and the firm or agency for which they work."[41]

Thus risk communication is heavily value-laden, consisting of judgments made by risk analysis experts, political leaders, communication specialists, and others who influence both the content and the presentation of risk information. Any comprehensive examination of a risk communication program that ignores the social, political, and cultural roots of the program risks overlooking biases in the presentation of information that may not be apparent on the surface. To avoid this problem, Slovic and his colleagues encourage a broad-based risk communication research effort that incorporates sociological, anthropological, and geographical studies, not only as a means of exploring the social and cultural roots of risk, but also as a way to examine the process of risk communication in a clearer light. This is a complex task, for

[t]he stakes in risk problems are high: industrial profits, jobs, energy costs, willingness of patients to accept treatments, public safety and health. Potential conflicts of interest abound. When subtle aspects of how (or what) information is presented can change people's behavior, someone needs to determine which formulation should be used. Making that decision takes one out of the domain of psychology and into law, ethics, and politics. The possibilities for manipulation suggest that informational programs cannot be left to any one group (e.g., employers, unions, physicians, toxicologists). Indeed, the way to get the most

balanced message may be to subject it to diverse critiques, with each group challenging features that it considers to be confusing or misleading.[42]

RISK COMMUNICATION AND NUCLEAR POWER

Perhaps no other risk communication effort in the United States lends itself better to a cultural analysis than the federal program to provide emergency information to residents living around the nation's commercial nuclear power plants. Born in the crisis of the accident at Three Mile Island in March 1979, nuclear emergency communication is one of the nation's most comprehensive technological risk communication programs, with nearly a decade of experience in providing pre-emergency information to what is now estimated at 3.4 million Americans.[43] Because of the rich, well-documented, and controversial history of commercial nuclear power development in the United States, nuclear risk communication is particularly well suited to a cultural analysis to see if elements of that history have become imbedded in the fabric of the risk communication process.

It was not until shortly after the Three Mile Island accident that a serious federal effort was begun to plan for off-site ramifications of an accident involving a commercial nuclear power plant. Prior to Three Mile Island, both the Nuclear Regulatory Commission (NRC) and the nuclear industry generally ignored off-site emergency planning. Richard T. Sylves suggests several reasons for this indifference. First, federal regulators and the nuclear industry believed that the probabilities of an accident were so low, due to engineering safeguards built into the plants, that planning for an accident was unnecessary and would create needless public concern. Beset by rising costs and increasing numbers of safety regulations necessitating major engineering changes at the plants, nuclear plant owner/operators tended to put off-site emergency concerns on the back burner. And, ironically, the anti-nuclear movement that developed in the late 1960s and early 1970s similarly tended to denigrate off-site planning, believing that full-scale evacuation of a large population living around a plant would be impossible in a serious accident.[44]

At the time of the Three Mile Island accident, the federal government did not require either the states or the nuclear plant owner/operators to have approved off-site emergency response plans as a condition of plant licensing. Instead, the NRC issued "guidelines" that encouraged but did not demand that states with radiological facilities submit emergency plans for NRC "review and concurrence." Pennsylvania was one of thirty-two states with nuclear facilities that did not have emergency plans meeting the NRC guidelines. Sylves suggests that Congress had allowed this situation to occur because it feared that state and local governments might use such a requirement to withhold plans and thereby block the licensing of plants.[45]

Both the presidential commission that investigated the Three Mile Island accident and the NRC's own review were highly critical, as was Congress, of the lack of off-site emergency planning around the plant.[46] For example, the presidential commission noted that there was a "lack of coordination and urgency" at all levels of government in planning for off-site emergencies and that the interaction between NRC, utility, state, and local emergency organizations was "insufficient to ensure an adequate level of preparedness for a serious radiological accident at TMI."[47] The key recommendation made by the commission was that federal responsibility for off-site emergency radiological planning be transferred from the NRC to the Federal Emergency Management Agency (FEMA), a step taken by President Carter in December 1979.[48]

The NRC retained federal responsibility for assessing the overall state of a nuclear plant's safety, in effect creating joint NRC-FEMA responsibility for emergency planning. That relationship evolved from a Memorandum of Understanding entered into between FEMA and the NRC in November 1980, and was spelled out in administrative rules issued by both agencies.[49] Here is a simplified version of how the joint FEMA-NRC responsibilities for emergency planning are shared:

- FEMA is responsible for coordinating all federal planning for the off-site impact of radiological emergencies. FEMA reviews and judges the adequacy of off-site plans and readiness of state and local emergency preparedness agencies and communicates its findings to the NRC.

- The NRC reviews the FEMA findings and determinations, in conjunction with its own findings on a utility's on-site emergency plan, and makes a determination on the overall state of emergency preparedness.

- From its overall findings, the NRC decides whether new plants should be licensed or existing plants should continue operating. However, the NRC has told the General Accounting Office that a finding by FEMA that offsite safety is not adequate to protect the public does not obligate the NRC to deny a license, withdraw a license, or take any other punitive action.[50]

The process begins when the governor of the state in which a nuclear plant is located submits state and local plans for review. Since March 1982, FEMA has been assisted in its review of those plans by a Federal Radiological Preparedness Coordinating Committee composed of representatives from FEMA, NRC, the Environmental Protection Agency, and the Departments of Agriculture, Commerce, Defense, Energy, Health and Human Services, Interior and Transportation. Ten regional assistance committees composed of officials from these agencies assist state and local government officials in developing their plans.[51]

Before an off-site emergency plan can be approved, it must first meet planning criteria developed jointly by NRC and FEMA and published in November 1980.[52] Known in the industry as NUREG–0654, the criteria consist of sixteen planning standards, fifteen of which relate to both on- and off-site safety and one related solely to on-site safety, that are further broken down into 196 elements describing the intent of the standards. The overall objective of NUREG–0654 is the development of emergency plans that reduce radiation exposure to people living within a ten-mile radius of a nuclear plant in the event of an accident and that address problems associated with radioactively contaminated food and water for a distance of fifty miles from the plant. Before FEMA will approve an off-site emergency plan, the nuclear plant owner/operator must conduct an exercise that tests the state and local governments' ability to implement the plan, followed by a public meeting in which both the plan and the exercise are discussed.[53]

Of particular relevance to this study is the planning standard for public education and information. In its report following the accident at Three Mile Island, the presidential commission recommended a program to "educate the public on how nuclear power plants operate, on radiation and its health effects, and on protective actions against radiation," no doubt believing that public education would lead to a more effective response during an emergency.[54] Under its public education and information planning standard, NUREG–0654 requires that nuclear plant owner/operators make information available to the public on a periodic basis that tells them how they will be notified and *what their actions should be* in an emergency. In evaluating whether an emergency plan meets the standard, NUREG–0654 specifies that information be provided the public living within ten miles of a nuclear plant. That information addresses the following topics:

1. Educational information about radiation.
2. Where the public can obtain additional information.
3. Radiation protection measures, such as evacuation routes and relocation centers, sheltering, respiratory protection, and radioprotective drugs.
4. Special needs of the handicapped.[55]

NUREG–0654 does not require that plant owner/operaters adopt any specific communication tools or techniques for disseminating such information, but does offer some suggestions, including publishing the information in telephone books and with utility bills; posting in public areas; and distributing the information annually in publications. Although a few local and state governments prepare these information materials, normally the nuclear plant owner/operator organizes the materials for review and approval by state and local governments. The form of these materials varies from plant to plant, but most are booklets or calendars, supplemented by telephone book inserts, posters, brochures, and other communication media (see Chapter 3 for a more complete description of these materials).

How effective are the nuclear industry's efforts to communicate emergency information to the public? A 1986 assessment by Philip L. Rutledge of the public education program for the McGuire Nuclear Station near Charlotte, N.C., found that less than one-half of the households living in the plant's ten-mile radius Emergency Planning Zone (EPZ) knew that upon hearing the plant's emergency warning sirens, they were to turn to the area's broadcast media for further instructions.[56] Instead, many respondents indicated that they would gather their families and evacuate the area without first determining the nature of the radiological emergency or even if they were at risk.[57]

Rutledge points out that this finding is consistent with other studies showing that spontaneous evacuation is a characteristic of nuclear plant emergencies. The classic example is the public's behavior around the Three Mile Island plant during the March 1979 accident. On the third day of the crisis, Pennsylvania Governor Richard Thornburgh issued an advisory recommending that pregnant women and pre-school children within five miles of the plant evacuate, and that everyone within ten miles of the plant take shelter. Post-accident studies indicate that had everyone evacuated who was advised to evacuate, only about 2,500 people would have left the area. Instead, 144,000 individuals living within fifteen miles of the plant evacuated.[58]

As several researchers have noted, the experience at Three Mile Island suggests that more people will evacuate during a radiological emergency than are advised to, a process that has been called the evacuation shadow phenomenon.[59] According to Houts et al., this is the reverse of what normally occurs in natural disasters when less people evacuate than are asked. They say the public tends to underreact in natural disasters because many people are familiar with the threat and overestimate their ability to deal with it, whereas radiological emergencies involve a threat that is invisible, associated in the public mind with cancer and bombs, and can cover a wide area geographically. Public disagreements among experts about the nature of the threat also cause people to underreact in natural disasters and overreact in radiological emergencies.[60]

Despite evidence that the evacuation shadow phenomenon may play a significant role in the public response to a radiological emergency, many nuclear plant emergency information programs are designed to educate the public on the specifics of participating in *zonal evacuations* in which only *portions* of the ten-mile EPZ would be evacuated depending upon the nature of the emergency, wind direction from the plant, the geography of the EPZ, etc. At plants that rely on zonal evacuation, education materials provided the public include a map of the EPZ divided into labeled zones. Presumably, officials would use the broadcast media to advise people living in zones downwind from the plant to evacuate and instruct people living in nonthreatened zones to take other protective measures (i.e., stay indoors) and avoid clogging routes of egress for those who are evacuating. This follows suggestions by several researchers that the goal of pre-emergency information programs should be to educate the public on the importance of listening to official instructions before making a decision to evacuate an area.[61] However, Rutledge's North Carolina findings, where less than one-half of the people surveyed indicated that their first response after hearing the warning sirens would be to turn on the radio or television for official instructions, questions whether this goal for public education is being achieved.

PROGRAM EFFECTIVENESS NOT ASSESSED

Because it does not attempt to assess the effectiveness of nuclear public education programs, the federal government has not generated evidence to contradict Rutledge's findings. Instead, FEMA, the federal agency charged with responsibility for assessing off-site nuclear emergency plans, confines its assessment of nuclear plant public education programs to determine only if EPZ residents have received the required information dealing with radiological emergency procedures. However, as a 1987 General Accounting Office (GAO) report noted, "these results do not necessarily mean that people understand this information or know what to do in such an emergency."[62]

FEMA bases its determination of whether EPZ residents have received public education materials on a survey conducted to assess the adequacy of nuclear plant emergency siren systems. Once the siren system has been installed and tested, a FEMA contractor telephones a sample of EPZ residents to determine the number who heard the siren test. As part of this telephone survey, residents are asked whether they recall receiving emergency preparedness information. According to GAO, as of November 1986 FEMA had tested the coverage of the siren systems for fifty-seven nuclear power plant sites and estimated that an average of 71.1 percent of the residents living within the EPZs around those plants recalled receiving emergency preparedness information. However, actual responses at the plants ranged from 31.5 to 84.5 percent, with many in the 50 to 60 percent range.[63]

As a result of the survey's findings that public education materials are apparently not attracting the attention of many EPZ residents, FEMA has devoted attention to improving the quality of materials being distributed by plant owner/operators. Under prodding from GAO, FEMA issued *A Guide To Preparing Emergency Public Information Materials* (FEMA-REP–11) in 1984 to help emergency management officials prepare or revise public education materials. The goal of the twenty-seven page guide is "to increase the comprehensibility of . . . public information documents so that if a notification is signaled, area residents will immediately tune in to EBS [Emergency Broadcast System]."[64] The document emphasizes the need to match the reading level of the materials with the comprehension level of the EPZ audience and suggests that emergency planners "analyze their target population and develop a style that is focused at a site-specific audience profile."[65] The document provides guidance on how to simplify content and organization, readability, comprehensibility, and graphic design, but emphasizes that its guidelines are only suggestions. "Setting standards for evaluating public information materials is very difficult because elements like graphics and design are not readily quantifiable," the document notes. "Producing public information is a creative process and the producers need a certain latitude in which to operate."[66]

FEMA also conducts a voluntary program under which it works through a contractor directly with plant owner/operators to improve their public education programs using standards like those listed above. According to GAO, FEMA had conducted extensive reviews of thirty-five owner/operator programs through November 1986. The GAO report noted that one plant participating in the review had replaced its information brochure with an attractive calendar, increasing the number of households that were aware of the information, while another plant rewrote its brochure to lower the reading level, also increasing the number of people who remembered receiving the information. But as the GAO report points out, "Neither FEMA nor the NRC determines whether—or to what extent—the public pays attention to the radiological emergency preparedness materials provided by the utilities that operate nuclear power plants."[67]

However, at one point in its history FEMA was willing to try to determine if EPZ residents understood the materials they received from nuclear plant owner/operators. In 1980, FEMA proposed to begin mailing an annual questionnaire to EPZ residents nationwide to assess both the effectiveness of the siren systems as well as how much the public knew about radiological emergency procedures. FEMA, which envisioned an initial mailing of 165,000 questionnaires in 1981 and about 300,000 each year thereafter, was required under the Paperwork Reduction Act (PL 96–511) to obtain approval from the Office of Management and Budget (OMB) before using the questionnaire. OMB denied FEMA's request in July 1981, on grounds that the survey was too large and was not required for FEMA to meet its responsibilities under NUREG–0654.[68]

FEMA could meet its oversight responsibility, OMB stated, by simply requesting copies of the emergency information sent out by nuclear plant owner/operators to the public. FEMA's responsibility, OMB emphasized, did not extend to making sure that people understood the information once they had received it. "It should not be necessary to ask ten percent of the affected population what they know about actions they should take in the event of nuclear emergencies," wrote OMB Deputy Administrator Jim J. Tozzi. "As to FEMA's proposal to assess the level of public understanding of the notification message, it could be argued that once the agency has assured that the warning signal was audible, and that the licensee has provided the population with emergency information, it has discharged its responsibility. FEMA should not be expected to make sure the public has read the material it has been given; that is an individual action. Nor should it be required to expand scarce resources supplementing the licensees' efforts."[69] Following the rebuff, FEMA modified the survey by removing the questions on public knowledge of radiological procedures and converting it into a telephone survey. OMB approved the modified survey in 1983.[70]

INDUSTRY ULTIMATELY RESPONSIBLE

Why has government chosen indirect involvement in nuclear power emergency communication programs? In an article describing efforts by the State of California to take a more active role in the public education component of nuclear emergency planning, Judy E. Rosener and Sallie C. Russell suggest two reasons: first, because the plant owner/operators are ultimately responsible for the public education programs as a condition for licensing, they can pass along the costs of these programs directly to ratepayers, absolving government of the program's expense. Second, government is reluctant to enter the nuclear power debate. "If they [state and local governments] disseminate materials that warn of a risk, they increase the possibility of opposition to nuclear plants and are dragged into the nuclear power debate. . . . By relegating public education to the utility, they effectively are able to 'lay low' with respect to the nuclear power plant risk issue."[71] By being handed the responsibility for public education by default, the owner/operators of the nation's nuclear power plants have been placed in the contradictory position of showing people what to do when a nuclear plant accident occurs while assuring them that such events are highly unlikely, notes Rosener and Russell. "Reconciling the need to assure citizens they have little to fear from nuclear power plants (which helps promote support for the industry) and the need to inform citizens of potential radiation threats (which is one of the goals of public education) poses an interesting dilemma," they write.[72] In effect, the government is asking an industry that has actively promoted a benign view of the safety of com-

mercial nuclear power for more than thirty years to produce materials
that raise significant questions about the ability of the industry to achieve
that level of safety. As a result, although many nuclear plant owner/
operators have made a serious effort to develop public education programs that accomplish the government's objectives for emergency communication, the industry has framed its risk messages with both
promotional rhetoric and images—images that mask the seriousness of
the information it is trying to communicate to people living around the
nation's nuclear power plants.

For example, as part of his study of the McGuire Nuclear Plant public
education program, Rutledge analyzed the content of both the McGuire
brochure and forty other nuclear plant emergency booklets from across
the United States. Rutledge first coded material in the booklets by paragraph under six themes—essential information (notification and protective actions); background information (introduction, glossary of
nuclear terms, etc.); radiation; plant design or operation; nuclear issues
(risks, benefits, and history); and non-nuclear information. He next classified the paragraphs under each theme on the basis of whether or not
each contained "reassurance" statements. According to Rutledge, reassurances presented information about nuclear energy in a favorable
light by either minimizing risks associated with nuclear power or emphasizing positive features such as the industry's safety record or the
role of nuclear energy in society. Finally, Rutledge further coded the
material on the basis on whether it was presented in a "normalcy" or
"crisis" content. Under his classification criteria, a crisis orientation "at
least implicity acknowledges that the plant poses some risk," while a
normalcy context "references the secure, everyday world of normal plant
operation."[73]

Rutledge concluded from his analysis that all of the booklets presented
the required information concerning the actions people living around
the plants should take when first warned of a radiological emergency
and that this "essential" information tended to reference a crisis context.
However, he found that only about one-third of the brochures devoted
more than one-half of their text to essential information, and that nuclear
power plant owner/operators chose to include vast amounts of non-
essential information that did not bear directly or indirectly on protective
actions.[74] Rutledge suggests that the amount of this non-critical information and the manner in which it is presented disguises the vital information. "This thesis is evident by both the context in which these
[non-essential] themes are discussed and by the numerous reassurances
in these booklets," Rutledge writes. "Some reassurances directly promote the benefits of nuclear energy, while others emphasize the safety
of the plant."[75]

Rutledge found that the brochures, rather than emphasizing the nature of the nuclear plant hazard, played down the risk. "Thus, a dual and conflicting message is present within most booklets: the protective action information is important but it will probably never be needed."[76] Rutledge argued, therefore, that nuclear education programs may serve both manifest and latent goals. While the manifest goal is to provide essential emergency information, the latent goal may be to "legitimate" the plant. "Efforts to legitimate the plant by persuading the public that it is safe (or beneficial) are consistent with the nuclear industry's efforts elsewhere," he noted.[77]

These findings, coupled with the government's reluctance to become more involved in nuclear emergency communication, lead me to suggest that the history of commercial nuclear power development in the United States—particularly the close, supportive relationship that once existed between the American nuclear industry, federal regulatory agencies, and Congress—is still functioning to seriously impede the effectiveness of modern nuclear risk communication. It is my contention that Americans living around commercial nuclear power plants are generally ill informed concerning the steps they should take to protect health and safety during a nuclear plant accident. This situation exists because federal regulatory agencies have allowed the owner/operators of the nation's nuclear power plants to frame risk communication materials in such a way as to mask the seriousness of the information contained within those materials, primarily through the use of historical message themes and/or images that are supportive of nuclear power development.

If, as communication research has shown, the *attitudes* of the participants in a communication process are a much more important determinant of *communications impact* than *message content*, examination of how those attitudes have been formed may provide insight into why nuclear plant risk messages are being framed as they are.[78] I believe that the way these messages are framed serves not to communicate the nature of the nuclear plant risk, but to reinforce in the public consciousness those images and rhetoric that the nuclear industry has historically used to affirm the worth of commercial nuclear power. Thusly, nuclear risk communication symbolically affirms societal values of safety and confidence, thereby masking the possibility of technological failure and protecting both the regulators and the owner/operators of nuclear power plants from public concerns over the safety of a high-risk technology. Under these conditions, the *latent symbolic role* of risk communication overwhelms its *manifest functional goal* to protect the health and safety of the public living around commercial nuclear power plants.

To confirm my hypothesis that important risk information contained within nuclear emergency communication is being masked or hidden by rhetoric and images that have been historically associated with commercial nuclear power, I will first examine the social history of nuclear power development to see if certain themes have dominated its historical discourse. Like physicist and science historian Spencer R. Weart, whose 535–page *Nuclear Fear* makes the definitive statement on the crucial role that imagery has played in the history of nuclear energy, I am convinced that the way we communicate risk information about nuclear power today is significantly influenced by rhetoric and images that have become imbedded in our cultural consciousness, some for many hundreds of years. "That fact is disturbing," says Weart, "for it shows that such thinking has less to do with current physical reality than with old, autonomous features of our society, our culture, and our psychology."[79] If we are to fully appreciate all of the ramifications of our efforts to communicate risk information to the public living around nuclear power plants, we must understand how that communication has been informed by the past history of nuclear power development before we can fix what's wrong with today's nuclear public education programs.

In the next chapter, I examine the central rhetorical themes that have dominated the discourse of commercial nuclear power throughout its history, as well as the institutions that have played significant roles in developing that discourse. In Chapter 3, I apply that analysis to the risk communication materials being distributed by nuclear plant/owner operators throughout the United States. I demonstrate in Chapter 4 how these materials are not meeting the government's goals for nuclear public education. Finally, I conclude this study with recommendations for improving our national nuclear risk communication effort.

Why is this study significant? First, I believe there is every reason to expect that within the next decade this country will experience a nuclear power plant accident requiring off-site evacuation of people living around the plant. Many of our nuclear power plants have operated for between fifteen and twenty years, and some are approaching thirty years of operation.[80] Although many of the operating and safety systems in these older plants have been modified or replaced, engineers are still learning new facts about the damaging effects of long-term radiation on metal and other materials used in plant construction. Press reports of the deteriorating condition of the thirty-five-year-old nuclear reactors at the Department of Energy's Savannah River military facility in South Carolina may prove to be a portent of conditions inside some of the nation's older nuclear power plants.[81] Despite improvements in the design of safety systems and training for nuclear plant operators, we must still be aware of the potential for human error in the operation of these complex technological systems. Part of the painful history of the development of commercial nuclear power has been the gradual awareness that it is impossible to completely engineer the human factor out of nuclear plant safety.[82]

Despite dire predictions that safety considerations and economics have "killed" the future development of commercial nuclear power in the United States, there is some indication that the industry may be on the brink of a rebirth. World concerns about the impact of carbon monoxide on global warming have resulted in making large-scale energy sources that do not rely on fossil fuels appear more attractive from an environmental standpoint, while new developments in reactor design are being touted as safer and more economical than previous designs.[83] Reports in the business media that demand for electricity is finally catching up with the utility industry's ability to meet that demand are being used by the nuclear industry as evidence that new nuclear power plants will be vitally needed in the future.[84] Of even more significance to the importance of this study is President Reagan's Executive Order of November 18, 1988, that directs FEMA to assume operational responsibility for off-site emergency planning should state and/or local governments refuse to cooperate in developing emergency plans.[85] The President's action was stimulated by the refusal of local and state authorities to cooperate in developing off-site emergency plans for the Shoreham plant on Long Island, N.Y., and the Seabrook plant in New Hampshire.[86] This has apparently removed a weapon from the arsenal of local officials who may want to use emergency planning as a tool to stop development of future nuclear power plants.[87] Finally, regardless of the outcome of the debate over the future of commercial nuclear power, there is no question that government has a responsibility to protect the safety of the estimated 3.4 million Americans who presently live within the shadow of more than 100 operating nuclear reactors.[88]

This study seeks to help increase that margin of safety.

NOTES

1. In December 1984 a chemical leak from the Union Carbide plant in Bhopal, India, overwhelmed people sleeping in the surrounding neighborhood. The Indian government now estimates that the accident killed 3,330 people and injured up to 200,000, many of whom the government says will die from their injuries. See *The New York Times*, 4 December 1988, 33.

2. It is important here to explain my use of certain terms. I follow W. David Conn and Nickolaus R. Feimer by defining a "hazard" as a threat that has the potential, at a certain magnitude, to produce negative consequences such as illness, death, or damage for an individual or a community. "Natural hazards" are those threats produced by events in nature, such as hurricanes, tornados, and floods. "Technological hazards" are threats produced by human activities and technologies, such as automobile accidents, toxic emissions from waste disposal sites, and radiation from nuclear power plants. "Risk" describes both the nature of the threat and the probability that the negative consequences resulting from the threat will occur. "Risk assessment" is the process of discovering that a risk exists and of estimating and measuring its magnitude and

probability of occurrence. "Risk management" are those activities taken to reduce either the probability that negative consequences will occur from a risk or
the damages that would result from those consequences, or both. Like Rae
Zimmerman, I define "risk communication" as the process of providing information on risks and their uncertainties in an effort to change perceptions, attitudes, and beliefs about risks, thereby achieving behavior modification toward
the risk. However, as my study shows, the ability of current risk communication
techniques to achieve behavior modification in emergencies is subject to considerable question. See W. David Conn and Nickolaus R. Feimer, "Communicating with the Public on Environmental Risk: Integrating Research and Policy,"
The Environmental Professional 7, no. 1 (1985): 40; and Rae Zimmerman, "A Process
Framework for Risk Communication," *Science, Technology & Human Values* 12,
nos. 3–4 (1987): 131.

3. Baruch Fischhoff et al., *Acceptable Risk* (Cambridge: Cambridge University
Press, 1981), 2.

4. Paul Slovic, Baruch Fischhoff, and Sarah Lichtenstein, "Regulation of Risk:
A Psychological Perspective," in *Regulatory Policy and the Social Sciences* (Berkeley:
University of California Press, 1985), 258; Robert S. Adler and R. David Pittle,
"Cajolery or Command: Are Education Campaigns an Adequate Substitute for
Regulation?" *Yale Journal on Regulation* 1, no. 2 (1984): 159–160; and Paul L.
Joskow and Roger G. Noll, "Regulation in Theory and Practice: An Overview,"
in *Studies in Public Regulation*, ed. Gary Fromm (Cambridge: MIT Press, 1981),
1–65.

5. Emergency Planning and Community Right-to-Know Act of 1986, Pub. L.
No. 99–499, 100 Stat. 1729 (1988).

6. The AIDS brochure was mailed to 107 million households between May
26 and June 15, 1988, at an estimated cost of $17 million. See *The Washington
Post*, 15 May 1988, 6(B).

7. Christine Russell, "Risk vs. Reality: How the Public Perceives Health
Hazards," *The Washington Post*, 14 June 1988, 14–18 (Health). Among the scholarly journals paying increased attention to risk communication are *Science, Technology & Human Values* (Summer/Fall 1987) and *Journal of Communication* (Summer
1987).

8. Ronald W. Perry and Joanne M. Nigg, "Emergency Management Strategies for Communicating Hazard Information," *Public Administration Review* 45
(January 1985): 76.

9. John H. Sims and Duane D. Baumann, "Educational Programs and Human Response to Natural Hazards," *Environment and Behavior* 15, no. 2 (March
1983): 183–184.

10. F. Reed Johnson and Ralph A. Luken, "Radon Risk Information and
Voluntary Protection: Evidence from a Natural Experiment," *Risk Analysis* 7, no.
1 (March 1987): 105.

11. Adler and Pittle, 160–161. Although Adler and Pittle do not include cost
figures for the CPSC program, the first two years of the NHTSC program cost
about $6.5 million and the California heart disease effort received about $4 million
in federal grants over five years; see pages 177, 185.

12. Sims and Baumann, 167–168.

13. Larry Christensen and Carlton E. Ruch, "Assessment of Brochures and

Radio and Television Presentations on Hurricane Awareness," *Mass Emergency* 3 (1978): 210–211.

14. Sims and Baumann, 167.

15. Herbert A. Simon, *Administrative Behavior* (New York: Macmillan, 1947).

16. Paul Slovic, "Informing and Educating the Public About Risk," *Risk Analysis* 6, no. 4 (December 1986): 403.

17. Paul Slovic et al., "Regulation of Risk," 263.

18. Ibid., 264. Although public opinion polls indicate that a sizable percentage of Americans regard commercial nuclear power production as a "risky" technology, technical estimates of the level of risk have been subject to considerable debate among both the scientific community and the various interest groups taking pro- and anti-nuclear positions. The best-known and perhaps most controversial estimate of nuclear power risk was commissioned by the Atomic Energy Commission and released in 1975. The Reactor Safety Study, also known as the Rasmussen report, established numerical estimates of the probability of reactor accidents. Directed by Dr. Norman Rasmussen of the Massachusetts Institute of Technology, the study concluded that the probability of a major reactor accident was about one in 20,000 per reactor-year. Although the study was used by the AEC, the NRC, and the nuclear industry to reassure the public that reactor accidents were highly unlikely, its methodology was discredited by the Union of Concerned Scientists, which characterized the analyses as being based on "thousands of potentially arbitrary and largely unverified assumptions," and by the American Physical Society. In January 1979, the Nuclear Regulatory Commission officially disavowed the validity of the study. Regardless of how the level of risk is quantified, the fact that the federal government requires that nuclear plant owner/operators take measures to protect the public from the effects of plant operations, including accidents, confirms that commercial nuclear power production is a "risky" technology. See *Reactor Safety Study: An Assessment of Accident Risks in U.S. Commercial Nuclear Power Plants* (Washington, D.C.: U.S. Nuclear Regulatory Commission, 1975). The Union of Concerned Scientists' critique of the study is contained in *The Risks of Nuclear Power Reactors: A Review of the NRC Reactor Safety Study* WASH–1400 (NUREG–75/014) (Cambridge: Union of Concerned Scientists, 1977).

19. Slovic, "Informing and Educating the Public About Risk," 408.

20. Good summaries of research on how heuristics influence risk assessments made by the public can be found in Conn and Feimer, 41–43; Slovic et al., "Regulation of Risk," 245–248; and Paul Slovic, Baruch Fischhoff, and Sarah Lichtenstein, "Facts and Fears: Understanding Perceived Risk," in *Societal Risk Assessment: How Safe is Safe Enough?* eds. Richard C. Schwing and Walter A. Albers, Jr. (New York: Plenum Press, 1980), 183–189.

21. Slovic et al., "Regulation of Risk," 248.

22. Johnson and Luken, 105.

23. Adler and Pittle, 160–161.

24. Harry Otway and Kerry Thomas, "Reflections on Risk Perception and Policy," *Risk Analysis* 2, no. 2 (1982): 69.

25. Ibid., 70.

26. Ibid., 69.

27. Alonzo Plough and Sheldon Krimsky, "The Emergence of Risk Com-

munication Studies: Social and Political Context," *Science, Technology & Human Values* 12, nos. 3–4 (Summer/Fall 1987): 6.

28. Ibid., 7.

29. Philip Selznick, "Foundations of the Theory of Organizations," *American Sociological Review* 18, no. 1 (February 1948): 25–35.

30. John W. Meyer and Brian Rowan, "Institutionalized Organizations: Formal Structure as Myth and Ceremony," *American Journal of Sociology* 83, no. 2 (September 1977): 340–363. For further refinement of the theory, see John W. Meyer, W. Richard Scott, and Terrence E. Deal, "Explaining the Structure of Educational Organizations," in *Organization and Human Services*, ed. Herman D. Stein (Philadelphia: Temple University Press, 1981), 151–179.

31. Gareth Morgan, *Images of Organizations* (Beverly Hills: Sage Publications, 1986), 134–135.

32. Meyer and Rowan, 350.

33. Perry and Nigg, 73.

34. Todd R. La Porte and Paula M. Consolini, "Theoretical and Operational Challenges of 'High Reliability Organizations': Air Traffic Control and Aircraft Carriers," Paper prepared for delivery at the 1988 Annual Meeting of the American Political Science Association, Washington, DC, 1–4 September 1988, 3.

35. Todd R. La Porte, "On the Design and Management of Nearly Error-Free Organizational Control Systems," in *Accident at Three Mile Island: The Human Dimensions*, ed. David L. Sills, C. P. Wolf, and Vivien B. Shelanski (Boulder, Colo.: Westview Press, 1982), 196.

36. Raphael G. Kasper, "Perceptions of Risk and Their Effects on Decision Making," in *Societal Risk Assessment: How Safe is Safe Enough?*, ed. Richard C. Schwing and Walter A. Albers, Jr. (New York: Plenum Press, 1980), 77.

37. Plough and Krimsky, 8.

38. Mary Douglas and Aaron Wildavsky, *Risk and Culture: An Essay on the Selection of Technical and Environmental Dangers* (Berkeley: University of California Press, 1982), 194.

39. Kasper, 75.

40. Slovic, "Informing and Educating the Public About Risk," 405–406. See also Slovic et al., "Regulation of Risk," 250–256.

41. June Fessenden-Raden, Janet M. Fitchen, and Jennifer S. Heath, "Providing Risk Information in Communities: Factors Influencing What Is Heard and Accepted," *Science, Technology & Human Values* 12, nos. 3–4 (Summer/Fall 1987): 98.

42. Slovic et al., "Regulation of Risk," 259.

43. General Accounting Office, *Nuclear Regulation: Public Knowledge of Radiological Emergency Procedures* (Washington, D.C.: GAO, 1987), 4.

44. Richard T. Sylves, "Nuclear Power Plants and Emergency Planning: An Intergovernmental Nightmare," *Public Administration Review* 44, no. 5 (September/October 1984): 394.

45. Ibid., 394–395.

46. President's Commission on the Accident at Three Mile Island, *The Need For Change: The Legacy Of TMI* (Washington, D.C.: GPO, 1979), 38–42; Mitchell Rogovin and George T. Frampton, Jr., *Three Mile Island: A Report to the Commissioners and to the Public* (Washington, D.C.: GPO, 1980), 1:129–137; and Congress,

House, Subcommittee of the Committee on Government Operations, *Emergency Planning Around U.S. Nuclear Powerplants: Nuclear Regulatory Commission Oversight*, 96th Cong., 1st Sess., 7, 10, 14 May 1979.

47. *The Need For Change: The Legacy Of TMI*, 39.

48. Sylves, "Nuclear Power Plants and Emergency Planning," 396. FEMA was created in 1979 under the Carter administration's Presidential Reorganization Plan No. 3, which was implemented by Executive Orders 12127 and 12148. FEMA replaced the Federal Disaster Assistance Administration within the Department of Housing and Urban Development as the agency responsible for national disaster relief, preparedness, and civil defense, and was also given responsibility for developing governmental policies to deal with earthquake hazards, dam safety, and natural disaster warning systems, and terrorist incidents. On December 7, 1979, President Carter directed FEMA to take the lead role in state and local emergency planning and preparedness activities associated with commercial nuclear power plants. See Alvin H. Mushkatel and Louis F. Weschler, "Emergency Management and the Intergovernmental System," *Public Administration Review* 45 (January 1985): 49–50. See also 44 C.F.R. § 350.3 (1987).

49. Nuclear Regulatory Commission, Emergency Plans, 10 C.F.R. § 50.47 (1988), and Federal Emergency Management Agency, Review and Approval of State and Local Radiological Emergency Plans and Preparedness, 44 C.F.R. § 350 (1987).

50. General Accounting Office, *Further Actions Needed to Improve Emergency Preparedness Around Nuclear Powerplants* (Washington, D.C.: GAO, 1984), 7. This issue was addressed in a June 1989 opinion of the United States Court of Appeals for the First Circuit in a case regarding the Pilgrim Nuclear Power Plant in Massachusetts. The Court ruled that the NRC, and not FEMA, has ultimate authority over the regulation of commercial nuclear power plants, including the determination of the adequacy of off-site emergency planning. The NRC is obliged to consider FEMA's findings and determinations regarding the adequacy of off-site emergency preparedness, but is not required to accept FEMA's determinations. See *Commonwealth of Massachusetts v. United States Nuclear Regulatory Commission*, 878 F.2d 1516 (1st Cir. 1989).

51. *Nuclear Regulation: Public Knowledge of Radiological Emergency Procedures*, 3–4.

52. Federal Emergency Management Agency, *Criteria for Preparation and Evaluation of Radiological Emergency Response Plans and Preparedness in Support of Nuclear Power Plants*, NUREG–0654, FEMA-REP–1, Rev. 1 (Washington, D.C.: GPO, 1980). Hereafter referred to as NUREG–0654. Page references correspond to printed copy available from the GPO.

53. *Nuclear Regulation: Public Knowledge of Radiological Emergency Procedures*, 4.

54. *The Need For Change: The Legacy Of TMI*, 77.

55. NUREG–0654, 49–51.

56. Philip L. Rutledge, "An Assessment of the Public Education Program for Nuclear Power Plant Emergencies" (Master's thesis, University of North Carolina, Greensboro, 1986), 38–40. Rutledge's study provided a good starting point for my examination of nuclear risk communication, although he limited his analysis to one nuclear plant and the promotional rhetoric, but not the images, contained in utility nuclear risk communication materials.

57. Under NUREG–0654, the physical means to effectively alert the public to a radiological emergency must be designed to communicate an alert signal and an informational message throughout the EPZ within fifteen minutes. In its criteria for evaluating alert and notification systems, FEMA suggests that fixed sirens be used to transit the alert signal, supplemented in remote areas with mobile sirens and tone alert radios. See Federal Emergency Management Agency, *Guide for the Evaluation of Alert and Notification Systems for Nuclear Power Plants*, FEMA-REP–10 (Washington, D.C.: Federal Emergency Management Agency, 1985), E–6–15.

58. James H. Johnson, Jr., and Donald J. Zeigler, "Distinguishing Human Responses to Radiological Emergencies," *Economic Geography* 59, no. 4 (October 1983): 390; and Peter S. Houts, Paul D. Cleary, and Teh-Wei Hu, *The Three Mile Island Crisis: Psychological, Social, and Economic Impacts on the Surrounding Population* (University Park: Pennsylvania State University Press, 1988), 19.

59. Donald J. Zeigler, Stanley D. Brunn, and James H. Johnson, Jr., "Evacuation From a Nuclear Technological Disaster," *The Geographical Review* 71, no. 1 (January 1981): 1–16; Johnson and Zeigler, 399; Houts et al., 14.

60. Houts et al., 14; Johnson and Zeigler, 389.

61. Susan L. Cutter, "Emergency Preparedness and Planning for Nuclear Power Plant Accidents," *Applied Geography* 4 (1984): 240; Johnson and Zeigler, 399; Perry and Nigg, 72.

62. *Nuclear Regulation: Public Knowledge of Radiological Emergency Procedures*, 7.

63. Ibid., 5–7.

64. Federal Emergency Management Agency, *A Guide to Preparing Emergency Public Information Materials*, FEMA REP–11, research and preparation by Education & Training Associates, Inc., Narragansett, R.I. (Washington, D.C.: FEMA, 1985), 3.

65. Ibid., 4.

66. Ibid., 3.

67. *Nuclear Regulation: Public Knowledge of Radiological Emergency Procedures*, 8.

68. Ibid., 4–5. Some critics contend that OMB uses the Paperwork Reduction Act to limit the collection of information by government agencies that might lead to new legislation or regulations. See "Watching the Watchdogs: How the OMB Helps Shape Federal Regulations," *Newsweek*, 20 February 1989, 34.

69. Jim J. Tozzi, deputy administrator, Office of Information and Regulatory Affairs, Office of Management and Budget, LS to Louis O. Giuffrida, director, Federal Emergency Management Agency, 13 July 1981, author's files.

70. Julius W. Becton, Jr., director, Federal Emergency Management Agency, signed letter to The Honorable Jack Brooks, chairman, House Committee on Governmental Operations, 11 August 1987, author's files.

71. Judy B. Rosener and Sallie C. Russell, "Cows, Sirens, Iodine, and Public Education about the Risks of Nuclear Power Plants," *Science, Technology, & Human Values* 12 (Summer-Fall 1987): 114.

72. Ibid.

73. Rutledge, 30.

74. Ibid., 84.

75. Ibid., 91–92.

76. Ibid., 92.

77. Ibid.

78. Scott M. Cutlip, Allen H. Center, and Glen M. Broom, *Effective Public Relations*, 6th ed. (Englewood Cliffs, N.J.: Prentice-Hall, 1985), 264.

79. Spencer R. Weart, *Nuclear Fear: A History of Images* (Cambridge: Harvard University Press, 1988), 421.

80. The nation's oldest operating commercial nuclear plant began operation in 1961 at Rowe, Mass. See U.S. Council for Energy Awareness, *Electricity from Nuclear Energy*, 1989 ed. (Washington, D.C.: USCEA, 1989), 16. Of the seventy-eight nuclear plant operating licenses granted by the NRC between 1959 and 1979, nearly 75 percent were issued in the decade of the 1970s. See John L. Campbell, *Collapse of an Industry: Nuclear Power and the Contradictions of U.S. Policy* (Ithaca, N.Y.: Cornell University Press, 1988), 41.

81. *The New York Times*, 30 November 1988, 1.

82. Some have argued that accidents are inevitable, even "normal," in complex technological systems. See, e.g., Charles Perrow, *Normal Accidents: Living With High-Risk Technologies* (New York: Basic Books, 1984).

83. Edmond Faltermayer, "Taking Fear Out of Nuclear Power," *Fortune*, 1 August 1988, 105. See also Matthew L. Wald, "The Nuclear Industry Tries Again," *The New York Times*, 26 November 1989), 1(F).

84. See, e.g., Richard Myers, "The Gathering Storm," *Nuclear Industry* (second quarter 1989), 6–7.

85. President, Executive Order 12657, "Federal Emergency Management Agency Assistance in Emergency Preparedness Planning at Commercial Nuclear Power Plants," 53 Fed. Reg. 47,513 (1988). FEMA published an interim rule to implement the president's order on February 28, 1989. See Commercial Nuclear Power Plants; Emergency Preparedness Planning, 54 Fed. Reg. 8512 (1988) (to be codified at 44 C.F.R. § 352).

86. *The New York Times*, 20 November 1988, 1.

87. On November 13, 1989, the NRC's Atomic Safety and Licensing Board unanimously ruled that emergency evacuation and shelter plans for communities around the Seabrook plant were adequate. The plans were developed by FEMA under the president's executive order after Massachusetts state officials refused to cooperate in the emergency planning process (a portion of the plant's EPZ lies within Massachusetts). The plant received its full power license on March 1, 1990. See *The Washington Post*, 14 November 1989, 14(A).

88. As of June 23, 1989, there were 112 commercial reactors with operating licenses in the United States. See U.S. Council for Energy Awareness, "Reactor Information Report," Energy Data press release, Washington, D.C., 23 June 1989.

Chapter Two

The Nuclear Ethic

It has been observed that "those who control the discourse on risk will most likely control the political battles as well."[1] If, indeed, social, political, and cultural factors have shaped modern discourse about risks associated with living around commercial nuclear power plants, a study that examines these factors is long overdue. This approach to nuclear risk communication is particularly appropriate given the rich and diverse body of information compiled about the history of commercial nuclear power development—information that frequently focuses on the complex relationships among Congress, the regulatory agencies, the nuclear industry, and the owner/operators of America's commercial nuclear power plants.

If risk messages often have symbolic meanings for those individuals and organizations that communicate information about risk, an examination of the historic discourse about atomic energy that took place during the development of America's nuclear power industry may help illuminate the hidden symbolic messages that exist within nuclear risk communication programs today—messages that may be *counterproductive* to regulatory goals for communicating such information. On another level, the history of nuclear power, and particularly an examination of how it was introduced into America's cultural consciousness, may yield valuable insights into the attitudes that affect how the message senders and receivers perceive nuclear plant risks. These attitudes have serious implications for the manner in which nuclear plant risk information is presently being communicated to the public.

Some researchers believe that the concerns many Americans have about the risks of nuclear power can be found in the social history of its development. Christoph Hohenemser, Roger Kasperson, and Robert Kates argue that modern attitudes about the atom rest in part in the heritage of atomic power as a weapon of terrible destruction:

Throughout its 30–year history, nuclear power has inspired some of the major hopes and fears of mankind. While it is difficult to describe this relationship except in terms of influence or anecdote, to ignore the social history of nuclear power is to misunderstand its present predicament. Many new technologies are born in wartime efforts. None have [sic] come to symbolize the destructiveness of war as has the atomic bomb. For better or worse, nuclear power was for many years tied to and overshadowed by the course of military developments.[2]

If America's cultural consciousness was first introduced to the destructive potential of the atom through news reports of the devastation of Hiroshima and Nagasaki, it seems incongruous that post-war America could begin construction of its first commercial nuclear power plant a mere decade after atomic bombs fell on Japan. Yet, a Gallup poll conducted one month after the war ended found that 47 percent of Americans surveyed believed that atomic energy would be developed within the next decade to supply power for industry, with only 19 percent saying it would not. By 1956, 66 percent of Americans surveyed by the Gallup organization believed that industries in their state would be using atomic energy in the next decade, and another survey found that 64 percent of Americans supported the generation of electricity from atomic energy, with only 6 percent opposed.[3]

Why was the atom so quickly transformed from a weapon of destruction to an instrument of progress in the minds of a majority of Americans? The answer goes to the very heart of the complex cultural relationship that we have had with atomic energy, a relationship that must be understood before present efforts to communicate nuclear risk information can be adequately assessed.

The rhetoric and images of nuclear risk communication have been heavily influenced by three institutions that have had a significant stake in the success of nuclear power—science, industry, and government. The combined efforts of these three to develop atomic energy as a positive force for humankind has created what I call a "nuclear ethic" that informs the rhetoric of nuclear risk communication today. The nuclear ethic puts its faith in the abilities of scientists and engineers to control the forces of the atom for positive rather than destructive ends. The roots of the ethic can be found in the atomic euphoria of the late nineteenth and early twentieth centuries that characterized early scientific discoveries about the nature and structure of the atom, a euphoria that lasted until the mid–1950s. As a result of the enthusiasm generated in the popular press, atomic scientists were seen as twentieth-century manifestations of the ancient alchemists; however, these "new alchemists" were not concerned with transmuting lead into gold but with unlocking and controlling the secrets of the atom.

The rhetoric of this period is significant in that it established within the culture, and particularly with those who would direct atomic development after the war, an image of the atomic scientist as a "magician-technician" who could transmute the destructive potential of the atom into an energy source that would benefit humankind. This view fitted in well with the already well-established idea within Western culture of science having power over nature, an idea that could easily be transferred to the engineers and technicians who designed and operated commercial nuclear power plants, and ultimately to the plants themselves. Thus nuclear power plants inherited from atomic scientists a symbolic legacy of having the power to release unlimited energy for the good of humankind. One might think of them as "magic castles of technology," a myth that, though shaken in the past decade or so by accidents, still functions as a powerful symbol within the culture and influences the tone and substance of nuclear risk communication today.

I demonstrate in this chapter that the values associated with the nuclear ethic were particularly appealing to scientists following World War II because most were feeling a deep sense of guilt over their contribution to the development of atomic weapons. That guilt provided an impetus to find something "positive" in post-war military research programs that could utilize the forces of the atom. When it became apparent to scientists such as Robert Oppenheimer, the "father" of the atomic bomb, that controlled atomic fission could be used to produce electricity to heat homes and run factories, the reactor became a powerful symbol of positive development of the atom. Both government and industry would rhetorically support that symbol throughout atomic power's commercial development phase of the 1950s and 1960s when both institutions used their considerable marketing resources to "sell" atomic power to electric utility systems at home and abroad. Although the economic and safety problems of the 1970s, capped by the accident at Three Mile Island, forced government and industry to re-evaluate their respective roles in nuclear development, the nuclear ethic has continued to exert an influence over the operation of nuclear power plants. This study examines how that influence has found its way into nuclear risk communication and functions to emphasize certain values about nuclear power at the expense of public safety.

ATOMIC ENERGY AND ALCHEMY

For many years prior to the development of the atom bomb, atomic energy had been a topic of discussion in both literature and the popular media. Led by the scientific community, the discussion was generally positive and hopeful, and pre-war rhetoric was filled with predictions about the atom's potential to improve people's lives. In their interesting discussion of how the "language" of nuclear power has helped shape political arguments over its place in American life, Stephen Hilgartner, Richard C. Bell, and Rory O'Connor note that the 1930s were filled with optimistic predictions about the development of atomic energy:

The discovery of X-rays and radium at the end of the nineteenth century brought forth visions of a technological *Garden of Eden*. The *philosopher's stone* and the *elixir of life* had been found at last. The discovery of nuclear fission in 1938 unleashed a torrent of similar imagery: nuclear-powered planes and automobiles would whisk us effortlessly around the globe, while unlimited nuclear electricity powered underground cities, farms, and factories.[4]

The references to atomic energy as the "philosopher's stone" and the "elixir of life" make an important rhetorical connection between the atomic scientist and the alchemist, a connection that was maintained throughout the first half of the twentieth century in the popular media and by the scientists themselves. Although with the passage of time we remember alchemists as charlatans who swindled people into believing they could transmute tin and lead into silver and gold, alchemy was a complex network incorporating religious, philosophical, and mystical ideas that sought to uncover the laws of nature, much like modern science. Alchemy existed in ancient China and India, but its main tradition emerged in Egypt about 100 A.D. It was practiced by the Greeks and enthusiastically adopted by the Arabs. When Arabic texts were translated into Latin after 1100, alchemy spread through western Europe, reaching its peak between the fourteenth and seventeenth centuries before the emergence of the scientific method began to dim the alchemist's star.[5]

In his account of how modern chemistry developed from alchemy, John Read acknowledges the broader role for alchemy, noting that it was a "philosophical system which aimed at penetrating and harmonising the mysteries of creation and life" and that transmutation of matter "was merely an incidental aim of alchemy, designed to afford proof on the material plane of its wider tenets, in particular that of the essential unity of all things."[6] According to Read, the search among alchemists for the philosopher's stone and the elixir of life is "the most enduring and romantic epic to be found in the whole history of science."[7] Although the guiding principles of alchemy were subjected to widely varing interpretations, it was generally assumed that the philosopher's stone functioned as a powerful transmuting agent or catalyst that was capable of curing "diseases" in the base metals so that they would be changed into the "noble" metals, silver and gold. Because the alchemist believed in the unity of all matter "it followed that such an agent should also be effective in healing the infirmities of man and prolonging his life. In this guise the Philosopher's Stone was regarded as the perfect medicine of man, under the name of the *Elixir Vitae*, or Elixir of Life."[8] Whereas descriptions of the physical processes required to produce the philosopher's stone and the elixir are both numerous and difficult to untangle, most were based on bringing together various elements in a hermetically sealed and heated glass vessel, known variously as the Vase of Hermes, the Vase of the Philosophers, or the Philosopher's Egg, where they were combined in the vessel with a liquid medium called either the Hermetic Stream, "philosophical water," or "heavy water."[9]

As Brian Easlea points out, early twentieth-century scientists were well aware of their alchemical legacy as they struggled to change the atomic structure of the elements:

In the very first years of the twentieth century the principal investigators of radioactivity saw themselves as taking the path that, in their eyes, had been so actively pursued by alchemists and natural magicians but which had been abandoned by the new philosophers as impossible; they were taking none other than the path leading to the discovery of the philosopher's stone and from thence to the elixir of life.[10]

For the modern scientist, transmutation of the elements would produce not silver or gold, but limitless energy, the modern-day elixir of life. In a widely read book published in 1908, Nobel prize-winning chemist Frederick Soddy declared that the energy derived from the transmutation of the atom would "make the whole world one smiling Garden of Eden."[11] Transmutation was but one of several comparisons made between alchemy and the new atomic science. The alchemist's hermetic vessel, which relied on tremendous heat to create the elixir of life, closely resembled in function the scientists' conception of the atomic reactor. "The material aim of the alchemists, the transmutation of metals, has now been realized by science, and the alchemical vessel is the uranium pile," wrote F. Sherwood Taylor, director of the London Science Museum, in 1949.[12] The "heavy water" used by alchemists as a medium for the creation of the elixir of life had its twentieth-century equivalent in deuterium, an isotope of hydrogen useful in sustaining nuclear chain reactions and termed "heavy water" by scientists because it weighed twice as much as hydrogen.[13] Massachusetts Institute of Technology President Karl Taylor Compton hammered home the comparison between alchemy and atomic science in a lengthy 1933 article:

Where have we left the alchemist? We left him dead, killed by the chemist who had destroyed his hopes of effecting the transmutation of elements. But now the physicist has brought him to life again, with renewed vigor and enthusiasm. For if the atomic nucleus is a structure of electrons and protons, it should be possible to break up this structure or to add to it, and thus to change one chemical element into another. The agencies are no longer earth, water, air, and fire, but electricity and probably electrical particles shot with tremendous speeds into nuclei. The goal is not gold or silver, but energy. And with the alchemist, who is a practical man trying to get something, is working the physicist, who is not an impractical man, trying to learn something. In fact they are one and the same man.[14]

The image became part of the scientific culture in 1937 when Ernest Rutherford, the Nobel prize-winning British physicist who expressed concern in 1902 about being compared with alchemists, named his book on atomic science *The Newer Alchemy*.[15]

By comparing themselves with alchemists, the early atomic scientists inherited an image of possessing "magical" power to control forces that the layperson could not understand. Alchemy, according to Read, was "a vast network in which the sparse strands of rudimentary chemistry were interwoven with threads derived from ancient and later religions, folklore, mythology, astrology, magic, mysticism, philosophy, theosophy, and other wide fields of human imagination and experience."[16] Alchemists distanced themselves from the layperson by protecting their secrets with obscure language and symbolic drawings, just as the work of the atomic scientist was shielded from public view at first by technical language and mathematics and later by the overwhelming secrecy of the Manhattan Project. "Just as the Vessel itself was hermetically sealed," writes Read, "so was everything pertaining to it guarded by the 'Sons of Hermes' as a sealed body of knowledge and ritual, sacred to these priests of 'the Divine Art.' "[17]

Alchemists generally protected their secrets not out of selfish motivations, but because they feared the dangers of placing such great power in the hands of those not properly trained to receive it. This idea was carried into the twentieth century through the medium of popular fiction and film, as many of the public prior to World War II were introduced to atomic energy by stories and movies that depicted scientists as "masters" of secrets locked inside the atom who could use their magic for either good or evil ends. "Anyone who could read a comic book or see a Saturday movie serial," notes Weart, "knew that vast amounts of energy were locked within atoms—energy somehow connected with the transmutation of elements, energy somehow connected with radiation, energy that might possibly be released someday for great benefit or destruction."[18]

Throughout its history, magical allusions have been used to characterize developments in atomic science. Easlea notes that as early as 1893, scientists were depicted as modern-day magicians, and that by 1898 the president of the British Association for the Advancement of Science was predicting that the energy locked inside the atom awaited only "the magic wand of science" to be set free.[19] By the 1930s, the atom was often described in the popular media as a "mysterious" force that scientists were trying to both "control" and "unleash." For example, a 1933 commentary from *The New York Times* talked of the future "less than a century away" in which the world would be "transformed by the atomic engineer ... at last the nucleus of the atom can be made to emit rays of energy by an instrument which man has invented and over which he has a crude control."[20]

The image of scientist as alchemist or magician who could use the atom as a magic wand to transform and improve daily life endured into the 1950s. As Hilgartner et al. point out, one of the image's more memorable representations occurred with the publication of the 1956 book *Our Friend the ATOM*, written by Heinz Haber and transformed by Walt Disney Productions into an animated cartoon version that was shown in movie theatres and on television. The story line was based on the legend of the genie and the bottle, with atomic energy personified as the wish-granting genie and the atomic scientist as the fisherman who first fears and then controls the genie.[21] The government capitalized on the power of the image when President Eisenhower used what *Life* magazine described as a "radioactive wand" to symbolically begin construction of the nation's first commercial nuclear power reactor at Shippingport, Pennsylvania, on Labor Day 1954.[22] In a speech to the National Association of Science Writers nine days later, Atomic Energy Commission Chairman Lewis Strauss used an alchemical allusion to describe the "new" magic of atomic power—the production of energy so inexpensive that it would not need to be metered, an image that would come back to haunt nuclear energy in the decade of the 1970s:

Transmutation of the elements—unlimited power... these and a host of other results all in fifteen short years. It is not too much to expect that our children will enjoy in their homes electrical energy too cheap to meter, will know of great periodic regional famines in the world only as matters of history, will travel effortlessly over the seas and under them and through the air with a minimum of danger and at great speeds, and will experience a life span far longer than ours.... This is the forecast for an age of peace.[23]

Although the atomic euphoria was generally confined to writers in the popular press throughout the early part of the twentieth century, some scientists were also caught up in the excitement. One of the most enthusiastic scientific spokesmen for atomic development during this period was R. M. Langer of the California Institute of Technology. Langer painted a bright picture of an atomic future in which scientists would

hand over the magical secrets of the atom to engineers for practical
application in everyday life:

We are about to enter a period of unparalleled richness and opportunities for
all. Privilege and class distinctions and the other sources of social uneasiness
and bitterness will become relics because things that make up the good life will
be so abundant and inexpensive. War itself will become obsolete because of the
disappearance of those economic stresses that immemorially have caused it.
Industrious, powerful nations and clever, aggressive races can win at peace far
more than ever could be won at war. This is not visionary. The foundations of
the happy era have already been laid. The driving force is within our grasp.
Reality is about to be handed from the scientists in their laboratories to the
engineers in their factories for application to your daily life. It is a new form of
power—atomic power. It will change our lives in a thousand ways. . . . Transportation anywhere on, over or beyond the earth will be at your personal touch.
The face of the earth will be changed—with rails, houses, and roads gone. Your
social and cultural and recreational life will have infinite variety. Everything—
your clothes, food, health—will be touched by the wand.[24]

   The popular press shared Langer's vision of a future positively shaped
by atomic power. *Time* magazine reported in 1940 that "the old dream
of sending a ship around the world on the energy in a pint of atoms . . .
seemed much closer than before,"[25] and John J. O'Neill noted in *Harper's
Magazine* that developments in atomic research " . . . may open a new
era for civilization." Looking at the impact of atomic energy on the
economy, O'Neill forecast that coal mining would cease as an industry
and oil would be exclusively devoted to chemical production. Railroads,
no longer required to ship large quantities of coal for power production,
would be hard hit by the atomic revolution, and electric energy production would be transformed. O'Neill also noted the beneficial uses of
atomic energy in medicine, particularly in the treatment of cancer, but
cautioned that the effect of atomic energy on the human body would
need to receive a "great deal of attention" because of the tendency of
scientists working with the new force to have low white cell counts.[26]
   With the exception of a flurry of interest in radium poisoning in the
late 1920s, rarely were the health risks associated with atomic energy
reported in the popular media prior to World War II, though tales of
radioactive "monsters" and "mad" atomic scientists did become popular
subject matter for pulp science fiction magazines and motion pictures.[27]
If dangers associated with the atom were mentioned in the media, they
were generally confined to descriptions of the heavy metal or water
shielding that scientists used to protect them from the "rays" produced
by the new force. A 1938 article in *Popular Mechanics* described work in
the radiation laboratory by the University of California at Berkeley and
pointed out that overexposure to the "rays" could be lethal, but the

article's focus was on the benefits of the rays in the treatment of cancer and other diseases.[28] Langer also briefly mentioned in his *Collier's* article that atomic energy rays were "deadly in character" and could be used as a weapon, but concluded that such a weapon "would be effective only for a few yards."[29]

ATOMIC SCIENTISTS EMERGE INTO SPOTLIGHT

Allusions to the atom as a "mysterious" force and the atomic scientist as the alchemist or magician who could produce the magic conveyed a symbolic image to the American public of the scientist as one who could, for the good of civilization, *control* the forces locked inside the atom. Already well established in the popular media before Pearl Harbor, the image was further enhanced by revelation of the contributions of the Manhattan Project scientists to the development of the bomb that ended World War II. "For some of the scientists," notes Peter Goodchild, "there were medals and letters of merit and, now that their secret was out, men who, for the duration of the war, had been thought by friends and relatives to have ducked out of the war effort, found themselves treated as heroes."[30] As nuclear power critic Daniel Ford points out, scientists, and particularly atomic scientists, emerged after World War II as "the high priests of a state religion that promised social progress by means of made-to-order technological advances."[31]

The successful completion of the Manhattan Project and the public disclosure of the role that atomic scientists had played in winning the war brought many scientists out of the laboratory and into the glare of the public spotlight for the first time. They became the country's first technical "experts" on atomic energy, and their advice was sought at the highest levels of government concerning what should be done with the new and terrible source of energy. As David E. Lilienthal observed several years after completing his term as the first chairman of the Atomic Energy Commission (AEC), the atomic scientist immediately after the war assumed a stature that was larger than life:

The Atom became all-important, and so therefore did the men who had called it into being, the atomic scientists. These men, whose skills lay in the handling of abstract concepts and inanimate physical materials, were suddenly catapulted into the very center of human affairs. Military men, politicians, business leaders, teachers—all categories of men who dealt with the more ornery and unpredictable affairs of human beings—were dwarfed by comparison. The scientist seemed to take on some of the attributes of his world-shaking creation; there was, in the public mind, something unearthly, something superhuman, something uncanny about him.[32]

But for many post-World War II atomic scientists, enjoyment of their celebrity status was tempered by recognition of their responsibility for unleashing forces powerful enough to destroy the world. V-J Day, as Goodchild points out, brought a sense of relief to the Los Alamos scientists who had designed the first bomb, but also feelings of guilt about what they had created:

There were those who, even on that jubilant evening [of VJ Day], felt that they were there celebrating a hollow victory. For years most of the men at Los Alamos had been caught up in the excitement of the technical challenge and had given so little thought to the consequences of their action. Their celebration marked the profound relief that a monumental task had been achieved, but at the same time there was a realisation of the awfulness of what they had done.[33]

The feelings of "awfulness" were exacerbated for some scientists because they had continued to develop the bomb after Germany, the foe thought most likely to produce atomic weapons, surrendered in May 1945. Richard Feynman, a physicist who would win the Nobel prize, was one of a number of scientists who joined the project because he believed the Germans were capable of producing atomic weapons: "What I did immorally was not to remember the reason why I was doing it. So when the reason changed, which was that Germany was defeated, not a single thought came to my mind that it meant I should reconsider why I was continuing to do this. I simply didn't think."[34] The realization that the blind search for scientific "truth" had unlocked the most destructive force known to humankind caused many atomic scientists to actively call for civilian control of atomic energy and an acceleration of the development of peaceful uses of the atom. "Science, which had theretofore been considered a progressive force for good, had revealed its essential neutrality and consequent potential for evil," observes Diane Carter Maleson. "The magnitude of the destructive force of the atom virtually mandated a showing that this force was also capable of conferring exceptional benefits upon mankind."[35]

A key figure in the scientist's search for atomic atonement was Robert Oppenheimer, who directed the special weapons laboratory at Los Alamos, New Mexico, where the first bombs were designed and assembled. Oppenheimer emerged after the war as a figure of popular acclaim with both the public and the scientific community for his accomplishments at Los Alamos and as an adviser of high regard among government policymakers who were setting the foundation of American nuclear policy.[36] From 1945 to 1954, according to James W. Kunetka, "Oppenheimer was one of the most important and influential consultants to the United States Government on matters of atomic energy."[37] During this period Oppenheimer served on several government committees and panels that helped develop post-war policy on atomic energy. He also contributed to the U.S. effort to establish international controls on atomic energy through the United Nations. His government career ended in 1954 when he lost his AEC security clearance following a hearing into his pre-war association with leftwing groups and his alleged activities to oppose development of the hydrogen bomb. He spent the final years of his life as director of the Institute of Advanced Studies at Princeton University. Ironically, the AEC gave Oppenheimer its Enrico Fermi award in 1963 for his contributions to the development of atomic energy. He died of cancer in 1967 at age sixty-two.

Although his final years as a government adviser were tainted by suspicion and doubt, Oppenheimer was representative of many scientists who provided a "bridge" between the atomic euphoria of the late nineteenth and early twentieth centuries and the period of intense industrial interest in atomic power that began in the 1950s. Oppenheimer the realist recognized that weapons development would always be associated with atomic energy, but he worked tirelessly after World War II to promote peacetime use of the atom through a combination of international controls, fundamental atomic research, and development of an AEC organization capable of creating a realistic atomic reactor development program. More importantly, Oppenheimer was the first in a generation of scientists-statesmen whose endorsement of commercial atomic power would lend scientific credibility to the nuclear ethic. By helping to effect the transformation of atomic energy from a weapon of war into a resource with the potential to produce cheap and abundant energy, Oppenheimer indeed became a "new alchemist."

Oppenheimer, like many Manhattan Project scientists, was torn between his feelings of guilt over the role science has played in the creation of the atomic bomb and the conviction that the pursuit of "pure" scientific research would ultimately produce societal good. "The designing and developing of a scientifically remarkable atomic weapon was a project that had interested and excited Oppenheimer as a scientist," observes Kunetka, "but the violent and devastating implications of the weapon presented another matter altogether. It was, perhaps, a situation that greatly complicated the scientist's life."[38] At the end of the war, he is quoted by Goodchild as saying, "In some sort of crude sense, which no vulgarity, no humour, no overstatement can quite extinguish, the physicists have known sin, and this is a knowledge which they cannot use." In 1948 he would tell President Truman, "Mr. President, I have blood on my hands."[39]

Oppenheimer was aware of the implications of his work while he labored on developing the bomb in the New Mexico desert, according to his colleague, Victor F. Weisskopf:

Long before the great test [of the first bomb at Alamogordo], the political and moral implications of the bomb were in the foreground of interest. Oppenheimer and [Niels] Bohr started many discussions about the dangers of atomic weapons and about ways and means of turning this new discovery into a constructive force for peace. All of us hoped that this great force of destruction might open the eyes of the world to the futility of war. It was in part Oppie's leadership that led to the formation of groups devoted to these problems and to a number of ideas and plans for an international approach to the exploitation of atomic energy, so that this new force would bring nations together instead of tearing them apart.[40]

But Oppenheimer was also convinced that scientists must be free to pursue their investigations into nature, regardless of what others would do with the knowledge of their discoveries. Speaking to the Association of Los Alamos Scientists in November 1945, he expressed his fear that national security restrictions on scientific exchange of information about the atom threatened the very existence of science:

If you are a scientist you believe that it is good to find out how the world works; that it is good to find out what the realities are; that it is good to turn over to mankind at large the greatest possible power to control the world and to deal with it according to its lights and its values. . . . It is not possible to be a scientist . . . unless you think that it is of the highest value to share your knowledge, to share it with anyone who is interested. It is not possible to be a scientist unless you believe that the knowledge of the world, and the power which this gives, is a thing which is of intrinsic value to humanity, and that you are using it to help in the spread of knowledge, and are willing to take the consequences.[41]

Unlike the ancient alchemists who were reluctant to share their secrets with others, Oppenheimer believed that it was incumbent upon scientists to freely provide information about atomic energy. If the promise of atomic energy would be achieved, the "new alchemists" must function effectively not only in the laboratory but also in the world:

We are not only scientists; we are men, too. We cannot forget our dependence on our fellow men. I mean not only our material dependence, without which no science would be possible, and without which we could not work; I mean also our deep moral dependence, in that the value of science must lie in the world of men, that all our roots lie there. These are the strongest bonds in the world, stronger than those even that bind us to one another, these are the deepest bonds—that bind us to our fellow men.[42]

Oppenheimer had defined what would later become the role of the "new alchemist" as a "scientist-statesman" after the war. In that role, he strongly pushed for peaceful development of atomic power as a means to erase in the public mind the spectre of atomic war. His most influential position in helping determine the course of peaceful development of

atomic power was as chair for five years of the influential AEC General
Advisory Committee.[43]

THE GENERAL ADVISORY COMMITTEE

The Atomic Energy Commission was created in 1946 following a bitter
political debate over whether control of the atom should remain in military hands or be turned over to a civilian administration. Most scientists
pushed hard for civilian control in the hope that future atomic research
would not be hampered by rigid security requirements.[44] They particularly liked the language in a bill introduced by freshman Connecticut
Senator Brien McMahon in December 1945 that loosened security controls over atomic research and forbade atomic weapons research that
was contrary to international agreements. The McMahon bill called for
a civilian commission appointed by the president subject to Senate confirmation that would oversee a complete government monopoly over
the development and use of atomic energy, including the ownership of
materials and production facilities. The debate continued throughout
the spring and summer of 1946 before a compromise bill was signed
into law by President Truman on August 1 as the Atomic Energy Act
of 1946. A significant product of the prolonged debate was the creation
of an eighteen-member congressional Joint Committee on Atomic Energy
(JCAE) to oversee military and civilian development of atomic energy
under the new commission.[45]

The Atomic Energy Act of 1946 directed the AEC to create an advisory
committee " . . . to advise the Commission on materials, production, research and development policies, and other matters."[46] Lilienthal was
President Truman's choice as the first AEC chairman, and he quickly
named Oppenheimer to the General Advisory Committee (GAC). Lilienthal and Oppenheimer had previously served together on an advisory
panel that helped the U.S. State Department develop its proposal to the
UN for international control of atomic energy. In working together to
produce the panel's final report, the two men agreed that the key to
eliminating military use of atomic energy was to increase public understanding of its peaceful applications. Lilienthal shared Oppenheimer's
belief that such a destructive force as the atom had to have a peacetime
use, and he was particularly impressed with Oppenheimer's mental
ability during the advisory panel meetings.[47]

Although not present at the GAC's first meeting in January 1947,
Oppenheimer was elected chair and soon occupied the most influential
position in the country for guiding the post-war development of atomic
power, second only to that of being an AEC commissioner.[48] Although
Oppenheimer recognized the importance of establishing a high priority
on the continued development of nuclear weapons for national defense,

it is clear that he reached that conclusion reluctantly. But Oppenheimer was above all else a realist, and he knew that national security priorities would relegate peacetime development of atomic power to a secondary position behind weapons development. Glenn T. Seaborg, one of his GAC colleagues who would later serve a ten-year term as AEC chairman, recalled that Oppenheimer approached the job fully cognizant of the difficulties ahead. "During those early GAC days Oppie also showed his great desire to foster the peaceful role of the atom," said Seaborg in a 1967 collection of essays written to honor Oppenheimer's memory. "Like most of us he wanted to see the early development of nuclear power. But, also like most of us at that time, he was overly pessimistic about the possibilities of rapid growth in this area."[49]

A major impediment to the peaceful development of atomic power was that the nation's limited supplies of fissionable material were vitally needed for the weapons program. A hope for the future might rest in reactors that would produce more fissionable material than they consumed—the breeders—but many technical difficulties confronted their commercial development.[50] Despite the negative prospects, Oppenheimer urged the GAC in its early meetings to support development of commercial nuclear reactors as a way to help mold public understanding of the peaceful potential of the atom, according to AEC historians Richard G. Hewlett and Francis Duncan:

After lunch, Oppenheimer began to think out loud on the subject. As well as he understood the value of weapons, he could not give reactors a second priority . . . he dwelt on the extraordinary opportunity to transform public understanding of atomic energy from a specter of war into a promise for peace by developing reactors for the production of power. Perhaps with a top priority it might be possible to obtain some power from a reactor in a year or two.[51]

When it was pointed out that the international situation precipitated by the Cold War required an increase in research and development of atomic weapons, Oppenheimer "was reluctant to accept the conclusion that the production of weapons and the development of improved models would be necessary in the postwar world." He tried to make a case for establishing a strong reactor research laboratory at Los Alamos that would have "greater appeal to the exceptional scientist than the development of thermonuclear weapons."[52] But in the end, the advisory committee assigned a high priority to weapons development, and Oppenheimer carried the discouraging report on commercial nuclear power development to the AEC commissioners in 1947.

Although weapons would be the committee's first priority, the GAC definitely determined that atomic reactors should be its second, according to Kunetka. "Reactor research was the key to increased fissionable materials production as well as for a myriad of scientific and technical achievements which might one day include cheap electrical power."[53] The GAC actively supervised a number of small AEC experimental reactor projects, and GAC members frequently visited remote laboratory locations where prototype reactors were being developed.[54] Oppenheimer, notes Seaborg, was particularly interested in how the AEC might support fundamental atomic energy research by universities and small laboratories—research not related to weapons:

During his leadership of the GAC, Oppenheimer spearheaded the move for strong AEC support of fundamental research. In no other era of human history had the world seen such a transfer of theory into application as in the events of the Manhattan Project. Perhaps better than any other person, Oppenheimer, who had overseen so much of this project, saw this transfer take place. And to a man of his depth and philosophical insight the realization of the future implications of fundamental research had a most profound effect. He saw the dawn of a new age of science and knew that the government's relationship to science could never be the same. Therefore, he argued brilliantly in GAC proposals to ensure that the AEC would play a leading role in fundamental nuclear research.[55]

Oppenheimer was unable to convince the GAC to place reactor development on an equal footing with weapons, but he was an effective advocate for peacetime development of the atom. His forceful personality undoubtedly exerted considerable influence over both his GAC colleagues and Lilienthal, who became a strong promoter of atomic energy commercialization after his tenure as AEC chairman.[56] In his journal, Lilienthal repeatedly praises the depth and clarity of Oppenheimer's thinking. For example, Lilienthal recalls that at his first meeting with Oppenheimer in 1946 he was "greatly impressed with his [Oppenheimer's] flash of mind" and considered him "a really *great* teacher" of atomic energy fundamentals [Lilienthal's emphasis].[57] Goodchild quotes Lilienthal on Oppenheimer: "He is worth living a lifetime just to know that mankind has been able to produce such a being. We may have to wait another hundred years for the second one to come off the line."[58] During Senate hearings on the McMahon bill, Lilienthal found Oppenheimer's testimony "brilliant" and made a later observation that Oppenheimer had "superior knowledge" and "special sensitiveness." Describing a one-hour Oppenheimer summation of GAC views on fundamental atomic research before the commissioners in 1947, Lilienthal called the report "as brilliant, lively, and accurate a statement as I believe I have ever heard. He [Oppenheimer] is pure genius. Even these great brains [the GAC] joined in the amazement and delight we all felt with this wonderful piece."[59]

Despite his keen interest in peaceful uses of the atom, Oppenheimer recognized that unrealistic claims about the potential of atomic energy would do more harm than good for future development. He was particularly concerned about public statements on the future of atomic energy made by respected figures of the day that ignored the infantile stage reactor technology development.[60] One such figure was John R. Dunning, director of the division of research at Columbia University, who predicted in 1946 that atomic energy would be used in ships and planes within three to five years, an estimate that the GAC members believed was off by at least a decade.[61] Even the normally cautious Maj. Gen. Leslie R. Groves, director of the Manhattan Project, was swept up in the post-war atomic euphoria, telling an audience that "Reports that limitless energy will be available from a superabundance of power, light and heat, that streamliners will be running across the continent on the atomic energy of a thimbleful of water are entirely within the realm of speculation; in fact, beyond it."[62]

Oppenheimer's solution to the problem of public education was to strongly encourage the AEC commissioners to release a statement that would reflect the "real" prospects for commercial development. But the commissioners were feeling increasing pressure from Congress, the scientific community, American industry, and some foreign governments in 1947 to meet inflated public expectations for commercial nuclear power development, and Lilienthal was afraid that a negative report would put the commercial reactor program further behind weapons development.[63] After negotiation between the AEC and the GAC, a statement was issued that was somewhat more positive in tone than Oppenheimer's original draft, but it indicated that the GAC still did not see any significant role for nuclear power in replacing the world's conventional power sources within the next twenty years.[64]

Although Oppenheimer believed that the public deserved a realistic appraisal of atomic energy development, he also led the GAC to take several concrete steps designed to make the reality of the AEC power reactor program move at least a little closer toward public expectations. Oppenheimer created a reactor development committee composed of representatives from each AEC research laboratory, believing that such a committee could help the commission focus and set priorities in a program that was spread out over a number of different projects.[65] Convinced that the AEC's organizational structure was too decentralized, Oppenheimer and the GAC issued a highly critical report in 1948 that called for the creation of five new staff positions to direct research, weapons, reactors, production, and administration. In Oppenheimer's typical no-nonsense fashion, the report's conclusion pointedly said that the GAC members "despair of progress in the reactor program and see further difficulty even in the areas of weapons and production unless a reorganization takes place."[66] Shortly thereafter, the commission an-

nounced a new organization with most of the major components recommended by the GAC in place.

The most significant step taken by the GAC under Oppenheimer to
further reactor development occurred shortly before the committee issued its negative 1947 statement on the prospects for commercial nuclear
power. In a meeting with the newly formed reactor development group,
the GAC heard a report on the lack of progress in power reactor development. At the same time, the navy and air force were petitioning the
commission to assign some priority to development of atomic power submarines and aircraft. The GAC saw in the navy and air force programs an
opportunity to give the reactor effort some direction, and assigned its
highest priority to the development of an atomic-powered submarine.[67]
That decision provided the spark that would lead first to the development
of the atomic submarine *Nautilus* and ultimately to the construction of the
first civilian nuclear reactor in the United States.

Whereas the GAC continued to help guide the reactor development
program throughout Oppenheimer's five-plus years as chairman, det-
onation of a Soviet atomic device in 1949 would force the committee to
return its attention to weapons, and it stimulated renewed interest by
U.S. leaders in production of the "Super" or hydrogen bomb. Although
Oppenheimer and the GAC recommended against pursuing the Super
for both political and humanitarian reasons, President Truman directed
the AEC in January 1950 to accelerate its development program toward
such a weapon. The outbreak of the Korean War in June further rein-
forced the government's determination to make more destructive atomic
weapons. By this time Oppenheimer was beginning to hear the first
rumblings of a concerted campaign to brand him as a leftwing sympa-
thizer and a security risk, allegations that would culminate in 1954 with
a four-week hearing before the AEC's Personnel Security Board that
produced 3,000 pages of testimony. Although the board's majority report
was contradictory, it recommended that Oppenheimer's security clearance be withdrawn.[68]

GOVERNMENT-INDUSTRY COOPERATION

Oppenheimer's well-publicized difficulties did not dim public credibility of the new alchemists who helped to establish commercialization
of the atomic reactor as a positive value within the nuclear ethic. However, if atomic power was to make a successful transition into American
society after World War II, it would need the support of two powerful
institutions—government and industry. That support came haltingly as
government had to overcome its desire to monopolize the atom's secrets
and industry had to be shown that atomic energy had the potential to

produce profits. But by the mid–1950s, both government and industry had overcome the political and economic problems that had initially blocked atomic development and were cooperating to make atomic power a positive symbol of American technological know-how. That cooperation would become another key component of the nuclear ethic.

The cooperative relationship between government and industry began during the Manhattan Project when several companies worked as government contractors in the bomb development program. Many of these contractors were interested in the commercial potential of atomic power at the end of World War II, but a number of impediments had to be removed before industry would invest the capital necessary to build atomic power plants. Chief among these was the veil of secrecy that was thrown up around atomic power during the war and that persisted into the Cold War years of the late 1940s and early 1950s. Despite the hopes of many scientists, the security requirements of the Atomic Energy Act of 1946, coupled with the Cold War conservatism of the Joint Committee on Atomic Energy, severely restricted the flow of information about atomic power. Only a limited number of companies able to obtain military contracts with atomic energy applications could gain any atomic expertise immediately after the war. Two such companies were Westinghouse and General Electric, and their vehicle for obtaining on-the-job atomic training was the navy program to develop a better way to power submarines.

Heading the U.S. Navy atomic reactor development effort was Captain Hyman G. Rickover, who would have tremendous influence over the direction of the civilian reactor program through the experience that private contractors gained by working on his submarine reactors. After a six-month assignment in 1946 at the Manhattan Project's Clinton Laboratories near Oak Ridge, Tennessee, Rickover became the navy's "expert" on atomic power. Like Oppenheimer and the GAC, Rickover recognized in 1947 that AEC research was not committed to a practical engineering program to develop an atomic power plant but would instead explore a number of options that might or might not prove feasible. Rickover believed that the only way for the navy to achieve an atomic-powered submarine was to remove its program from the laboratory physicists and put it into the hands of industry engineers under close navy supervision.[69]

Inspired by Rickover's vision of an atomic-powered navy, Westinghouse President Gwilym A. Price established in 1946 a separate division within the company to develop a submarine reactor, and Westinghouse signed a contract with the navy in 1948 to begin work on a reactor system code-named "Wizard," forerunner to the atomic power plant that would power the *Nautilus* in 1954.[70] General Electric was also pursuing basic atomic research at its Knolls Atomic Power Laboratory near the company's Schenectady, New York, corporate headquarters. The laboratory had been financed by the Manhattan Project in exchange for GE's agreement to take over operation of the government's plutonium production facilities at Hanford, Washington, shortly after the end of World War II. GE scientists expended considerable effort at Knolls in trying to develop a "breeder" reactor—so-called because it theoretically would produce more fuel than it consumed—but when that project stalled, the company agreed to join the navy's reactor development effort in a project named "Genie." The Genie reactor system would eventually be installed in the U.S. Navy's second atomic submarine, *Seawolf*, launched in 1955.[71]

Westinghouse and General Electric gained a tremendous advantage over the rest of industry through their navy work, an advantage that helped them ultimately dominate the domestic reactor manufacturing market.[72] But the security requirements of the Atomic Energy Act, aggressively enforced by the Joint Committee on Atomic Energy, severely limited the access of most American companies to technical information generated by the AEC's reactor research program. Hewlett and Oscar E. Anderson, Jr., advance two reasons why Congress placed such tremendous emphasis on control of atomic technology—control that at the time seemed to fly in the face of the American free enterprise system. One was to keep "atomic energy firmly under the government's thumb" until international controls could be established. The second was to keep the new atomic technology from "swamping" the free enterprise system:

What stirred . . . unprecedented Government intervention in the economic process was the anticipation of substantial if not spectacular innovations in non-military uses of atomic energy. Most of the scientists probably would have agreed with Oppenheimer's conclusion that technological advances in the foreseeable future would fall within the area of existing scientific knowledge; but lawyers and legislators had to allow for every eventuality, scientists only for the plausible. Who could be sure that someone would not invent a pill which could be dropped in a pail of water to heat a house or even a community for a year? Could the Government permit such a revolutionary invention to remain in the hands of a single individual or company?[73]

Because they were denied access to the classified atomic research being conducted under military contracts and in AEC laboratories, American business adopted a wait-and-see attitude toward commercialization of atomic energy throughout the late 1940s. The economic realities of the new technology also made industry cautious. Lawrence Hafstad, director of reactor development for the AEC, noted in a November 1950 speech to oil industry executives that the cost of electric power produced by the atom would have to become competitive with fossil fuels before commercial development would begin: "We can *justify* heavy commitments to reactors producing electric power only if and when the cost of this power bears a reasonable relationship to the cost under comparable conditions of power available from conventional fuels."[74] Projected costs of atomic power compared poorly with power produced from oil and coal, a conclusion reached in a widely publicized 1950 study by the University of Chicago's Cowles Commission for Research in Economics.[75] Indicative of the general lessening of enthusiasm for atomic power was a *Newsweek* report on the Chicago study that began, "As yet no deserts have burst into bloom, no polar icecaps have melted away. Indeed the brave new world of cheap and abundant atomic power seems far more remote then it did just after the war. And estimates of the atom's industrial future are becoming less extravagant."[76]

Although the AEC commissioners recognized that commercialization would not proceed until the private sector had sufficient information on which it could make informed judgments about the economic potential of atomic energy, the Cold War mindset of the late 1940s kept atomic research under the lock and key of national security. The commissioners did recruit a committee of business leaders in 1947 to investigate industrial opportunities for nuclear power, but there is evidence in Lilienthal's journal that the committee was little more than a public relations ploy to quiet industry concerns about secrecy.[77] After a year of study, the committee made a few feeble recommendations that did nothing to lower the wall of secrecy.

CHANGE IN NATIONAL ATOMIC POLICY

As America entered the 1950s, however, world affairs prompted the AEC to alter its position of secrecy and improve the flow of research information on reactor technology into the private sector. Korean War electricity requirements began taking up a larger proportion of U.S. power supplies, making civilian power reactor development more attractive to American policymakers. Because of the war, the AEC staff found it prudent to encourage development through private industry rather than through its contractors such as Westinghouse and GE who were preoccupied with military programs.[78] Evidence by the end of 1952 that the Soviet Union and Great Britain were actively working to develop the atom's industrial potential also introduced foreign policy considerations into the commercial reactor program. As AEC Commissioner Thomas Murray pointed out in a 1953 speech, the United States could not afford to fall behind in the race to develop the industrial atom, or power-hungry developing nations might be tempted to move toward those countries with the most developed reactor systems.[79]

Finally, national policy toward private atomic development significantly changed after the death of JCAE Chairman McMahon in the summer of 1952 and the election of President Dwight Eisenhower the following November. McMahon had vigorously pushed for a government monopoly in atomic energy for security reasons, and his death, coupled with the return of Republicans to power, resulted in reorganization of the JCAE and reduced influence for those members concerned with the security implications of providing atomic information to industry.[80] President Eisenhower's famous "Atoms for Peace" speech before the General Assembly of the UN in December 1953 also publicly signaled the new administration's positive attitude toward commercial development of atomic power. Among the ideas expressed by the president was the role that atomic energy could play in meeting the electric power needs of developing nations.[81] Shortly after Eisenhower's inauguration, the National Security Council decided that a vigorous national industrial program in atomic power development was in the interest of national security.[82]

By permitting greater industry access to reactor information, the AEC gave commercialization of atomic power a much-needed boost, and in 1951 the commission received a positive, though qualified, report about the potential of atomic energy for power production from a Dow Chemical-Detroit Edison team that had been given limited access to classified reactor information.[83] Interest in commercialization was further stimulated by news at the end of the year that an experimental reactor at the AEC's testing facility in the Idaho desert had produced the first electricity from atomic power.[84] Now industry had a working demonstration of the potential of the atom. By 1952 enthusiastic reports about atomic power had been received from three other industrial study groups, and by the end of 1954 the AEC had authorized studies by eighteen teams representing forty-one utilities, twenty-nine private engineering or manufacturing concerns, one federal agency (the Tennessee Valley Authority), and one trade association (National Association of Railroad and Utilities Commissioners).[85]

But industry needed more than access to information to make the commitment to commercialization. The Atomic Energy Act of 1946 restricted ownership of reactors and fuels to the government. If industry was going to participate in the development of atomic energy, it wanted to own and operate its own nuclear facilities. By 1953 the pressure had built to amend the 1946 act to provide industry with incentives that would encourage its participation in atomic power development, although the number and kind of those incentives were extensively debated. For example, public power advocates and organized labor were concerned that amending the act to benefit industry would result in a private monopoly of atomic power. But the scientific community, the AEC commissioners, and the JCAE were equally convinced that atomic energy would not take its rightful place in American society without fundamental changes in the law that would allow the private sector wider participation in power reactor development.[86]

As the push for legislation gained momentum in Congress, the pace of atomic technological development also gathered speed. In January of 1954 the *Nautilus* was launched, powered by the reactor developed by Westinghouse and brought to fruition by Hyman Rickover. But the most significant development for commercial nuclear power occurred on September 6, 1954, when ground was broken for the nation's first full-scale reactor project at Shippingport, Pennsylvania. The AEC had entered into a contract with Westinghouse nearly a year earlier for development, design, and construction of the reactor that would have a capacity of 60,000 kilowatts and be operated by the Duquesne Light Company. The reactor's pressurized-water design was based on work that Westinghouse had done for the navy.[87]

These events, coupled with AEC and JCAE interest in a greater role for private industry in atomic power development, culminated in the passage of the Atomic Energy Act of 1954, a wholesale revision of the 1946 statute that, according to Frank G. Dawson, "paved the way for a new relationship between the AEC and industry in developing commercial nuclear power."[88] The key provisions of the new legislation allowed private ownership of nuclear facilities under AEC licensing and provided more normal patent rights for private equipment manufacturers. Whereas the law required that the government maintain ownership of fissionable materials, the AEC was allowed to lease these to private industry. The legislation also provided greater industry access to government information about atomic power and directed the AEC to develop programs necessary to introduce atomic energy into the private sector. In effect, Congress was asking the commission to *promote* atomic power with one hand and, through licensing of reactors, *regulate* it with the other—a pattern that would have important implications for the industry's later risk communication efforts. The JCAE also firmly established itself as the most powerful element in Congress on atomic power issues by including a provision in the new law giving the committee power to authorize appropriations for federal atomic plant construction and real-property acquisitions, although civilian power reactors were still beyond the scope of the JCAE's authorization power.[89]

With the passage of the 1954 legislation, a mechanism was in place that should have provided the impetus for the growth of commercial atomic power, but industry was still reluctant to make the necessary investments. The AEC tried to involve industry in the construction of new atomic power plants through a joint program in which government and industry would develop the plants together. Once the reactors were built, the AEC would step out of the project and industry would shoulder the financial responsibility. But industry, although encouraged by the commercial prospects, was still unwilling to absorb the costs and risks associated with construction of power plants, and response was luke-warm to the AEC program.[90] Fear of liability from nuclear reactor accidents had scared off most utilities from ordering reactors, although by 1955 the insurance industry had created insurance pools that provided up to $60 million each for property damage and liability arising from atomic energy activities. This coverage was viewed as inadequate by the fledging nuclear industry, which would not risk bankruptcy to move ahead with civilian reactor development.[91]

Congress' solution was passage of the Price-Anderson Act of 1957 that limited industry liability for accidents to $560 million and provided some compensation to the public. The $560 million ceiling was arrived at by totaling all of the private insurance that the nuclear industry could raise, $60 million, with the government putting up the remaining $500 million. It was obvious even in 1957 that the consequences of a serious nuclear plant accident would far exceed the $560 million ceiling, but the JCAE recognized that no commercial nuclear plants would be built without a financial safety net to protect industry from an accident. Most observers agree that Price-Anderson removed the last major roadblock to com-mercialization of nuclear power in the United States.[92]

With the passage of Price-Anderson, the American nuclear industry was poised and ready to take off. Congress and the AEC were coop-erating fully with the industry and reactor manufacturers and owner/operators were no longer bound by liability concerns should the tech-nology fail. But, as Daniel Ford notes, one major obstacle still remained before nuclear power plants would dominate the American landscape—economics:

Economically, nuclear power did not look like a winner. Coal, the major fuel used by the electric utilities, was in plentiful supply. Improvements in the ef-ficiency of coal-burning power plants, moreover, had been dramatically reducing the cost of the electricity they generated. Even under the most favorable as-sumptions, nuclear power appeared to be decidedly more expensive than the electricity generated using this orthodox fuel.[93]

In an effort to stimulate sales and compete with coal, the reactor man-ufacturers, led by GE, offered "turnkey" contracts to utilities in which the manufacturers guaranteed delivery of a complete plant by a specified date and at a firm price that was competitive with coal-fired plants. The contracts were called "turnkey" because all a utility had to do when the plant was completed was turn the key, walk in the door, and begin operations. The turnkey contracts resulted in huge losses for the man-ufacturers, but they achieved their purpose of stimulating sales and creating confidence in the market that atomic power plants could compete competitively with coal plants. Once sales began to pick up, manufacturers switched from turnkey contracts to "cost-plus" contracts in which the utilities began paying for cost overruns.[94] Encouraged by a steady national demand for electricity that averaged 7–8 percent per year from 1960–72, utilities ordered 211 reactors between 1965 and 1974, more than ten times the total number of reactor systems ordered prior to 1965.[95]

"SELLING" ATOMIC POWER

It is beyond the scope of this book to explore all of the ramifications of the cooperative effort by the AEC, the JCAE, and the private sector to develop atomic energy. There is ample evidence to suggest that one significant consequence of the AEC's close relationship to industry was neglect of the agency's regulatory function, particularly in the area of reactor safety.[96] Indeed, Elizabeth Rolf points out that the issue of public health and safety was noticeably absent from the 1956 bill. "While many of the hazards of radiation were clearly apparent in 1946," she writes, "no one viewed the potential threat of an evolving nuclear technology as intolerable or something good engineering could not acceptably control."[97] A more significant consequence of the cooperative relationship to this examination of nuclear risk communication is the extensive effort made by government and industry to establish a climate of public opinion conducive to the growth of the new industry through a variety of public relations activities.

The government public relations effort began initially as a campaign to "sell" President Eisenhower's "Atoms for Peace" program to foreign nations. At the first International Conference on the Peaceful Uses of Atomic Energy held in Geneva in 1955, the AEC sponsored several exhibits containing models of different types of atomic reactors, radiation-detection instrumentation, and other assorted atomic "hardware." Highlight of the U.S. exhibit was a small working research reactor that had been purchased from the United States by the Swiss government. Conference attendees were able to look down in the reactor while it was operating and observe the blue glow of the Cerenkov effect caused by reactor radiation.[98] Many of the AEC exhibits developed for the conference were returned to the United States and reassembled to help educate American citizens about atomic energy.

The AEC relied principally on press releases, speeches by commissioners, and interviews with the news media to keep the positive aspects of atomic energy in the news, but the agency also took some innovative measures to reach the American public directly with positive information. Five mobile exhibits detailing various phases of atomic energy development began traveling throughout the United States in 1956 and were offered free of charge to exhibitors. These were the first in a series of exhibits that were seen by millions of Americans throughout the 1950s and 1960s. The AEC also established the American Museum of Atomic Energy in Oak Ridge, Tennessee, and began assisting colleges and universities to develop programs in nuclear science and engineering.[99] Perhaps its most productive effort was the distribution of numerous films about atomic power. In 1960 alone, an estimated 2,500,000 people viewed these films, and throughout the decade, more than 200 million people watched them, either at direct screenings or on television.[100] As Ford notes, the films were generally positive, upbeat productions about atomic energy that tapped into the now common theme of atomic scientists controlling the "magic" of atomic energy:

The scientists in the A.E.C. films did not discuss the risks and, indeed, hardly ever said anything. They were shown in scenarios—handling nuclear materials by remote control, pressing buttons to turn on equipment, or sitting behind drafting tables working on the blueprints for the atomic future—while A.E.C. announcers described how "the sure hand of science brings power unlimited from the magic of the atom."[101]

Private industry cooperated fully with the AEC. More than eighty U.S. companies, including all of the major reactor equipment manufacturers, contributed equipment and other resources to the U.S. exhibits in Geneva. General Electric was one of the most enthusiastic promoters of the atom. *A Is for Atom*, a GE-produced film, was shown at Geneva and then later included in the AEC film catalogue for distribution to the American public. The company also used the three-minute commercial advertising segment of its popular GE Television Theatre to "sell" atomic power to television viewers.[102] Although GE and the atomic industry supported the AEC's public relations effort, it also felt the need for its own public relations arm, and in 1953 it created a trade association that has since functioned as a powerful tool for the dissemination of positive information about atomic power.

The idea for an industry-sponsored association of atomic industries was conceived by Dr. T. Keith Glennan, president of Case Institute of Technology and a former AEC commissioner. Glennan proposed in a speech to manufacturing chemists in 1952 that " . . . those industrial concerns, institutions, and individuals that are today actively engaged in atomic energy research, development, and operations form—voluntarily and without governmental urging or subsidy—a national association of atomic industries."[103] Taking his cue from Glennan, Walker L. Cisler, president of the Detroit Edison Company, organized a meeting of thirty industrial leaders, scientists, and engineers in January 1953 that resulted, four months later, in the establishment of the Atomic Industrial Forum, Inc. (AIF), a non-profit membership organization designed to "facilitate the continuing development of atomic energy for the common good."[104] The founding members included nearly 170 atomic equipment manufacturers, engineering and construction companies, electric utilities, and other organizations interested in atomic development.[105]

Over the next three decades, the AIF became a powerful force for molding public opinion about atomic power through a well-planned and implemented campaign that combined close and frequent contacts with the news media, Congress, regulatory agencies, and the owner/operators of the nation's atomic power plants. Indicative of the AIF's close relationship was the fact that it was designated as the AEC's first official depository for atomic energy information in 1954 and was recognized by the United States Information Agency (USIA) for its contributions to the Atoms for Peace public relations effort in Europe.[106]

The AIF is particularly significant to this study of the rhetoric of nuclear risk communication because much of its public relations effort on behalf of atomic power has been directed at helping nuclear plant owner/operators communicate with their electric ratepayers and other publics about issues involving atomic energy. As early as 1960, the AIF began to articulate in its annual report what became the dominant public relations philosophy of the organization; i.e., that public *understanding* of atomic energy is equivalent to public *acceptance* of atomic energy:

The Forum is acutely aware that the peaceful utilization of atomic energy, to which it is exclusively dedicated, can survive and grow only in the context of basic acceptance by the general public. Concern has recently been growing that a generally favorable climate of public opinion may be jeopardized by continued sensational news and public media treatment of events relating to atomic energy and radiation, and by the activities of several groups devoted for various reasons to emphasizing the dangers of radiation to the public.

It is the belief of the Forum that the atomic industry can be proud of its remarkably good safety record, and that a proper public understanding of radiation should encompass not only its hazards but the safeguards against them, the benefits of radiation for public welfare, and the perspective of radiation hazards set against the hazards associated with other more familiar servants of humanity such as fire, electricity, gravity, and the automobile.[107]

Although research has shown that new knowledge serves to confirm rather than shape attitudes and that opposition to nuclear power stems from factors other than ignorance, the philosophy that public education equals public acceptance has dominated the AIF's public affairs program since its inception.[108]

The AIF's concern about media reports of radiation was stimulated by a series of events beginning in 1955 that began to question the safety of atomic power plants.[109] As noted above, safety was not a major issue for either Congress or the AEC during the commission's early years as the nation grappled with developing a stockpile of atomic weapons and getting the fledgling industry underway. The navy reactor program under Rickover had set a standard for safety that most in the industry thought could be maintained in the civilian program. "Nobody ever thought that safety was a problem," former AEC lawyer Harold Green is quoted as saying. "They assumed that if you just wrote the requirement that it be done properly, it would be done properly."[110]

According to Rolph, the first safety controversy involving atomic reactors began in 1955 when a consortium of utilities made a proposal under the AEC's demonstration program to build and operate the so-called Fermi breeder reactor about twenty miles from Detroit. The proposal came just as a small experimental breeder reactor suffered an accidental core meltdown at the AEC's Idaho laboratory facilities. Despite contrary advice from its own Advisory Committee on Reactor Safety (ACRS), the AEC decided to issue a conditional construction permit for the Fermi project, triggering lengthy public hearings by the JCAE in 1957 that questioned the safety of the design and the advisability of locating the plant so close to a major city. According to Rolph, the debate called "public attention to the fact that there continued to be substantial gaps in our information about the hazards imposed by nuclear technology and that where some information existed, experts could still differ."[111]

A second important safety issue surfaced in 1957 when the AEC released, from its Brookhaven National Laboratory, the first major study to detail the implications of a serious atomic plant accident. The study was requested by the JCAE in 1956 to determine potential industry liabilities in preparation for its consideration of legislation that would ultimately become the Price-Anderson Act of 1957. Known by its AEC nomenclature as WASH–740, the study estimated that a major accident at a nuclear plant located near a large city could produce $7 billion in property damage, 3,400 deaths, and 43,000 injuries.[112] The publicity surrounding the study caused public relations problems for the atomic industry and further raised the level of public concern over atomic power.[113] That concern was elevated in May of 1957 when the JCAE held several days of hearings on setting national radiation protection standards and criticized the AEC for its failure to educate the public about the dangers.[114] A few months later, the world's first major reactor accident occurred at the Windscale plutonium plant in Great Britain, when a fire in the reactor core released large amounts of radioactive isotopes into the atmosphere, contaminating an area of 500 square kilometers and requiring the destruction of two million litres of milk.[115] About one year later, an incident at the AEC's Oak Ridge, Tennessee, operations was widely publicized when eight employees received excessive radiation exposures.[116] Local opposition to the proposed construction of plants at Bodega Head north of San Francisco and at Ravenswood in the Queens section of New York City also attracted national attention.[117]

The cumulative effect of these events caused the AIF and the atomic industry to pay particular attention to public opinion polls conducted by member organizations in 1960 that indicated increasing concern by Americans about the safety of commercial atomic power. A General Electric-sponsored survey of 1,500 households nationally showed that larger numbers of Americans favored government development over private development of atomic power. Less than one-half believed that working in a atomic power plant was as safe as working anywhere else. The AIF report on the study noted that the survey produced a "significant" percentage of respondents (25 percent) who gave "negative" replies when asked the question, "What does atomic energy mean to you?" GE concluded that the findings indicated "the need for an organized, integrated and intensified effort" to solve problems of negative public reaction to atomic power, and stepped up its own public relations effort by designing a Sunday newspaper supplement on atomic energy and creating a "Citizen Atom" literature campaign. Findings from a second survey of 1,000 people living in the power service area of Consolidated Edison Company of New York were generally in accord with the GE results. The AIF report on that survey noted that it "showed a relatively consistent hard core of negative attitude responses—a small percentage—to questions bearing on whether it is a good idea for a company to build a nuclear power plant, and whether there is danger from such a plant to the individual or the community."[118]

Concerned that American public opinion was turning against commercial development of atomic power, the AIF began in 1960 to increase what it called "public education" activities. It established a Committee on Public Understanding to coordinate the education effort and began to assist member organizations in developing informational materials that would "present for the general public in a straightforward and meaningful way the benefits and hazards associated with atomic energy development."[119] Over the next decade, these public education activities were many and varied. They included publishing a newsletter to keep the industry informed about activities supporting the promotion of atomic power. A series of articles under the general title of "The Busy Atom" were written and distributed to newspapers throughout the United States. Numerous "fact" booklets were churned out and distributed to schools, organizations, and anyone interested in atomic power. The AIF completed a twenty-eight-minute film for public distribution entitled "Atomic Power Today: Service with Safety" and established an annual program to recognize journalists and others who made "significant contributions to public understanding of atomic energy."[120] And in an effort to disconnect atomic power from atomic bombs, AIF and industry publicists began encouraging everyone to use the more scientifically accurate term "nuclear" when writing or speaking about atomic power.[121]

By 1969 the AIF had tripled its public affairs and information program budget to meet what it termed "increasingly sharp attacks on the [atomic] industry by dissidents who are seeking to spread misinformation about the impact of nuclear energy on the environment."[122] Those "attacks" were the product of a growing national concern for the environment— a concern reflected in the passage of major environmental laws like the National Environmental Policy Act (1969) and the Water Quality Improvement Act (1970).[123] By 1970, "People were no longer complacent with nuclear power safety and environmental claims made by industry and government," notes Joseph P. Tomain. "Even though Congress left the 1954 enabling legislation intact except for some 1964 amendments, the consciousness raising accomplished through the environmental movement made people aware of radiological hazards."[124]

But the increasing public relations problems faced by nuclear power in the late 1960s and early 1970s were also generated by a conflict within the AEC itself. The conflict began in the mid–1960s when manufacturers began increasing the size of reactors sold to utilities in an effort to utilize economies of scale to make nuclear power competitive with coal. According to Rolph, average reactor generating capacities increased from 550 to 850 megawatts (MW) between 1963 and 1967. Utilities, seeking to further lower their costs, increasingly petitioned the AEC to allow reactors to be built closer to major cities and thereby reduce transmission line costs.[125] As the number of nuclear power plants increased, so did the probability of an accident, whereas the larger reactors and the proximity of new plants to cities significantly increased the consequences of such an accident.

The number and variety of safety issues resulting from these developments put the AEC on the horns of a dilemma. AEC technical staff recognized in the early 1960s that locating large reactors close to cities was a potentially dangerous combination and had urged the administrative staff to slow new plant licensing until the agency's safety research could catch up with developments in reactor technology and resolve the emerging safety questions. But the administrative staff, under pressure from Congress, the JCAE, and the industry to promote commercial development, ignored or suppressed technical staff concerns and adopted a policy that allowed continued licensing of nuclear reactors. The policy effectively put the responsibility for safety on the back of industry. Frustrated by the lack of regulatory action, AEC technical staff began to raise safety issues outside the confines of the agency in technical publications read by environmental groups, and by the early 1970s these issues were starting to receive widespread coverage in the popular news media.[126]

As media attention to safety issues increased, the AIF refocused its efforts to counterbalance criticism by concentrating on key groups within American society that it believed could influence the nuclear debate. Chief among these groups were members of the news media, and the AIF established as one of its major objectives the provision of "accurate and timely information about nuclear energy to the mass media."[127] The organization began publishing in 1970 a special press edition of its monthly membership newsletter *INFO*. This new newsletter gave the media the AIF's perspective on a variety of nuclear energy issues as well as critiques of books, articles, and news stories about nuclear power. By 1971, *Press Info* was being sent to 1,100 reporters who covered energy issues. The AIF also began a series of workshops around the nation specifically designed to "educate" news media representatives to its position on various energy issues.[128] Held under the joint sponsorship of local nuclear plant owner/operators and the AIF, the workshops were effective in establishing the organization as a credible source of information about nuclear power. AIF moved its public relations operation to Washington to be closer to policymakers and influential news media, and by 1973 it could boast that it was a principal source of information for the first hour-long network television documentary on nuclear power, ABC's *The Nuclear Alternative*.[129]

While the AIF was establishing itself as a source of nuclear information for the news media, the AEC was rapidly being overwhelmed by the criticisms of the growing anti-nuclear power movement. The movement had begun to take shape in the late 1960s when the Union of Concerned Scientists, an independent group of scientists worried about technical deficiencies at nuclear power plants, began questioning the AEC's assumptions about the adequacy of emergency systems that cool the reactor's core and prevent a meltdown during certain serious accidents.[130] Much of the information critical of those assumptions was provided to the scientific group by AEC technical staff, and, in addition to raising serious safety issues, generated considerable negative publicity about AEC efforts to ignore or suppress its own technical staff in the rush to promote nuclear power. At the same time, utilities were starting to reconsider the nuclear option due to skyrocketing cost overruns resulting from a combination of licensing delays, construction mismanagement, and more stringent regulatory safety standards.[131] In 1974 consumer advocate Ralph Nader convened Critical Mass '74, a gathering of 1,200 anti-nuclear activists that attracted national attention and galvanized public opposition against nuclear power, and a host of regional groups began actively taking their case against nuclear plants to the public in films, leaflets, and at public forums.[132]

The controversy convinced Congress that the AEC's dual mission of promotion and protection was clearly not in the public interest, and it passed the Energy Reorganization Act of 1974. The act created two organizations—the Nuclear Regulatory Commission (NRC), responsible for safety and licensing, and the Energy Research and Development Administration (ERDA), responsible for promotion and development of nuclear power and later absorbed by the Department of Energy. However, as Tomain points out, the dissolution of the AEC into two separate units had little effect on the government's promotion of nuclear power because the pattern of federal promotion had been set and the split failed to eliminate a basic regulatory conflict between the NRC's responsibility for licensing and the protection of public safety. "If the commission too vigorously exercises its safety role," notes Tomain, "then the attendant compliance costs act as a disincentive to invest in nuclear plants and cut across the NRC's promotional grain."[133] Thus promotion and protection remained linked within the nuclear ethic, a linkage that continues to shape risk communication literature within the industry.

NEW PR STRATEGIES EMERGE

It would be four more years until the accident at the Three Mile Island nuclear plant in Pennsylvania would shake the NRC's legacy of nuclear power promotion. But the dissolution of the AEC, coupled with criticism of its zeal in promoting nuclear power, did reduce the level and effectiveness of the government's public relations effort for nuclear power, leaving private industry to take up the slack. According to *The New York Times*, the AIF doubled its public education program in 1975 primarily because of the AEC's demise.[134] President Carl Walske told his board of directors that the increased funding would be used to influence the views of key government officials, newspeople, labor organizations, and women's groups. One part of the new effort would provide "balanced" information on nuclear power to legislative decision makers at the federal, state, and local levels, whereas the second part would generate "positive news events . . . to counter the pseudo-press conferences held regularly by the national critics, and to provide a news peg for media attention."[135]

The AIF strategy was no doubt influenced by a 1975 report prepared for the electric power industry by Cambridge Reports, Inc., a national polling organization. Based on national surveys of public attitudes, the report suggested that support for nuclear power was particularly weak among women, young people, and those of low socioeconomic status. The report suggested that the industry develop "messages" about nuclear power that would be directed at each group. For women, Cambridge Reports proposed that the message emphasize that nuclear power is safe for women and their children, and suggested that women be used as spokespersons to address other women on the issue. For young people and those in low socioeconomic status groups, the report recommended that the industry emphasize how nuclear energy was essential for continued economic growth and point out the impact of a no-growth society on jobs and opportunities for the young and the poor. Cambridge Reports proposed that scientists, particularly young, articulate, ecology-minded scientists, be used as spokespersons for nuclear energy because "the public has faith in science, believes scientists and would listen."[136] Labor leaders would also be effective in reaching low socioeconomic groups, the report added.

Analysis of the AIF annual reports after 1975 indicates the extent to which the Forum took to heart the Cambridge Reports' recommendations. Here are just a few of the public relations activities conducted by the AIF during the four years preceding the trouble at Three Mile Island in 1979:

- Completed and distributed a twenty-five-minute film entitled *Now That the Dinosaurs Are Gone* featuring Dr. Dixie Lee Ray, chairman and only female member of the Atomic Energy Commission.
- Organized a tour of the Salem nuclear plant in New Jersey for a group of women's magazine editors.
- Developed a new series of videotapes entitled "Nuclear Power: An Introduction" and "The Need for Nuclear: Our Energy Options" narrated by scientists from the University of Texas and the University of Missouri.
- Worked with five other energy organizations to sponsor Nuclear Power Assembly, two days of briefings and contact meetings with congressional staff for several hundred senior utility officials.
- Conducted numerous special briefings for members of Congress, committees, and staff on nuclear subjects, developed programs for organized labor and the labor media, and provided speakers for groups of university faculty and students, editors, and high school teachers.
- Expanded the operation of Nuclear Energy Women, a taskforce of female scientists and utility personnel, and conducted special programs on nuclear energy for numerous women's groups, including the American Legion Auxiliary, American Medical Women's Association, League of Women Voters, American Association of University Women, National Organization for Women, American Women in Radio and Television, and the National Federation of Democratic Women.[137]

The 1979 Three Mile Island accident had little effect on the industry's already intense public relations effort except, perhaps, to give it an added impetus. In its annual report for that year, the AIF noted that one of the industry's major goals for its public education effort after the accident was to "restore public confidence in the nuclear option and to inform the public that the lessons of Three Mile Island will result in a safer nuclear industry."[138] A special report issued by the AIF's Public Affairs and Information Program in 1980 summarized the industry's public education strategy following the accident:

- To put Three Mile Island into its proper perspective, by providing authoritative information about the accident and its effects.

- To demonstrate to the media and national opinion leaders that the nuclear industry has taken seriously—and applied—the lessons learned from Three Mile Island.

- To show that the industry was far from immobilized by the Three Mile Island accident, that amidst the turmoil surrounding that event the industry remained vigorous and a substantial contributor to the nation's energy supply.

- To explain how nuclear energy can play a far larger role than its critics contend in freeing America's dependence on foreign oil—if the difficult financial problems confronting the entire utility industry can be solved.[139]

Ironically, the accident also helped to thrust AIF spokespeople into the national spotlight where they could provide industry's perspective on the future of nuclear energy.

Three Mile Island was a serious setback, but it did not dampen the American nuclear industry's faith in its technology. And with billions invested in commercial nuclear power, the industry resolved to fight back. Its first step was to create a special industry public relations group called the Committee on Energy Awareness with responsibility to deal with the public relations demands imposed by the accident. The AIF worked closely with the CEA while focusing on other problems facing the nuclear industry, including the serious issue of radioactive waste disposal. It also began a concerted effort shortly after Three Mile Island to counter anti-nuclear organizations directly at the grassroots level. The strategy was motivated by the increasing prevalence of anti-nuclear measures on state referenda and the growing tendency of state public service commissions not to approve new nuclear power plants until questions about storage of radioactive waste and used reactor fuel were resolved.[140] By 1979 the AIF was assisting more than 100 "independent" groups active in opposing anti-nuclear forces in legislative hearings, schools, civic clubs, and the press. These "voices speaking out for energy adequacy" included most of the groups that the AIF had targeted for several years—labor, ethnic groups, and academicians—as well as large energy users and their employees.[141]

In the aftermath of Three Mile Island, the American nuclear industry has settled on a public relations strategy of showing how a continued nuclear development effort will help free the country from its dependence on foreign oil. The strategy grew out of the industry's discovery that its messages about nuclear safety immediately after the accident were generally not well received by the American people. "We found it was very difficult to communicate nuclear-power safety effectively," one industry spokesman is quoted as saying in a public relations trade magazine. "It seemed our messages raised more concerns, instead of alleviating them."[142]

Although the long gas lines resulting from the Arab oil embargo of 1973 had become a distant memory in the minds of most Americans by the 1980s, television coverage of the Iranian hostage crisis was a reminder that the unsettled Middle East was an area on which the nation depended for much of its energy. The industry took advantage of the situation by running television advertisements in the spring of 1980 that used the hostage crisis to focus national attention on the role that nuclear energy could play in loosening the grip of Arab oil. Just getting television stations to run the pro-nuclear ads was a major victory, the committee pointed out in a report on its advertising campaign. Broadcasters had been reluctant to run ads on nuclear power because they feared that anti-nuclear organizations would demand equal time for non-nuclear viewpoints under the Federal Communication Commission's Fairness Doctrine. The committee was able to convince broadcasters to run the 1980 advertisements as a counter to what it regarded as unbalanced coverage of the Three Mile Island accident. "Now, because of the CEA breakthrough, electronic advertising is a viable tool in the nuclear industry's arsenal of communications weapons," the committee said in its report on the $760,000 national advertising campaign. "The surprisingly widespread broadcaster acceptance of the pro-nuclear ads has paved the way for the industry to use the powerful electronic media to its full advantage."[143]

As the AIF noted in its 1981 annual report, the public relations effort of the American nuclear industry since the Three Mile Island accident has focused on "returning the nuclear option to normalcy. This has meant explaining how nuclear power used for the generation of electricity can assume an expanding role in meeting our nation's future energy needs, and at the same time, reduce our dependence on imported oil."[144] The message has been delivered by the AIF and the Committee on Energy Awareness, and the two organizations ultimately merged their public relations efforts into the U.S. Council for Energy Awareness in 1987.

The audiences for this message are essentially the same as they were before Three Mile Island—news media, government leaders, labor unions, women, ethnic groups, and minorities. For a brief period after the April 1986 accident at Chernobyl, the industry focused its advertising on demonstrating the differences between the Soviet reactor design and those in the United States, pointing out that U.S. reactors rely on containment structures surrounding the reactor vessel to keep radioactive materials from entering the atmosphere outside the plant. According to a USCEA spokesperson, public anxiety over Chernobyl was reduced enough by September 1986 to enable the industry to return to its traditional advertising themes.[145]

The promise of nuclear energy, so bright in the 1950s, has dimmed considerably over the past three decades due to a combination of circumstances. In addition to the safety considerations that have dogged nuclear power since the early 1960s, the costs of building plants have skyrocketed as the demand for electricity has declined. Due to more stringent safety and environmental requirements for licensing, plants under construction have been delayed by several years, resulting in still higher costs. As a result, there has been a de facto moratorium on orders for new nuclear power plants since 1978. Well-publicized problems at government nuclear weapons plants—at Hanford in Washington, Rocky Flats in Colorado, the Idaho National Engineering Laboratory, Savannah River in South Carolina, and the Feed Materials Production Center in Fernald, Ohio—have also helped fuel public opposition to nuclear power that has risen dramatically since the halcyon days of the 1950s.[146]

THE NUCLEAR ETHIC

In his critique of the American nuclear industry, Mark Hertsgaard provides considerable insight into the philosophy of industrialists who guided the development of commercial nuclear power from its infancy in the late 1940s to its current struggle with safety issues, economics, and government intervention, a philosophy he terms the "nuclear imperative." Within this philosophy it is possible to trace the values that have coalesced into what I have termed the "nuclear ethic." That philosophy can be envisioned as triangular. At one point rests the industry's faith in science to provide information necessary to liberate the energy from the atom; at another sits faith in the ability of technology through engineering to use that information to safely control atomic energy; and at the third point of the triangle rests industry's belief that nuclear energy is necessary for the continued growth, and even survival, of Western civilization. Surrounding this philosophy is a conviction that government exists to support the private sector by creating the social, political, and technological climate necessary to achieve the promise of nuclear power.

Hertsgaard points out that in the minds of these industry executives, "what is at stake in the struggle over nuclear power is not just the profitability of their own corporations but the future of American capitalism, technological society, and indeed Western civilization."[147] Through interviews with industry executives, Hertsgaard provides a clear picture of the mindset of those who run the American nuclear industry. It is a mindset that sees the nation's very survival as dependent upon abundant supplies of nuclear energy. Without nuclear power, these executives paint a dark picture of a nation in danger. The danger results from energy shortages caused by depletion of native supplies of fossil fuels and the whims of hostile nations controlling the world's major petroleum resources. The energy shortages produce extreme social consequences, including massive unemployment, leaving people without jobs to freeze in the dark. The resulting domestic turmoil prompts the government to take drastic measures to free up supplies of foreign oil or other sources of power, creating the conditions for a massive and disastrous war. Only continued development of nuclear power can save the nation from this fate. There is no other alternative.

On a more philosophical level, these executives believe that nuclear power is the "very embodiment of progress and enlightenment"—the key ingredient in the natural evolution of human civilization.[148] Abundant energy through nuclear power is the nation's only hope of maintaining the advances that a technological society has produced for its people. And even if the creation of that energy produces risk, it is a minimal risk that the nuclear industry executives can control. For them, "the scientific method, carefully applied, can permanently triumph over human fallibility."[149] The risk of nuclear power cannot be eliminated, but it can be managed to such a degree that it becomes insignificant when compared to the other risks associated with daily life.

These insights into the thinking of nuclear industry executives complete my search for the values of the "nuclear ethic." It is an ethic that draws its psychological power from the myth of the ancient alchemist—a myth that reaffirms the power of science to unlock and control the mysteries of the atom to produce energy for the benefit and survival of American society. The energy can be destructive, but the scientists-statesmen who emerged from the atomic laboratories at the end of World War II—the new alchemists—instilled positive values in the new energy source by promising and promoting peaceful development of that energy through the atomic reactor. Thus the credibility of the new alchemists succeeded in "transmuting" the atom from an instrument of war to a tool for peace, and the power of that conversion helped to convince government and industry that the philosopher's stone of unlimited energy had been found. In the cooperative effort to develop atomic power, government and industry conveyed these values into the culture through a vast public relations effort. Government's participation in that effort has become tempered by the problems of safety, but private industry still devotes considerable resources to communicating the values of the nuclear ethic to public opinion leaders, the news media, and ultimately the American public.

The concern of this book is to show how those values have become imbedded in the rhetoric of nuclear risk communication. The next chapter examines risk communication materials provided by the nation's nuclear plant owner/operators to see how the themes of the nuclear ethic have become interwoven with the essential messages of nuclear risk communication, thereby masking information vital to public safety in the event of a serious nuclear plant accident.

NOTES

1. Alonzo Plough and Sheldon Krimsky, "The Emergence of Risk Communication Studies: Social and Political Context," *Science, Technology, & Human Values* 12, nos. 3–4 (Summer 1987): 4.

2. Christoph Hohenemser, Roger Kasperson, and Robert Kates, "The Distrust of Nuclear Power," *Science* 196, no. 4285 (1 April 1977): 26.

3. George H. Gallup, *The Gallup Poll* (New York: Random House, 1972), 1:527, 1400, and Stanley M. Nealey, Barbara D. Melber, and William L. Rankin, *Public Opinion and Nuclear Energy* (Lexington, Mass.: D. C. Heath, 1983): 3–4.

4. Stephen Hilgartner, Richard C. Bell, and Rory O'Connor, *Nukespeak* (San Francisco: Sierra Club Books, 1982), xiii–xiv.

5. My understanding of alchemy is taken from John Read, *Through Alchemy to Chemistry: A Procession of Ideas & Personalities* (London: Bell and Sons, 1957); F. Sherwood Taylor, *The Alchemists* (New York: Henry Schuman, 1949; reprint, New York: Arno Press, 1974); and Mircea Eliade, *The Forge and the Crucible: Origins and Structures of Alchemy*, trans. Stephen Corrin (New York: Harper & Row, 1962). Page references to Taylor are to reprint edition.

6. Read, 14.

7. Ibid., 28.

8. Ibid., 15.

9. Ibid., 35, 20.

10. Brian Easlea, *Fathering the Unthinkable: Masculinity, Scientists and the Nuclear Arms Race* (London: Pluto Press, 1983), 42. For an interesting discussion of the influence of alchemy on a pioneering figure in atomic science, see Richard E. Salove, "From Alchemy to Atomic War: Frederick Soddy's "Technology Assessment' of Atomic Energy, 1900–1915," *Science, Technology & Human Values* 14, no. 2 (Spring 1989): 163–194.

11. Frederick Soddy, *The Interpretation of Radium*, 3d ed. (London: Murray, 1912), 225; quoted in Spencer Weart, *Nuclear Fear: A History of Images* (Cambridge: Harvard University Press, 1988), 6.

12. Taylor, 179.

13. *McGraw-Hill Encyclopedia of Science & Technology*, 5th ed., S. V. "Heavy Water."

14. Karl Taylor Compton, "The Battle of the Alchemists," *The Technology Review* 35, no. 5 (1933): 168.

15. Ernest Rutherford, *The Newer Alchemy* (New York: Macmillan, 1939).

16. Read, 14.

17. Ibid., 36.

18. Weart, 72.

19. Easlea, 41–42.

20. *The New York Times*, 31 January 1933, 16.

21. Hilgartner et al., 39.

22. "A Wand Wave, A New Era," *Life*, 20 September 1954, 141.

23. Lewis Strauss, remarks prepared for delivery at Founders' Day Dinner, National Association of Science Writers, New York City, 16 September 1954, quoted in Daniel Ford, *The Cult of the Atom: The Secret Papers of the Atomic Energy Commission* (New York: Simon and Schuster, 1982), 50; revised and reissued as *Meltdown* (New York: Simon and Schuster, 1986). All citations are from *The Cult of the Atom*. See also Richard Pfau, *No Sacrifice Too Great: The Life of Lewis L. Strauss* (Charlottesville: University Press of Virginia, 1984), 187.

24. R. M. Langer, "Fast New World," *Collier's*, 6 July 1940, 18.

25. "Atomic Power in Ten Years?" *Time*, 27 May 1940, 46–47.

26. John J. O'Neill, "Enter Atomic Power," *Harper's Magazine*, June 1940, 1–10.

27. Weart, Chapters 3 and 4.

28. "Putting the Atom to Work," *Popular Mechanics*, May 1938, 690.

29. Langer, 54.

30. Peter Goodchild, *J. Robert Oppenheimer: 'Shatterer of Worlds'* (London: BBC, 1980), 169.

31. Ford, 24.

32. David E. Lilienthal, *Change, Hope, and the Bomb* (Princeton, NJ: Princeton University Press, 1963), 63–64.

33. Goodchild, 169–170.

34. As quoted in Easlea, 83–84.

35. Diane Carter Maleson, "The Historical Roots of the Legal System's Response to Nuclear Power," *Southern California Law Review* 55 (1982): 600–601.

36. Goodchild, 174.

37. James W. Kunetka, *Oppenheimer: The Years of Risk* (Englewood Cliffs, NJ: Prentice-Hall, 1982), vii.

38. Ibid., 5.

39. Goodchild, 174, 176.

40. I. I. Rabi, Robert Serber, Victor F. Weisskopf, Abraham Pais, and Glenn T. Seaborg, *Oppenheimer* (New York: Charles Scribner's Sons, 1969), 27.

41. Alice Kimball Smith and Charles Weiner, eds., *Robert Oppenheimer: Letters and Recollections* (Cambridge: Harvard University Press, 1980), 317. See also Kunetka, 84.

42. Smith and Weiner, 325.

43. The GAC was a prestigious group of educators and scientists, all of whom had wartime experience with atomic energy. In addition to Oppenheimer, the original nine members included Harvard University President James B. Conant, Cal Tech President Lee A. DuBridge, physicists Enrico Fermi and Isidor I. Rabi, and Glenn T. Seaborg, who would later serve a ten-year term as AEC chairman. The GAC's recommendations were extremely influential on the AEC commissioners during the commission's formative years. For a complete discussion of the GAC's historic role in advising the AEC, see Richard T. Sylves, *The Nuclear Oracles: A Political History of the General Advisory Committee of the Atomic Energy Commission, 1947–1977* (Ames: Iowa State University Press, 1987). See also Rich-

ard G. Hewlett and Francis Duncan, *A History Of The United States Atomic Energy Commission* (University Park: Pennsylvania State University Press, 1969), vol. II, *Atomic Shield, 1947/1952*, 15–16, 46, hereafter referred to as *Atomic Shield*.

44. Ironically, Oppenheimer publicly testified in support of early atomic energy legislation, supported by the military, that placed very strict controls over scientific and technical information. He supported the "May-Johnson Bill" because he believed its prompt passage would avoid further delays in atomic research and international agreement on control of atomic weapons, but his lobbying for the bill was criticized by many atomic scientists. For a discussion of Oppenheimer's role in the debate over control of the post-war atom, see Richard G. Hewlett and Oscar E. Anderson, Jr., *A History of the United States Atomic Energy Commission* (University Park: Pennsylvania State University Press, 1962), vol. I, *The New World, 1939/1946*, 428–455, hereafter referred to as *The New World*. See also Alice Kimball Smith, *A Peril and a Hope: The Scientist's Movement in America: 1945–47* (Cambridge: The M.I.T. Press, 1965), 128–173; Goodchild, 174–178; and Kunetka, 87–99.

45. For a discussion of the legislative battle that led to the passage of the Atomic Energy Act of 1946, see Chapter 14 of *The New World*.

46. Ibid., 507.

47. Kunetka, 101. See also Lilienthal, *Change, Hope, and the Bomb*, 109–110.

48. Sylves, *The Nuclear Oracles*, 11.

49. Rabi et al., 50.

50. *Atomic Shield*, 29–30.

51. Ibid., 31.

52. Ibid., 31–32.

53. Kunetka, 122.

54. Sylves, *The Nuclear Oracles*, 241.

55. Rabi et al., 50–51.

56. Sylves, *The Nuclear Oracles*, 32. For an example of Lilienthal's post-AEC views on commercialization, see David E. Lilienthal, "Free The Atom," *Collier's* 17 June 1950, 13, and "Toward the Industrial Atomic Future," *Collier's*, 15 July 1950, 14.

57. David E. Lilienthal, *The Journals of David E. Lilienthal* (New York: Harper & Row, 1964), and *The Atomic Energy Years*, 13, 14.

58. Goodchild, 178.

59. Lilienthal, *The Atomic Energy Years*, 33–34, 70, 186; *Atomic Shield*, 82; and Kunetka, 122.

60. *Atomic Shield*, 83.

61. *The New York Times*, 8 January 1946, 21.

62. *The New York Times*, 27 February 1946, 25.

63. *Atomic Shield*, 101.

64. Ibid., 116–117.

65. Ibid., 117–118.

66. Ibid., 337–338.

67. Ibid., 118–121; Frank G. Dawson, *Nuclear Power: Development and Management of a Technology* (Seattle: University of Washington Press, 1976), 38.

68. Goodchild, 259–269, and Kunetka, 248–260.

69. The story of how Captain Hyman Rickover mobilized the resources of

the navy, the civilian government, and private industry to develop atomic-powered propulsion systems for submarines and large ships is a fascinating chapter in the development of commercial nuclear power. The story is well documented in Richard G. Hewlett and Francis Duncan, *Nuclear Navy* (Chicago: University of Chicago Press, 1974).

70. Ibid., 66. See also Mark Hertsgaard, *Nuclear Inc.: The Men and Money Behind Nuclear Energy* (New York: Pantheon Books, 1983), 21.

71. *Nuclear Navy*, 66; Hertsgaard, 22–24; and *Atomic Shield*, 629.

72. Of the 246 nuclear reactor systems ordered in the United States through 1985, Westinghouse supplied 86 and General Electric supplied 74. The next closest competitor was Combustion Engineering with 37. See John L. Campbell, *Collapse of an Industry: Nuclear Power and the Contradictions of U.S. Policy* (Ithaca, N.Y.: Cornell University Press, 1988), 33.

73. *New World*, 494–495.

74. Lawrence R. Hafstad, "Reactor Program of the Atomic Energy Commission: Outlook for Industrial Participation," *Vital Speeches of the Day*, 1 February 1951, 251.

75. Sam H. Schurr and Jacob Marschak, *Economic Aspects of Atomic Power* (Princeton, N.J.: Princeton University Press, 1950).

76. "The Atom and Industry," *Newsweek*, 27 November 1950, 72.

77. Lilienthal, *The Atomic Energy Years*, 242.

78. *Atomic Shield*, 492, 509, 590.

79. Hertsgaard, 25–26.

80. Harold P. Green and Alan Rosenthal, *Government of the Atom: The Integration of Powers* (New York: Atherton, 1963), 12.

81. Dawson, 59–60.

82. Hertsgaard, 26.

83. *Atomic Shield*, 512.

84. Ibid., 497–498.

85. Dawson, 49–53. See also Atomic Energy Commission, *Seventeenth Semiannual Report* (Washington, D.C.: GPO, 1955), 26–27.

86. For an example of the arguments advanced for private sector participation, see the statement by F. K. McCune, general manager of GE's Atomic Products Division, in Congress, Joint Committee on Atomic Energy, *Atomic Development and Private Enterprise: Hearings Before the Joint Committee on Atomic Energy*, 81st Cong., 1st Sess., 26 May 1949, pt. 1, 301–306.

87. Successful completion and operation of the Shippingport reactor in December 1957 marked a significant milestone in the development of commercial atomic power in the United States. Hundreds of engineers from throughout the United States attended seminars at the plant and thousands of technical reports were distributed on every facet of the project. This dissemination of knowledge, coupled with the plant's successful operation, firmly established the "light water" reactor design (so named because the design used ordinary water to transfer heat from the reactor core to the electricity-producing turbine) as the dominant reactor design in the United States, and Westinghouse and GE as the dominant light water reactor manufacturers. Through an accident of fate, the Shippingport reactor design has originally been conceived as a large ship propulsion reactor, so that when the project was converted to a civilian power

reactor project by the AEC, Hyman Rickover was put in charge of design and construction under a complex arrangement between the navy, the AEC, and Westinghouse. The success of the Shippingport project can be attributed to Rickover's commitment to excellence in engineering and construction of atomic reactors. Joseph G. Morone and Edward J. Woodhouse further suggest that the emphasis placed on Rickover's submarine program also helped make the light water reactor the dominant design in the U.S. commercial reactor program and caused work on other designs to be scaled back or cancelled, to the ultimate detriment of the nuclear industry. See Chapter 2 in Morone and Woodhouse, *The Demise of Nuclear Energy? Lessons for Democratic Control of Technology* (New Haven: Yale University Press, 1989). For an informative discussion of how the light water reactor technology became dominant, see Irvin C. Bupp and Jean-Claude Derian, *Light Water: How the Nuclear Dream Dissolved* (New York: Basic Books, 1978); reissued as *The Failed Promise of Nuclear Power: The Story of Light Water* (New York: Basic Books, 1981). For Rickover's role in the construction of the Shippingport project, see Hewlett and Duncan, *Nuclear Navy*, 247–257.

88. Dawson, 72.

89. Ibid., 72–75, and Green and Rosenthal, 168–172.

90. Dawson, 93–101; Ford, 58; and Hertsgaard, 31–32.

91. Dawson, 123, 129, and Joseph P. Tomain, *Nuclear Power Transformation* (Bloomington: Indiana University Press, 1987), 9.

92. In 1975 the act was amended so that reactor owners effectively paid the total insurance bill, and further amendments in 1988 increased to $150 million the amount of private insurance required for each reactor, raising the ceiling on liability to $7.2 billion. For the impact of the 1975 amendments, see Tomain, 9. For the recent amendments, see Price-Anderson Amendments Act of 1988, P.L. 100–408, 102 Stat. 1066 (1988). The amendments are discussed in the *Wall Street Journal*, 8 August 1988, 23.

93. Ford, 59.

94. Hertsgaard, 42–44, and Tomain, 9–10.

95. Tomain, 11, and Campbell, 33.

96. Elizabeth S. Rolph, *Nuclear Power and the Public Safety: A Study in Regulation* (Lexington, Mass.: D. C. Heath, 1979), 26–29, and Michelle Adato, James MacKenzie, Robert Pollard, and Elyn Weiss, *Safety Second: The NRC and America's Nuclear Power Plants* (Bloomington: Indiana University Press, 1987), 1–8. See also Campbell, 50–51, and Tomain, 6–12. Morone and Woodhouse point out that safety was not ignored by the AEC, but that reactor designs were first selected for development for other reasons (mainly economic) before safety considerations entered the picture. See Chapter 4 of *The Demise of Nuclear Energy? Lessons for Democratic Control of Technology*. For an excellent discussion of the AEC and NRC reactor safety programs from the end of World War II until the Three Mile Island accident in 1979, see David Okrent, *Nuclear Reactor Safety: On the History of the Regulatory Process* (Madison: University of Wisconsin Press, 1981).

97. Rolph, 22.

98. Atomic Energy Commission, *Nineteenth Semiannual Report* (Washington, D.C.: GPO, 1956), 17–21.

99. Atomic Energy Commission, *Twentieth Semiannual Report* (Washington, D.C.: GPO, 1956), 64–68, and Hilgartner et al., 74.

100. Hilgartner et al., 74, and Ford, 48.

101. Ford, 48–49.

102. Atomic Energy Commission, *Eighteenth Semiannual Report* (Washington, D.C.: GPO, 1955), 16–17, 155–60, and Weart, 168.

103. Atomic Industrial Forum, Inc., *Annual Report* (New York: Atomic Industrial Forum, 1954), 5.

104. Ibid., 2.

105. Ibid., 18–19.

106. Atomic Industrial Forum, Inc., *The Forum Memo to Members* 1 (May 1954): 3.

107. Atomic Industrial Forum, Inc., *Annual Report* (New York: Atomic Industrial Forum, 1960), 8.

108. Roger E. Kasperson et al. "Public Opposition to Nuclear Energy: Retrospect and Prospect," *Science, Technology & Human Values* 5, no. 31 (Spring 1980): 19.

109. Public concerns about the dangers of radioactive fallout from aboveground testing of atomic weapons began to emerge in the mid–1950s. See Sylves, *The Nuclear Oracles*, Chapter 7.

110. Adato et al., 3.

111. Rolph, 38–42.

112. Adato et al., 3.

113. Ford, 68.

114. Green and Rosenthal, 205.

115. Peter Pringle and James Spigelman, *The Nuclear Barons* (New York: Holt, Rinehart and Winston, 1981), 225–226.

116. Atomic Industrial Forum, Inc., *The Forum Memo to Members* 5 (August 1958): 39–40.

117. Kasperson et al., 13.

118. Atomic Industrial Forum, Inc., *The Forum Memo to Members* 7 (September 1960): 47–48.

119. Atomic Industrial Forum, Inc., *Annual Report* (New York: Atomic Industrial Forum, 1961), 8.

120. For a detailed description of these activities, see the *Annual Report* for the Atomic Industrial Forum, Inc., for the years 1960 to 1968.

121. Weart, 168.

122. Atomic Industrial Forum, Inc., *Annual Report* (New York: Atomic Industrial Forum, 1969), 39–40.

123. Rolph, 101.

124. Tomain, 11.

125. Rolph, 59–60, 79, and Campbell, 52.

126. Rolph, 101–116, and Campbell, 50–63.

127. Atomic Industrial Forum, Inc., *Annual Report* (New York: Atomic Industrial Forum, 1971), 8.

128. Atomic Industrial Forum, Inc., *Annual Report* (New York: Atomic Industrial Forum, 1972), 15.

129. Atomic Industrial Forum, Inc., *Annual Report* (New York: Atomic Industrial Forum, 1973), 12.

130. Adato et al., 4.

131. Between 1974 and 1982, utilities canceled orders for more than 100 nuclear plants, some of which were well under construction. See Campbell, 3–4.

132. Hertsgaard, 70–71, and Campbell, 5.

133. Tomain, 12.

134. *The New York Times*, 17 January 1975, 34.

135. Hertsgaard, 71–72.

136. Hilgartner et al., 78–80.

137. See the *Annual Report* for the Atomic Industrial Forum, Inc., for the years 1975 to 1979.

138. Atomic Industrial Forum, Inc., *Annual Report* (Washington, D.C.: Atomic Industrial Forum, 1979), 24.

139. Atomic Industrial Forum, Inc., Public Affairs and Information Program, *Report to Subscribers 1980–1981* (Washington, D.C.: Atomic Industrial Forum, 1981), 2.

140. Campbell, 86.

141. Atomic Industrial Forum, Inc., *Annual Report* (Washington, D.C.: Atomic Industrial Forum, 1979), 24.

142. Mark Jacobs, "Closing the Generating Gap," *Public Relations Journal* (May 1987): 22.

143. U.S. Committee for Energy Awareness, *Electronic Advertising* (Washington, D.C.: U.S. Committee for Energy Awareness, 1980), 3, and Hertsgaard, 190–191.

144. Atomic Industrial Forum, Inc., *Annual Report* (Washington, D.C.: Atomic Industrial Forum, 1981), 24.

145. Jacobs, 22.

146. Campbell, 3–6, and Tomain 22–24. See also Connie De Boer and Iuke Catsburg, "The Impact of Nuclear Accidents on Attitudes Toward Nuclear Energy," *Public Opinion Quarterly* 52, no. 2 (Summer, 1988): 254–261. For an interesting comparison of the problems of operating nuclear weapons plants in the Soviet Union and the United States, see *The New York Times*, 16 July 1989, 2(E).

147. Hertsgaard, 165.

148. Ibid., 173.

149. Ibid., 176.

Chapter Three

"Our Friend the Atom": The Reassuring Message of Nuclear PR

The preceding chapter examines the historical forces that combined to produce the "nuclear ethic"—a set of values, fostered by atomic scientists, the federal government, and private industry, that undergirded development of a commercial nuclear power industry in the United States. Now let us see how those values have become part of the rhetoric and images of modern nuclear risk communication. To do so, we return again to the early days of nuclear development when the industry began to focus on the importance of public acceptance of the peaceful atom. Modern nuclear risk communication messages have become clouded by rhetoric and images historically associated with the promotion of commercial nuclear power, but these images have also become so much a part of the culture of nuclear power that we must go back to the beginnings of nuclear power promotion to see how the images were created and later modified as economic and political conditions dictated. My "texts" for this analysis are the words, publications, advertisements, films, and photographs that the American nuclear industry has produced in support of commercial nuclear power development. A careful reading of these "texts" compared with today's materials will show how the promotional history of the industry and the values of the nuclear ethic have influenced modern risk communication messages.

GATHERING THE PR FORCES

New York City was gripped by an unseasonably late snowstorm on the morning of Monday, March 19, 1956, when nuclear industry executives gathered in the Plaza Hotel for what would be the first industry

conference on public relations.[1] The conference, called by the Atomic
Industrial Forum (AIF), the trade group formed three years earlier to
promote development and utilization of nuclear energy, marked a recognition by the industry that a negative connection still remained in the
public mind between atomic bombs and atomic reactors. Public opinion
had moved to the top of the industry's agenda because, after several
years of frustration, nuclear power appeared ready for a commercial
breakthrough. The nation's first full-scale power-producing reactor at
Shippingport, Pennsylvania, was only one year away from operation,
other reactors had been ordered, and Congress was actively considering
legislation to limit the industry's liability for nuclear plant accidents, a
step believed crucial for further commercial development. Although the
commercial prospects for nuclear power did seem brighter in 1956 than
at any time in the past, the executives were concerned about what their
pollsters were learning about American public opinion. Optimistic about
peaceful uses of the atom, Americans were extremely anxious about
nuclear weapons, and by 1956 public opinion had coalesced into what
Weart calls "the polarity of weapons versus peaceful uses, the atomic
genie who could be either menace or servant."[2] The question for the
industry's public relations specialists, pointed out AIF Executive Manager Charles Robbins in his opening statement to the conference, was
"how do we overcome the doubts and apprehensions of the wartime
atom and replace these with confidence and a ready acceptance of peaceful atomic enterprise?"[3] Industry executives knew that, for economic
reasons, they eventually would have to locate nuclear reactors close to
large population centers. A concerned and worried citizenry would make
it much more difficult to convince local officials and state utility commissions that such plants were safe.

The problem for the public relations specialists was how to send messages about nuclear power that would help Americans make a strong
distinction between bombs and power reactors, or, to use a *Time* magazine phrase, between "Good & Bad Atoms."[4] Because polls had shown
that the public was poorly informed about private industry's role in
developing the peacetime atom, the executives were also concerned that
the knowledge gap would strengthen the hand of public power advocates who wanted all nuclear facilities operated by the federal government. This concern with public opinion no doubt determined the choice
of a pollster as the principal speaker on the Monday evening program.
Lebaron R. Foster, vice president of Opinion Research Corporation, told
the group that the story of private industry's role in the development
of atomic energy "is largely untold or unregistered so far as the people
at large are concerned."[5] People were also unsure of the proper role for
government in the development of atomic energy, Foster said, and were
"groping for some kind of a social framework or social answer to atomic

development.'"[6] Foster reported that a substantial percentage of the public was either pro-public development of nuclear energy or had not yet formed an opinion on the public versus private development question. And whereas people had very positive hopes for peaceful development of the atom, they had very little knowledge about even the most elementary technical details of how nuclear power could be produced.

Other speakers throughout the two-day seminar reiterated the message that the industry's public relations mission must be to erase in the public mind the specter of the atomic bomb and replace it with an image of the atom's "positive" benefits. Dr. Frank K. Pittman, deputy director of the AEC's Division of Civilian Application, suggested that even the most basic change, such as replacing the word *atomic* with the more scientifically correct term *nuclear*, might go a long way toward helping people to understand that atomic energy did not necessarily mean atomic explosions.[7] However, in a remarkably prescient statement, Pittman cautioned that if the industry was to maintain credibility with the public, it should not mask the potential dangers associated with commercial development of nuclear power. "I think it's really important for people in your position to continuously get across to the public the idea that some day something is going to happen," Pittman said. "Then, when it does happen, you don't have an hysterical reaction by the public, which would really set back the whole nuclear energy industry."[8]

Pittman's prophetic concern about the impact of a serious accident on the future growth of the nuclear industry was not lost on the executives. One of nuclear power's greatest strengths in the battle for public opinion in the 1950s was its good safety record. There had been no serious accidents at any of the nuclear test and development facilities, and although there was some limited public concern about radiation, it was mainly associated with radioactive fallout from bomb tests and not from operation of nuclear facilities.[9] General Electric's Harold A. Beaudoin cited a 1950 University of Michigan study indicating that the public regarded the nuclear industry "as just another industry—with the risks and technical problems known to exist in the industrial world generally."[10] The survey's authors stressed that a serious accident could cause the public to recognize the uniqueness of the hazards posed by nuclear energy in the industrial field:

One incident happening in one company's facilities could have a most damaging effect on the entire industry program and its rate of progress. Looked at in this way, we in this industry have a mutual stake in what happens and how it is interpreted to and by the public. In terms of each company's interests, it would seem wise to evaluate the public relations risks—as we do other risks—and set up a program to reduce such risks in so far as is possible.[11]

Such a public relations program, Beaudoin pointed out, would involve "education on a low-pressure basis" of the public and local officials and opinion leaders prior to the construction of a nuclear plant, including providing information on radiation, safety measures, and waste disposal. "A good, positive educational approach on the local scene at the time of announcement of plans will forestall fears and the spread of 'scare' or misleading information as the project progresses."[12]

Beaudoin was GE's farsighted manager of advertising, sales promotion, and public relations, and had become a leading figure among the industry's public relations executives due to his company's experience with nuclear energy. Whereas in 1956 the industry was just beginning to recognize the important role that public opinion would play in future nuclear development, GE had well underway a strong program that involved a combination of print and broadcasting advertising, education of the news media, and community relations around GE nuclear facilities. For example, the Federal Communications Commission (FCC) allowed GE three minutes of commercial time on the popular "GE Television Theatre" to promote activities such as nuclear energy development, enabling the company to reach twenty to thirty million viewers with its nuclear message. The commercials were narrated by highly credible Don Herbert, television's famous "Mr. Wizard," and were designed to instruct the audience about science and technology as well as promote GE's efforts in various scientific endeavors.[13] In addition to television, the company feature film, *A Is for Atom*, would be seen by five million people by 1956 and was among several films distributed by the AEC to schools as part of a government effort to educate young people about nuclear energy. GE's "opinion leader" advertising series in *Time, Fortune, Newsweek, Harper's*, and the *Wall Street Journal* reached more than nine million readers each week, and more than twelve million copies of the comic book *Inside the Atom* would be distributed to secondary, high school, and college students between 1948 and 1965.[14]

Beaudoin told his audience that as early as 1948, when GE built its first developmental reactor, the company had recognized that "it was both desirable and necessary to tell local civic and municipal leaders, and the press, the full story [about company nuclear facilities] with the greatest possible speed." GE quickly discovered, Beaudoin said, that "public enthusiasm for pioneering with the atom completely outweighed questions about the potential hazards."[15] For Beaudoin, the job of nuclear public relations could be summarized in one word: education. "It is important that we tell the townsfolk and the city folk our stories so that they can understand something more of what a nuclear power plant is, how it works, as well as its advantages to the community." Beaudoin termed GE's program "a massive dose of preventive medicine, of atomic vaccine" and characterized as its purpose "to inform, and thereby to condition the public mind to familiarity and, ultimately, acceptance."[16]

For the industry as a whole, Beaudoin noted, a strong public relations effort would establish a climate of public trust, making future development of nuclear energy that much easier. "It's far easier to borrow money from a friend if he knows, from past experience, that you won't play the horses with it," Beaudoin concluded. "Likewise, if the mind is strongly conditioned on a continuing basis, then the public problem of a particular moment—locating a reactor in a populated area, for example—can be superimposed with a far better chance of understanding."[17]

SEPARATING "GOOD" FROM "BAD" ATOMS

Although Beaudoin and the other executives recognized that intensive public education programs might convince even the most skeptical that nuclear power plants were not atomic bombs waiting to explode, a much more difficult public perception problem remained—radiation. Like so many facets of nuclear power, radiation exemplified the classic dichotomy of "good and bad atoms." By 1956 the public was intimately familiar with the benefits of X-rays for medical diagnostic purposes and the use of radiation treatments for cancer and other diseases. However, people had also read news media reports from Japan shortly after the end of World War II about the "mysterious" deaths of Japanese who initially survived the blast and heat from the bomb dropped on Hiroshima, reports initially dismissed by the American military as propaganda.[18] The AEC's decision to allow news media coverage of bomb tests in the South Pacific in 1946 and later at the Nevada Proving Ground in the early 1950s increased media attention to radiation as technicians continually scanned reporters with Geiger counters following each blast.[19] When in 1954 a Bikini test showered the Japanese fishing ship *Fukuryu Maru* (*The Lucky Dragon*) with radioactive ash, resulting in the death of one fisherman from radioactive poisoning, the protest from the Japanese received considerable publicity in the United States.[20]

The industry's public relations executives recognized that people were beginning to develop an "irrational" fear of radiation that might inhibit the development of commercial nuclear power. William A. Stenzel, manager of public relations for Tracerlab, Inc., a company that produced various gauges and instruments containing radioactive sources, said that if the nuclear industry was going to "develop consumer acceptance of radioactivity," it would have to convince the public that radiation was "another industrial hazard over which we have spread a net of protection."[21] It was imperative, Stenzel emphasized, that the industry develop a "policy" for telling the public that radiation raises " . . . no more of a hazard than any other industrial hazard, when adequately protected against." He noted that such a policy should emphasize the "scientific, pragmatic control of peaceful applications of radioactivity" in contrast to the "uncontrolled dangers of the bomb."[22]

By the time the AIF conference ended, a picture had emerged of what would become the industry's public relations strategy for the next two decades. One element of the strategy would place emphasis on education about nuclear energy, primarily as a means to separate commercial nuclear power in the public mind from the image of atomic bombs. Because polls had shown the American public to be ignorant about how nuclear power was produced, the industry would devote considerable resources to instruction about nuclear fission, the structure of the atom, and how electricity was manufactured, at the same time pointing out the differences between nuclear power and nuclear explosions. Bombs were the product of "bad" atoms and were produced for destructive purposes, so education would hammer home the "positive" aspects of nuclear energy, and particularly how "good" atoms were daily touching the lives of people in industry, agriculture, and through the use of radioactive isotopes for the treatment of disease. "You must implant in the minds of our people the picture of the constructive atom—working for them," emphasized one conference speaker. "You must minimize the mental picture of mass destruction and misery whenever the words atomic energy are mentioned."[23] And as another speaker noted, education would put "the real, objective story of the atom over to the public so that the atomic age can be ushered in with the benefit of public understanding rather than misapprehension."[24] Better public understanding of nuclear energy would be the key to public acceptance.

The second prong of the industry's public relations strategy would be to provide the public with visual images and rhetoric that would help nuclear power blend in and become part of American technological life— what I call the "naturalization" of nuclear power. Stuart Hall has argued that certain codes, or meanings, may be "so widely distributed in a specific language community or culture, and be learned at so early an age, that they appear not to be constructed . . . but to be 'naturally' given." These codes, according to Hall, produce apparently "natural" recognitions that conceal "the practices of coding which are present."[25] Thus when nuclear publicists produced rhetoric and images to reinforce the idea that electricity production from nuclear power plants was no different from other industrial processes and that the risks, particularly from radiation, were no greater, they were attaching certain meanings, or codes, to nuclear power that were already "naturalized" in America's industrialized culture. Such a strategy carried with it certain dangers, as the publicists recognized. A serious accident involving a large release of radiation into the environment would quickly dispel the image of "naturalness" and might even create a backlash among the public. But of greater concern to the industry was the connection between the power plants and bombs—a connection that would be broken if the public accepted nuclear power as part of the "natural" march of progress.

Finally, it was important to create in the public consciousness a connection between the scientists who had unlocked the secrets of the atom in their laboratories and the engineers/technicians who were putting the atom to work in nuclear power plants. The development of nuclear power was the fulfillment of a great scientific quest dating back some 2,000 years to the ancient alchemists and such thinkers as Democritus and Aristotle. These early scientists and their successors had transferred the secrets of the atom to the engineers and technicians who would build and operate nuclear power plants. And the key secret that had been transferred was "control"—the scientists had gained their control over the atom in the laboratory and the research reactor, and engineers would maintain that control in the power plant. Furthermore, an emphasis on technological control in the power plant would further dispel the connection between peaceful uses of the atom and atomic bombs, whose destructive power was created by uncontrolled "bad" atoms.

One of the first ways in which the nuclear industry sought to educate the public was through traveling exhibits that visited county fairs, public buildings, and school rooms to demonstrate the peaceful benefits of nuclear energy. The AEC pioneered in the use of such exhibits, having designed the U.S. technical exhibit at the First International Conference on the Peaceful Uses of Atomic Energy in 1955. That exhibit was brought back to the United States in 1956 and viewed by several hundred thousand people at showings in New York and Oklahoma before being permanently installed at the Museum of Science and Industry in Chicago. By 1958 the AEC exhibit inventory included three large, eighty-six-panel "Atoms for Peace" exhibits; five mobile vans that were utilized in the agency's "This Atomic World" lecture series at high schools; ten eighteen-panel exhibits that could be shipped and shown without an attendant; three eight-panel exhibits entitled "The Useful Atom" that were designed for libraries and encouraged students to read about nuclear energy; and one booth exhibit for trade shows. The exhibits provided information on nuclear raw materials, reactors, nuclear power in the United States, industrial applications through the use of radioisotopes, and beneficial uses of nuclear energy in medicine and agriculture.[26] By June of 1958, the exhibits had been seen by more than nine million Americans.[27]

Reaching schoolchildren with information about nuclear power was a major part of the AEC's public education effort. More than 1.2 million schoolchildren had seen the "This Atomic World" program by 1958.[28] The program, conducted by AEC personnel, allowed students to come face-to-face with a model of a power reactor, a "visual and auditory chain reaction device," a Van de Graff generator, a Geiger counter, and other equipment.[29] The AEC had also put seven specially trained high school teachers on the road in government-provided station wagons to visit high schools and conduct programs stimulating interest in science courses. By 1957 the teachers had visited 186 schools in all forty-eight states plus the District of Columbia.[30] Requests by elementary and high school students and their teachers for kits of published material on nuclear energy exceeded 2,000 per month.[31] Years later, the nuclear industry would still use exhibits to reach target audiences at a variety of locations. For example, in 1983 some 43,000 people saw AIF exhibits on nuclear energy at many meetings, including those of the National Education Association, the American Association of University Women, and the American Association for the Advancement of Science.[32]

"NATURALIZING" THE ATOM

A more subtle technique for gaining acceptance of the new industry was to reassure the public that commercial nuclear power was no different from any other industrial process. "Nuclear energy is an industry just like the chemical industry or any other fabricating industry in which accidents will occur," one speaker had emphasized at the Plaza Hotel meeting. "Working in nuclear energy will not harm people."[33] Making nuclear power seem like just another industry required the public relations specialists to create an image of an industry that could coexist with the natural environment. By associating nuclear power with images and rhetoric that tapped into the normal, everyday environment with which people were familiar, the technological process of producing nuclear energy could appear to be a natural extension of the technological advances that Americans had come to expect in the post-war years—advances that had made the world a better place in which to live. And because that technological progress was identified by the public with science and scientists, nuclear power could be shown to be under the "control" of these same scientists, and, by proxy, the engineers and technicians who built and operated nuclear power plants. The scientific "magicians" who had used their magic to release the energy from the atom could also put that magic to work and control the energy.

The "naturalization" of nuclear power was accomplished both through the images that publicists selected for public view and through the language used in articles, booklets, and press releases describing the new technology. For example, General Electric chose to "market" nuclear power with the same photographic strategy that it had used since the turn of the century to market electricity and the electric light bulb. In his study of General Electric's use of photography between 1890 and

1930, David Nye points out how the photograph became a mechanism for helping GE tie new technological developments in with the past:

Through photographs it [GE] sought to reshape the structure of the social world. Yet these changes were continually presented as small conveniences or clear developments from the past, not as revolutionary shifts in the ways Americans illuminated their streets, lived in their homes, traveled, or communicated. Photography helped to smooth these transformations, suggesting landscapes of desires and wants.[34]

Similarly, General Electric used photography to show how nuclear power was a logical, orderly extension of technological progress, not a radically different way of making electricity. For example, a GE insert in a 1955 edition of *Senior Scholastic* entitled "Atoms At Work" used text, photographs, and drawings to tell the story of the company's role in nuclear power development. The cover photograph showed two clean-cut, white male engineers leaning over an architectural model of a nuclear power plant. The photograph is shot so that the large, round reactor containment sphere—a piece of equipment not found at conventional electric generating plants—is placed in the background and partially hidden by an engineer's arm, whereas the more common electric transmission line towers are placed in the foreground. The photograph thus conveys an image that nuclear power plants produce electricity and are no different from conventional power plants.[35]

Photographs of engineers towering over nuclear power plant models conveyed the image that those who designed and built the plants had inherited the mantle of control from those who first unlocked the power of the atom. These young engineers, the GE ads said, were "pioneers" who would "harness" and "tame" the atom.[36] A 1958 AEC publication made the connection between the scientists and the engineers crystal clear for a public that was still awed by the mystery of nuclear energy:

Today's 'atomic scientist' may be a physicist or chemist, but he is as likely to be a mathematician, metallurgist, meteorologist, medical scientist, biologist, geologist, engineer, or even an oceanographer. Nor is it uncommon to find an engineer working as a reactor physicist, or a physicist working as a reactor engineer. In fact, the transmutation of disciplines is as much a part of the alchemy of atomic energy as the transmutation of elements.[37]

Similarly, a full-page advertisement in a 1955 edition of *General Electric Review*, a magazine that went primarily to engineers both inside and outside the company, shows two engineers leaning over an architectural model of GE's first commercial nuclear power plant for Commonwealth Edison in Chicago. One man, the older of the two, points to the plant in an instructive pose, while the younger man leans forward and looks on with interest. The headline reads that "The Atomic Age Is Now" and the advertising copy, after stressing America's need for more electricity, points out that "the many-sided atom is already working its magic for the good of mankind. As we see it, the Atomic Age is *now*." Even when the company had a "real" reactor to photograph, as when it opened the research reactor at its Vallecitos Atomic Laboratory in Pleasanton, California in 1957, GE chose to photograph two executives in the foreground on a hillside overlooking the laboratory and research reactor, making the men appear larger than the nuclear facilities they managed.[38] Many GE advertisements of this period also carried a phrase across the top reading "Engineering Leadership Key To Atomic Progress."[39]

The use of architectural models in the GE advertisements illustrates a problem for nuclear publicists prior to the completion of the Shippingport plant in 1957—there were no full-size nuclear power plants to photograph. Therefore, many of the advertisements were illustrated with drawings. As Nye points out, in certain situations the drawings enabled GE to help the viewer make connections that would have been difficult or impossible with a photograph.[40] For example, a two-page GE ad in the October 1956 issue of *Harper's* entitled "What General Electric is doing to help bring America atomic-electric power" uses twelve drawings of equal size to illustrate the company's history in the nuclear field. Most of the drawings reproduce visual themes with which Americans were familiar in the 1950s. Scientists are depicted in their laboratories. The company's contribution to the military effort, and by implication its patriotism, is illustrated by drawings of the Manhattan Project complex in Oak Ridge and the launching of the nuclear-powered submarine *Seawolf*. Happy, smiling natives in tropical dress are shown near electric transmission lines to illustrate GE's efforts to sell reactors outside the United States, and a large, electric light bulb superimposed over a nuclear plant makes a direct connection between nuclear power and electricity—a connection that could not have been made at that time in a photograph. Only two of the twelve drawings—one of workers in protective radiation clothing and the other of a GE experimental reactor—do not convey familiar images.[41] In later industry publications, schematic drawings of the inner workings of both fossil-fueled and nuclear power plants would help the industry show how similar the electrical production processes were.

No doubt in an effort to maintain the image of engineering "control" over the atom, GE deviated from historic company practice in the composition of photographs that showed equipment necessary for the construction and operation of nuclear power plants and other nuclear technology. Nye points out that a random analysis of photographs contained in editions of the *General Electric Review* published in the 1920s and 1930s showed that 70 percent were pictures of machines *without* people, and the photographs that included people used them to illustrate the size of the machines. "The photographs overwhelmingly emphasized machines cut off from human involvement and from their social implications," Nye notes.[42] Conversely, photographs of nuclear equipment used in *GE Review* in the 1950s rarely showed the equipment without showing people in an active, operational state. Photographs that showed technicians handling radioactive materials with remote-controlled arms (known as "master-slave manipulators"), engineers testing reactor safety equipment, radiation technicians in protective clothing, and environmental specialists collecting samples of flora and fauna around nuclear facilities all conveyed an image of scientists, technicians, and engineers who were comfortable with the nuclear equipment and in total control of the nuclear process.

Another technique used by the industry to "naturalize" nuclear power plants was to photograph the buildings so that they blended into the natural environment, what Weart calls "the machine in the meadow."[43] For example, the front and back color cover of a 1958 AEC publication extolling nuclear energy shows GE's Vallecitos research reactor at the base of a green hill with yellow wildflowers, a pond in the foreground, and the leaves from a nearby tree gracefully framing the reactor containment vessel.[44] The perspective provided by aerial photographs helped minimize the tremendous size of reactor buildings, and such photographs were frequently used in promotional publications. For example, eleven of thirteen full-view shots of power plants in a 1964 AIF publication were taken from the air.[45] When ground-level photographs of plants were taken, a frequently chosen camera angle reduced the visual impact of the large, round spherical containment buildings common on GE plants. Because most plants were located near large bodies of water for reactor cooling purposes, photographs were taken with the water in the foreground and the reactor buildings well in the background. Weart points out that a 1969 AEC film included girls fishing near a white reactor building, and many an industry publication took advantage of the positive effect that warm water discharged from the plant had in attracting fish to include at least one shot of fishing boats near the plant cooling towers.[46]

USING COMICS AND FILMS

Another technique the industry used to "naturalize" nuclear power was to educate the public about the new technology through cartoon characters and drawings. Although research indicates that cartoons do not enhance learning, there is some evidence to suggest that they make learning more enjoyable and tend to reduce anxiety, making them an ideal teaching tool for a subject that was born under a mushroom cloud.[47] Perhaps the industry's most ambitious effort in this regard was the publication in 1955 of GE's comic book *Inside the Atom*.[48] Widely circulated in the school systems, *Inside the Atom* told of the development of nuclear energy through the eyes of Ed, an older man who functioned as a teacher for Johnny, a boy of about twelve. Like many popular accounts of nuclear energy development produced in the 1950s, *Inside the Atom* begins with an explanation of early atomic theories, and connects the work of well-known modern scientists such as Bohr, Rutherford, and Einstein to the legends surrounding the alchemists and the early atomic theories of Democritus and Aristotle.[49] This is followed by a detailed explanation of the structure of the atom and the principle of nuclear fission, and concludes with Ed's explanation of how the atom is making "wonderful things possible" in power production, transportation, medicine, industry, and agriculture.[50]

By using a comic book to educate schoolchildren about nuclear energy, General Electric was able to present strange and unfamiliar information in a context that was both noncontroversial and enjoyable to children. "Adopting the style of a particular kind of publication can be used both to present a point of view in a striking form and, perhaps, to bring it to the attention of readers who would not otherwise be made aware of it," notes Edward Booth-Clibborn and Daniele Baroni in *The Language of Graphics*. "The fantasy world of comic books, for instance, seems remote from political controversy, but their graphic techniques have been called to the aid of many causes. In the process, the stereotypes of popular imagery become the format of an analytical message."[51] In *Inside the Atom*, the message is clear. "When we've solved all the problems [of developing commercial nuclear power]," Ed tells Johnny, "the energy potential locked inside the atom will provide enough power for everybody—everywhere."[52] Ed doesn't mention the problems associated with "bad" atoms; there is no discussion in the book of atomic bombs, just a brief reference to GE's role in helping develop uranium separation facilities during the war. Ed tells Johnny that the safety of workers in the nuclear industry is assured through several measures—training, rules, protective features of the plants, and "sensitive instruments" that "warn" workers of dangerous developments. "The result: Folks living nearby are in no danger at all . . . and workers are as safe as they'd be in their own homes."[53]

Because cartoons and drawings allowed publicists to create images that could not be reproduced in photographs, they were frequently used to both educate and promote. For example, the AEC relied on cartoon characters to educate workers in the early years of atomic development about safe practices in handling nuclear materials. "Radiation . . . a new Hazard is born!" began the AEC's *Radiation Safety Primer*, with an accompanying illustration showing a "baby" whose head was the familiar atomic symbol (a small ball ringed by whirling electrons) being pushed in a stroller by an engineer, a doctor, and a scientist.[54] The pamphlet tells workers that radiation is a "natural force like electricity" and that "radiation like electricity can be harmful in large amounts." Through a series of simple cartoon illustrations and text, the primer shows industry workers how they are protected from overexposure to radiation by special shielding, instrumentation, and regular medical checkups, and instructs them on techniques they must use to avoid radiation contamination. So workers would not be left with the impression that radiation is their only job-related hazard, the primer concludes with an illustration of workers in various accident situations whose attention is being distracted by an attractive woman in a swimsuit. The accompanying caption reads "Radiation is New and Interesting . . . But Don't Forget the old reliable . . . Killers."

Although produced for educational purposes, these cartoon drawings tended to "naturalize" radiation by depicting it symbolically as a woman, a baby, or the more common phenomenon of electricity. A similar purpose was achieved in a 1966 AIF publication entitled *The What and Why of Atomic Power* in which a cartoon character named Harry Gibbs is instructed by an "information specialist" named Burt Blake about nuclear energy.[55] When Harry first "meets" nuclear energy on the publication's cover, the AEC's radiation "baby" has grown up into an atomic power "adult" with the familiar atomic symbol still being used as the character's head. Harry Gibbs functions as a sort of "Everyman" in the publication who asks questions about nuclear energy, according to the introduction, that the reader would want answered. Cartoon characters and drawings use familiar themes to make nuclear power production appear simple and natural. Fission is depicted as a magic show in which a magician, "The Great Neutron," throws neutrons at the atomic character and "splits" the character into two identical characters. The multiple levels of nuclear plant safety are illustrated by a baseball player who attempts to field a ground ball while being backed up by several other players and a large safety net. The atomic character links hands with other characters depicting coal, oil, and gas to "help utilities keep down electricity prices." The publication concludes with a drawing of a man resting comfortably in a hammock with a nuclear plant nearby as the text concludes that "atomic power plants make good neighbors." More recently, cartoon characters have proven useful in helping the industry make further connections between ideas that are beyond the capability of photographs. A 1980 print media and television advertising campaign by the U.S. Council for Energy Awareness used a cartoonlike stick figure to illustrate how nuclear energy could help the country satisfy its need for electricity and lower its dependence on foreign oil.[56]

Films have also occupied an important position in the industry's public education effort. In 1952 the AEC began making available to private film studios and others black-and-white stock film footage showing the use of nuclear energy in medical, biological, and agricultural research and a variety of other peaceful applications.[57] Films were a particularly effective way to reach students, and in 1953 the agency began distributing the GE-produced film *A Is for Atom* into classrooms around the country. Other AEC films produced during the period included *The Magic of the Atom* (1954), *Atoms for Peace* (1959), and *Atoms for the Americas* (1963).[58]

A. Costandina Titus points out that these AEC films presented basic information about the atom and its positive uses to public school science classes and contained very little information about the use of nuclear weapons. "Their significance lies in their very existence, which demonstrates an attempt by the government to launch an extensive campaign to present atomic power to the American public as a positive, beneficial, non-threatening phenomenon as long as it was understood and controlled by the proper authorities," he notes.[59] Most of the films used animated cartoon characters that tended to greatly simplify and even trivialize atomic science. For example, in a 1964 version of *A Is for Atom*, Dr. Atom, a cartoon character whose head was the familiar atomic symbol, explains the internal structure of atoms while other similarly drawn characters jump happily about in a community called "Element Town." Radium, the film explained, was a highly "active" or radioactive element, so the cartoon character depicting radium was shown frantically dancing. When the discussion turned to positive applications of nuclear power, a Geiger counter was transformed into a cartoon character resembling the famous fictional detective Sherlock Holmes, who busily began "tracking down" radioactive tracers in plants and people.[60]

The film also depicted nuclear energy as a faceless, muscular giant, straddling the United States with arms crossed, symbolically representing what Weart calls the "transcendental power" of the atom to be both the savior and destroyer of humankind.[61] The image of nuclear power as a powerful giant capable of being both "good" and "bad" was perhaps best depicted in the 1957 Walt Disney film *Our Friend the Atom*, which was produced for the Disney television series "Disneyland" on ABC and later released to theaters in Europe.[62] Much of the film is narrated by Heinz Haber, a scientist hired by Disney as a consultant to the studio on nuclear energy.[63] Haber, who spoke with a heavy German accent, is surrounded throughout the film by white-coated technicians in the Disney "science laboratory," giving the production an aura of scientific credibility. Haber explains that the scientific search for the secrets of the atom is reminiscent of the ancient story of the fisherman who finds a genie in the bottle, and this story becomes the device through which *Our Friend the Atom* traces the development of nuclear energy. In an animated sequence at the film's beginning, the fisherman removes the lead stopper from the bottle, releasing a malevolent-looking purple genie who rises high above the scared fisherman in a mushroom-shaped cloud. The genie threatens the fisherman with death, but the clever fisherman tricks the genie back into the bottle, and the genie agrees to grant the fisherman three wishes for his release. In the Disney version of this ancient story, the fisherman chooses for his first two wishes to use the genie's "magic power" to produce energy and provide health and food. The fisherman's third wish is that the atomic genie forever remain the friend of humankind.

In *Our Friend the Atom*, Disney demonstrated the difference between "good" and "bad" atoms by juxtaposing the image of the atomic mushroom cloud with a nuclear reactor. In one sequence, three atomic bomb tests are shown in sequence while Haber describes how, like the fisherman, society may wish it had never found the vessel containing the genie. But Disney then shows a bomb blast in reverse motion with the mushroom cloud being sucked down into the fisherman's bottle. The scene dramatically illustrates the control that the film's producer believed society could have over the atomic genie. Later in the film, a now benevolent genie rises in a cloud from a nuclear reactor, while Haber describes the "magic power" of the reactor to make materials radioactive for use in research and medicine. As the film ends, the now "tamed" genie towers over the land, and from his giant hands society receives the "fire" of atomic power and the "magic tools for research" in agriculture, medicine, and industry. The final image is a view of the world as the nucleus of the atom.

Both of these films, and others produced by the industry, told the story of atomic energy development as one of choices. Society had been given the power to control the atom by its scientists, and that power could either serve or destroy. There was very little in the films to suggest that there were risks or tradeoffs associated with the peaceful atom. When radiation was discussed, it was always characterized as being under the control of those "experts" who held the secrets of the atom. In *A Is for Atom*, for example, the narrator explained that nuclear reactors could control radioactivity "in complete safety," and drawings of various commercial nuclear power plants were presented with cows shown grazing in the fields next to the cooling towers while farmers plowed the land on tractors. Films have continued to be a vehicle for public education by the nuclear industry. In its 1981 annual report, AIF reported that more than ten million people had seen its film *A Play Half Written: The Energy Adventure* on commercial and public television and in school and community showings.[64]

Although photographs, drawings, films, and cartoons helped to create a visual image of nuclear power as a normal, natural, and logical extension of modern science and technological progress, the language of promotion often relied on simile and metaphor to connect the atom to familiar images in American life. No doubt because radiation was so feared by the public, publications discussing it were marked by language that stressed science's "control" of radiation and the positive impact radiation was having on the treatment of disease and in industry and agriculture. As one AIF publication assured nuclear industry workers, radiation was "strictly regulated, effectively controlled, carefully monitored, and precisely quantified."[65] An AEC publication noted in 1958 that radiation film badges and other detection devices "are today as familiar to workers in this field as water coolers and pencil sharpeners."[66] Publicists also went to great lengths to show that even without nuclear power plants, "natural" or background radiation was a part of the environment, and that man-made radiation contributed very little to the radiation already present in nature. The comparison between the two radiation categories was most often made by producing charts showing both natural and man-made radiation sources, with nuclear power located at the bottom of the list. An industry film released in 1982 was aptly named *Radiation . . . Naturally.*[67]

A comparison of 1951 and 1960 editions of an AEC publication designed to provide the public with "nontechnical" information about radiation provides in microcosm an example of how government and industry publicists changed their treatment of radiation as commercial nuclear power plants entered American culture.[68] Both pamphlets rely on a question-and-answer format, but by 1960 such questions as "Is It Safe to Live Near Atomic Energy Plants?" and "Can Radiation Injuries Be Cured?" had been dropped. Reflecting the concerns of some publicists that the word *atomic* was automatically connected in the public mind with bombs, the 1960 report substituted *nuclear.* Only three photographs showing radiation handling equipment and a worker in protective clothing were included in the 1951 report; the 1960 edition included photographs of a patient being treated with cobalt, the nuclear-powered submarine *Nautilus,* the use of radiation in agriculture to study plants and eradicate pests such as the screwworm fly, and other "positive" applications.

Although some of the differences in the two publications can be explained by the passage of time and technological developments in the nuclear energy field, the comparison also reveals the efforts that publicists made to "naturalize" radiation and emphasize its benefits, at the same time minimizing its harmful effects. For example, compare the opening paragraphs of the two publications:

1951

Light is a kind of radiation; so are radio waves. The word radiation, as used in the atomic energy enterprise, applies to one particular kind—*nuclear radiation.*

It is called "nuclear" radiation because it comes from the core, or the nucleus, of atoms.

1960

Nuclear radiations are types of energy that occur naturally in the world we live in, just as do other more familiar radiations such as light, heat, radio waves, and X-rays. General interest in nuclear radiations is comparatively new, and our unfamiliarity with the term and what it means may make these particular radiations seem mysterious, just as electricity once was mysterious to most people. We now know electricity as a familiar and indispensable servant of mankind; it has been controlled and put to work. Nuclear radiation, likewise, is being controlled and put to work for man's good. Handled carelessly, however, nuclear radiation, like electricity, can be destructive.

In 107 words, the 1960 paragraph established the following ideas:

- Radiation occurs *naturally* in the environment.
- Radiation is a type of energy, just like light, heat, radio waves, and X-rays.
- Radiation may be unfamiliar and mysterious, but once so was electricity and, by implication, so were other technological phenomena that we now take for granted.
- Radiation can be controlled, just like electricity.
- Radiation has been put to work for the benefit of humankind, just like electricity.
- Radiation's dangers are like those of familiar electricity, but danger occurs only if the two (very similar) forces are "handled carelessly."

The 1960 pamphlet also discussed national defense applications of nuclear energy, although in most references "bombs" were transformed into "weapons." According to these publications, the difference between weapons and reactors was "control." Bombs were examples of atoms reacting in an "uncontrolled" fashion, whereas in nuclear reactors "the rate of the reaction is under strict control." Using a strained comparison, the 1960 publication sought to show that nuclear energy was no different than any other power source if handled properly: "Similarly, gasoline can explode, but also can be burned in a stove or in an automobile engine."[69] References in the 1951 report that atomic bombs can "kill and injure thousands" and that two government workers had been killed by radiation in laboratory accidents were also dropped from the 1960 report.[70]

Although directed at the layperson, many of the publications about nuclear power contained a high level of technical detail. Weart notes that in Europe and the United States, industry publicists created rational "information" campaigns with a multitude of technical facts and detail.

Even though much of the public did not understand all the technical details about nuclear power, the volume of information served a symbolic function by projecting "confidence that matters were safe with the experts who understood what it was all about."[71]

For example, the 1960 AEC publication on radiation provided a detailed and specific discussion of the four principal kinds of radiation, complete with drawings of alpha, beta, and gamma rays and neutrons. A section on radioactive decay provided decay rates for various nuclear materials and contained a glossary defining the ten different units for measuring radiation exposure, including discussion of roentgens, rads, rems, and curies.[72] A 1964 AIF publication on reactor safety devoted several pages to features of reactor operation such as the "Doppler effect," nuclear "excursions," fuel rod cladding, "safe geometry" in the reactor core, "zero"-leakage containment shells, and other technical issues that projected scientific concern with safety.[73] To demonstrate the level of federal control over nuclear power, detailed descriptions of how plants were licensed by the AEC were included in some publications, and one added drawings of cartoon characters who "smiled" as they worked their way through the multiple levels of the federal licensing process.[74]

As the industry moved into its growth years in the 1960s, publicists continued to use language that educated, "naturalized" nuclear power, and emphasized control. Through drawings and schematic diagrams, the industry sought to show how nuclear plants produced electricity in the same manner as coal and hydroelectric plants, and that only the fuel source was different. It was "physically impossible" for a nuclear power plant to behave like an atomic bomb, emphasized one publication, and then explained the differences in detail.[75] The amount of radiation exposure to the public from living near a nuclear power plant was compared to that received from watching television, wearing a luminescent watch, or having an X-ray,[76] and another publication equated the number of "man-hours" required to build the pyramids with the same amount of effort devoted to research in nuclear energy.[77] Substances placed in the reactor controlled neutrons "much as a blotter soaks up ink,"[78] and nuclear fuel could be stored "in a space not much larger than your living room."[79] Used nuclear fuel became "spent."[80] Cooler water discharged from nuclear power plants was "feebly radioactive," whereas releases of radioactive gases into the environment were "controlled" to meet AEC regulations.[81] The laws of physics governing the combination of nuclear fuel in water-cooled reactors (all but one commercial U.S. reactor are cooled by water) created "natural safety features" that limited accidents. But should the "natural" features fail, operators could rely on "control rods," "safety mechanisms" that operated in a "fail-safe" manner, "multiple physical barriers," and other "special safeguards" to limit accidents.

To further "naturalize" the technology, publicists sometimes gave nuclear reactors human characteristics. For example, the physical laws governing the operation of nuclear reactors caused these devices to have a "stubborn streak" that naturally prevented accidents.[82] Neutrons were the "life's blood" of nuclear reactors and there were various "generations" of reactor designs in the "atomic power family."[83] And with all of their advantages, nuclear power plants made "good neighbors."[84] Sometimes, the industry carried the machine-human comparisons too far, as in a 1976 trade publication advertisement that posed the provocative question, "Why is a woman like a nuclear power plant?" "In order to remain beautiful she must take good care of herself . . . she schedules her rest regularly . . . when she is not up to par she sees her doctor . . . she never lets herself get out of date . . . she is as trim now as she was ten years ago . . . in other words, *she is a perfect example of preventative maintenance.*"[85]

As criticism of the industry began to escalate in the 1970s, publicists recognized that they would have to confront the now actively debated issues associated with safety and the environmental effects of operating the plants. A 1970 publication turned the environmentalists' argument about nuclear power on its head by pointing out that unlike coal-fired generating plants, nuclear plants were "clean" because they did not introduce bulk combustion products such as fly ash into the atmosphere. The same report characterized many of the environmental problems associated with nuclear power as "imagined," but where real problems existed, such as the potential damaging effects on aquatic life by warm water discharged from the plants, the industry could engineer solutions to the problem (cooling towers). Nuclear plants were pleasing aesthetic additions to the environment compared to coal-burning facilities; plants had a "streamlined" look, resembling "light industry."[86]

By the mid–1970s, the industry was openly acknowledging the growing public distrust of nuclear power. One AIF pamphlet began: "People tell pollsters that their greatest worry about nuclear power is that reactors will explode. A housewife asks if the electricity generated by a nuclear plant is radioactive. A Congressman refers to the 'nuclear explosions' that produce energy at these generating stations." The solution to these "misconceptions," according to the pamphlet, was education. "Actually, nuclear plants are not as different from other power plants as these misconceptions imply. Understanding what they are and how they work is important to forming judgments and attitudes about nuclear power."[87] But whereas education about the mechanics of nuclear plant operations and safety would continue to be an industry theme throughout the 1970s,

a second theme began to emerge as consumers started becoming pain-
fully educated to the world energy situation through the oil embargo of
1973. AIF publications began to stress the country's "dependence" on
electricity as a measure of an "improved" standard of living. The country
had an "insatiable appetite" for electrical energy, an appetite that could
not be realized if America continued its dependence on foreign oil. The
solution was heavier reliance on the nation's most plentiful fuels—coal
and uranium. Increasing reliance on nuclear power "is vital to our way
of life," one publication concluded, noting that "distinguished American
scientists, including 11 Nobel Prize winners," agreed with the industry
that the situation was "critical."[88]

Although preoccupied with the political and economic fallout from
the accident at Three Mile Island in 1979, the industry continued to
expand on an overall public relations theme of making America "energy
independent through nuclear power." The public relations posture following the accident was to demonstrate that nuclear power was now
even safer as a result of the lessons learned and that more than ever the
country must meet the challenge of foreign oil. Indeed, support of nuclear power was deemed patriotic, and industry publications and advertising began to be marked by symbols that reflected patriotic ideals.
For example, in 1980 a major national advertising campaign begun by
the U.S. Council for Energy Awareness (CEA) relied heavily on red,
white, and blue designs and a "stars and bars" color scheme to reinforce
the message that nuclear energy was a necessary weapon in the battle
to reduce America's dependence on foreign oil.[89]

NUCLEAR RISK COMMUNICATION TODAY

It is unlikely that the nuclear industry executives who met in the Plaza
Hotel on a snowy March day in 1956 could even have begun to imagine
the twists and turns that the industry's public relations strategy would
take over the next three decades. And although their prophetic concern
that a major accident would drastically change public attitudes has been
dramatically confirmed, few in that room would have ever guessed that
their industry would one day publish information warning about how
the public could avoid the dangerous consequences of serious nuclear
plant accidents. There is an old adage in the practice of public relations
that one should "never repeat a negative" when discussing issues affecting one's client or employer, but among the sweeping changes forced
on the industry after Three Mile Island was just such a directive. Nuclear
utilities, working with state and local officials, would be required to
discuss a subject they had historically avoided or minimized—accidents
involving radiation releases and their impact on the public. How has an
industry intent upon speaking no evil managed to convey the idea that

nuclear power is a "risky" technology . . . and how effective has it been in raising the level of public consciousness about those risks?

As of June 1989, there were 112 commercial nuclear reactors with NRC operating licenses at seventy-three locations in thirty-four states. During the first three months of that year, those plants provided more than 18 percent of the electricity produced in the United States. Illinois has twelve operating reactors, the most of any state; ten states have one reactor. The reactors are operated by fifty-two utilities, although many are jointly owned by several utility companies. For example, the Arizona Public Service Company is the operating utility for the three-unit Palo Verde plant in Wintersburg, Arizona, but the reactors are also owned by six other utilities.[90]

Under the criteria developed jointly by the NRC and FEMA to assess radiological emergency plans and preparedness around nuclear power plants (NUREG–0654), the owner/operators, in conjunction with state and local agencies, develop emergency plans to reduce radiation exposure to people living within a ten-mile radius and address potential problems from radiation contamination of food and water for a distance of fifty miles from the plant. The ten-mile Emergency Planning Zones (EPZs) are normally circular with the plant located at the center, but the shape may vary due to geographical features at the plant site. The NRC and FEMA criteria allow two small water-cooled reactors of less than 250 megawatts and the Fort St. Vrain gas-cooled reactor in Colorado to establish EPZs of about five miles in radius. Because reactors at multiple-unit plants are located close together, only one 10–mile EPZ is required per plant.[91]

As part of the utility/state/local emergency plan, nuclear plant owner/operators are required periodically to make information available to the public living within the EPZ (and transients passing through the area) concerning how they will be notified and what their actions should be if a nuclear plant emergency occurs. As noted in Chapter 1, the NUREG–0654 criteria for evaluating whether the public education planning standard has been met specifies that the information provided EPZ residents include, but not be limited to, educational material on radiation; a contact for additional information; radiation protection measures such as evacuation routes, sheltering information, and respiratory protection; and information for the benefit of the disabled and others with special needs. The planning standard does not require plant owner/operators or state and local officials to adopt a specific communication format or method to provide the public with this information, but does suggest posting the information in public areas, placing it in telephone books, and mailing it with utility bills and in annual publications.[92]

To determine the communication materials that nuclear utilities use to meet the NUREG–0654 planning standard for public education and

Table 1
Utility Emergency Communication Materials

Material	Utilities (N = 46)
Booklets	32
Telephone Book Ads	27
Calendars	18
Newsletters	17
Letters	12
Posters	12
Print Ads	11
Broadcast Ads	10
Stickers	7
Brochures	6
Signs	3
Maps	2
Annual Reports	1
Leaflets	1

information, a questionnaire was mailed to the fifty-two nuclear utilities in May 1989. It was addressed to the heads of utility public information offices or others who had been identified as having responsibility for nuclear public education within the ten-mile EPZ. In many cases, the completed questionnaires were returned by utility communication and emergency planning specialists who were physically located at the nuclear plant site rather than at the utility's headquarters address. A total of forty-seven questionnaires were returned by utilities operating ninety-three reactors in thirty states, representing 83 percent of the licensed operating reactors in the United States. Two utilities operating separate nuclear power plants that are geographically close together were counted as one because both plants share a combined EPZ and the utilities use the same principal communication tool, thereby reducing, for the purposes of the study, the number of participating utilities to forty-six.[93] (Utilities that returned questionnaires are identified in Appendix A.) The total combined estimated EPZ populations for forty-four of the forty-six utilities is more than three million people; two utilities did not provide estimates of EPZ populations. EPZ populations served by the utilities ranged from a high of 420,919 to a low of 1,200.

Each utility was asked to indicate the communication material or materials it used to meet the NUREG–0654 criteria for public education. The utility responses are shown in Table 1. It shows that the most popular communication material used by the utilities is the booklet, followed by telephone book advertisements, calendars, newsletters, letters to EPZ residents, and posters. Utilities were then asked to indicate

Table 2
Primary Utility Emergency Communication Materials

Material	Utilities (N = 46)
Booklets	26
Calendars	17
Telephone Book Ads	2
Brochures	1

which *one* of these communication materials they primarily relied on to meet the NUREG–0654 criteria for providing *EPZ residents* with emergency information. Table 2 shows that the majority rely on booklets and calendars; two utilities rely on telephone book advertisements and one on a brochure.

Advertisements in telephone books serving the EPZ contain essential emergency information placed by the utilities. Although a number of utilities prepare the advertisements, their low ranking as a *primary tool* for meeting the NUREG–0654 criteria suggests that most utilities use the advertisements for reaching *transient* populations who pass through the EPZ but do not reside there.

It is important to note that this study sought to identify utility communication materials that went directly to EPZ residents without being filtered through an information "gatekeeper" such as the news media. Most utility public education programs also involve communicating messages to EPZ residents through the news media via press releases and new conferences, interviews, and other media relations techniques. In addition, some nuclear utilities have extensive public speaking programs about nuclear power and/or hold meetings in neighborhoods at which EPZ residents can receive information and ask questions. These neighborhood meetings are normally informal sessions for which transcripts are not kept, but utilities that hold such meetings generally provide participants with printed materials such as the booklets and calendars mentioned above.

Forty-one of the forty-six utilities, nearly 89 percent, said they took *primary responsibility* for seeing that their principal communication material was distributed to EPZ residents; the remaining five utilities relied on either state or local governmental agencies to handle the distribution. All but two of the utilities said that their materials were distributed by mail, but ten utilities indicated that they used several distribution methods, including hand delivery to EPZ residents, central pickup points, and placement at public buildings and other locations where EPZ residents were likely to visit. All of the utilities responding to the question-

Table 3
Utility Estimates of State/Local Governmental Effort in Emergency Material
Preparation

Effort	Write/Edit (N = 46)	Photography (N = 46)	Graphics (N = 46)
> 50 percent	5	2	3
25-50 percent	11	4	5
< 25 percent	30	40	38

naire said they annually update their primary communication material for EPZ residents.

To determine the level of involvement by state and local government in the preparation of emergency communication materials, utilities were asked to estimate the *percentage of effort* that governmental agencies contributed to the development of these primary materials. As shown in Table 3, state/local governmental involvement is extremely limited. Only 35 percent of the responding utilities reported that state/local governments contributed 25 percent or more of the effort required to write and edit the materials; governmental involvement in photograph selection and graphic design was considerably less.

It should be noted that the overall emergency planning process requires state and local agencies responsible for emergency planning to review and approve these materials, and those agencies are listed in the materials as points of contact for the public during emergencies. But these findings do indicate that, with few exceptions, state and local governmental agencies do not actively participate in the preparation of utility public education materials for EPZ residents.

The survey also indicates that federal involvement in the development of nuclear public education materials is more extensive than state/local involvement. All but two of the forty-six nuclear utilities responding to the survey reported that their communication materials had been reviewed by FEMA, which has an ongoing program to improve the quality and effectiveness of utility public education programs. FEMA has told the General Accounting Office that its review program has caused some utilities to revise the format and style of brochures and change the reading level to coincide more closely with that of a plant's geographic area. This survey confirms that FEMA has been active in suggesting changes for utility communication materials. Of the forty-four utilities who said FEMA had reviewed their communication materials, twenty-eight, or nearly 64 percent, said that the federal agency had suggested changes in the format and organization of the materials; 50 percent reported that FEMA had proposed changes in the graphic design of the materials.

Table 4
Utility Knowledge Assessment and Communication Material Selection by EPZ Size

Assessment/Material	< 50,000 (N = 25)	≥ 50,000 (N = 19)[1]
Made Assessment	13	12
No Assessment	12	7
Calendars	13	4
Booklets	12	12
Brochure	0	1
Telephone Book Ads	0	2

[1]Two utilities did not provide EPZ size.

However, the survey findings support the GAO's concern that not enough attention is being devoted to determining whether EPZ residents actually read and understand the emergency communication materials they receive from nuclear plant owner/operators.[94] Twenty utilities, 43 percent of those responding to the survey, said they do not assess whether EPZ residents understand their material. Of the utilities that did make such an assessment, only one-third did so on an annual or more frequent schedule. The most popular assessment method was a survey of EPZ residents (eighteen responses), followed by analysis of letters and informal comments (twelve responses). Three utilities indicated that they met with "focus groups" of EPZ residents to discuss emergency communication materials; one utility used reading experts to determine readability of the publications; and one utility relied on the FEMA survey of the emergency notification system as a measure of residents' understanding. One utility noted that it had been able to assess the understandability of its communication materials when emergency evacuations were conducted within the plant EPZ for both a chemical plant problem and a hurricane.

Because the cost of communicating to a large EPZ population might influence a utility's public education strategy, an analysis was conducted to see if EPZ population size might be a factor in (1) choice of primary communication material and (2) whether a utility assessed the level of understanding of that material within its EPZ population. Table 4 shows that calendars were the communication material of choice for utilities with small EPZ populations; EPZ size does not appear to be a factor influencing whether utilities assess their residents' understanding of the content of emergency communication materials.

Although the survey did not attempt to gather information from the utilities about factors affecting their selection of materials, common sense may suggest why thirteen of the seventeen utilities that used calendars have EPZ populations of 50,000 or less. Emergency calendars are similar to those produced for commercial sale in that they rely on full-color photographs, special folding and binding, and other graphic techniques that increase production expense. Most of the booklets analyzed in this study do not use full-color photographs, special bindings, or complicated graphics, and are therefore less expensive to produce than calendars. Thus utilities having to communicate with large EPZ populations may find it too expensive to utilize calendars; utilities with small populations are better able to absorb calendar costs.

It might be assumed that utilities serving small rather than large populations would be more likely to assess EPZ residents' knowledge of emergency materials information. However, 63 percent of the utilities with large EPZ populations assessed EPZ residents' knowledge compared with 52 percent of the utilities serving small populations. Because 88 percent of the utilities serving small EPZ populations also indicated that they are responsible for only one EPZ, it may be that communication specialists serving small populations feel that they obtain an adequate assessment of their communication programs through normal community contacts such as speaking engagements, complaint letter monitoring, and simply living and/or working in the affected communities. For these specialists, more formal assessment mechanisms are not necessary because of more frequent contact with residents; while utilities serving large EPZ populations often must communicate in multiple geographic locations. For example, nearly one-half of the utilities with large EPZ populations have two or more EPZs for which they must provide emergency materials. Communication specialists for these utilities may feel that more formal techniques, such as surveys, are necessary to assess knowledge levels across varying EPZ populations.

This study of nuclear plant public education programs shows that whereas nuclear plant owner/operators use a variety of materials to communicate emergency information, they rely principally on annual mailings of booklets and calendars to meet the NUREG–0654 criteria. The materials are prepared with minimal input from state and local governmental agencies, although these agencies approve the materials before they become part of the emergency plan. And although the federal government reviews and suggests improvements in the readability and graphic design of the materials, the study confirms that a substantial number of utilities still do not assess whether EPZ residents understand the information. Thus the content of important emergency information distributed to EPZ residents by nuclear plant owner/operators is essentially the product of utility communication specialists, and many utilities do not assess whether this information contributes to the public's knowledge about what to do in a nuclear plant emergency.

In an effort to better understand the content and design of these important communication materials, I reviewed more than forty booklets, calendars, brochures, and telephone book inserts provided by nuclear plant owner/operators since 1986. Although the content and design of the materials vary greatly even within specific categories such as calendars and booklets, the images and rhetoric associated with the promotional history of nuclear power have become imbedded in many materials. Before turning to the specific informational content of these materials and the images they project, it is important to explain how this information is "packaged" to provide a more complete picture of the impact that the words, pictures, and graphic designs have upon the level of knowledge that EPZ residents must have to survive a radiological emergency.

Booklets. As noted above, booklets are the most popular communication vehicle. I examined twenty-three booklets published between 1986 and 1988 that were obtained by writing to nuclear plant owner/operators. The booklets were published in various sizes, ranging from about 38 square inches (about 5 x 7 inches) to a maximum of nearly 94 square inches (8.5 x 11 inches). There was no "typical" booklet cover size; the two most preferred were 8.5 x 11 inches and 5.5 x 8.5 inches. All of the booklets were stapled and, with a few exceptions, the booklet spine ran vertically. Counting both the front and back covers, the booklets ranged from four to thirty-two pages. Fourteen booklets contained between ten and twenty pages, and eight booklets contained more than twenty pages. No doubt to save printing costs, a majority of the booklets examined were printed with only two ink colors; four booklets were printed in four colors. One booklet printed in two colors did include an inserted map printed in four colors. Thirteen of the booklets were printed on textured paper; the remainder were printed on glossy, coated paper.

Calendars. Calendars are becoming increasingly popular as tools for communicating emergency information to EPZ residents. FEMA believes that calendars are more likely to be retained by residents than other materials, and at least one utility communication specialist said informally that FEMA encourages utilities to use calendars in conjunction with other materials.[95] I examined sixteen utility emergency communication calendars published in 1988 and 1989. Full-size calendars ranged from about 94 square inches (8.5 x 11 inches) to 154 square inches (11 x 14 inches); one desk calendar was about 47 square inches (5.5 x 8.5 inches). With the exception of the desk type, which was bound by staples on its vertical spine, the calendars were bound along the horizontal spine with either staples or spiral plastic and metal binding. All but the desk calendar came with pre-cut holes for wall mounting. Counting both the front and back covers, they ranged from twenty-four to forty-eight pages, with thirteen of the fifteen calendars having thirty or more pages.

As attractiveness is no doubt one significant function of a wall calendar, thirteen utilized four-color photographs either on the cover or inside, and all but two were printed on glossy, coated paper.

Because so few utilities rely on brochures and telephone book advertisements as their primary communication tool for EPZ residents, I did not conduct an extensive analysis of their content, so this description is limited to their physical characteristics.

Brochures. Although utilities have traditionally relied on brochures to communicate information on a variety of topics, very few use them as the primary communication tool for EPZ residents (see Table 2). For the purposes of this study, a brochure is defined as a printed sheet folded into multiple pages, or panels, that are not bound at the spine. I obtained only two brochures published later than 1986 that contained emergency information for EPZ residents. One brochure had a cover panel that was 50 square inches (5 x 10 inches) and unfolded into sixteen panels; the second was 36 square inches (4 x 9 inches) and unfolded into twenty panels. Both brochures used four-color photography on glossy, coated paper. One functional design feature was that the brochures contained large, easily read evacuation maps printed on one side of the full unfolded sheet of paper.

Telephone Book Advertisements. FEMA considers telephone book advertisements to be excellent emergency communication materials because they reach into most homes, business, public buildings, and hotel and motel rooms within the EPZ. Utilities purchase space in either the front or back of the commercial telephone book to print information and maps detailing the emergency action plan for the EPZ. The two advertisements reviewed did not contain photographs or other graphic devices and reproduced basic emergency information without elaboration.

CATEGORIES OF INFORMATION

The thirty-nine booklets and calendars examined for this study organized emergency information into several general categories, although not all categories were contained in every material examined. Table 5 shows how the categories were distributed between booklets and calendars.

Here is a summary of the information content of each theme:

Notification. All of the materials contained information on how EPZ residents would be notified in the event of a radiological emergency and what residents' actions should be in such a case. Most utilities use one of two warning strategies—sirens or weather alert radios—and the materials contained information describing the nature of the warning signal or message. Sirens are generally used in heavily populated areas; weather radios are provided for EPZ residents who live where the pop-

Table 5
Content Categories of Booklets and Calendars

Category	Booklet (N = 23)	Calendar (N = 16)	Total (N = 39)
Notification	23	16	39
Sheltering	23	16	39
Evacuation	23	16	39
Radiation	22	15	37
Introduction	21	15	36
Problem Class.	18	15	33
Special Needs	19	12	31
Children	20	10	30
Special Needs Card	18	12	30
Plant Description	18	11	29
Summary	14	12	26
Planning Rationale	16	5	21
Glossary	6	8	14

ulation is more scattered. At least one utility also relies on a computerized telephone system to automatically call residents with an emergency message. The communication materials listed radio and television stations that residents should tune to for emergency instructions upon hearing the emergency warning signal.

Sheltering. All of the communication materials contained information on what EPZ residents should do if advised by emergency officials to stay indoors ("sheltering"). This advice included gathering family members and pets inside the home, closing windows and doors, turning off air-conditioning and other ventilation systems, closing fireplace flues, etc.

Evacuation. All of the communication materials contained specific instructions on how residents should prepare for evacuation of their homes if necessary. This information included turning off lights, electrical appliances, and other equipment; packing items such as bedding, prescription medications, clothing changes, etc.; and securing the home. Many of the materials recommended that residents leave pets at home with adequate food and water. All of the booklets and calendars also contained an evacuation map showing the appropriate transportation routes for leaving the area and locations of reception centers and shelters outside the ten-mile EPZ where residents could wait out the emergency.

Radiation. All of the calendars and all but one of the booklets contained information on radiation. The level of detail varied greatly but generally included a definition of radiation, an explanation of how it is produced, comparisons of human exposure to radiation from both "natural" and "man-made" sources, and health effects associated with various levels of exposure.

Introduction. All but three of the communication materials examined contained an introduction that explained the purpose of the booklet or calendar and encouraged EPZ residents to read the information carefully. In sixteen of the materials examined, the introduction was in the form of a "Dear Friend" or "Dear Neighbor" letter from either the utility management, local emergency management agency officials, local governmental officials, or the governor of the state in which the plant was located.

Problem Classification. All but one of the calendars and more than three-fourths of the booklets contained a description of the NRC system for classifying radiological emergencies at nuclear power plants. The system ranks problems into four classes depending upon their severity and their potential effect outside the plant boundary.

Special Needs. Eighty-three percent of the booklets and 75 percent of the calendars prominently displayed information directed at persons with physical impairments that might make it difficult for them to respond quickly in an emergency. Slightly more than three-quarters of the publications contained tear-off cards that individuals could mail to emergency planning officials so that residents with special needs could be identified.

Schoolchildren. Although most of the materials contained some reference to evacuation of children who might be away at school, this information was prominently featured in 87 percent of the booklets and 63 percent of the calendars. The instructions varied from plant to plant, but generally EPZ residents were told not to travel to schools to pick up children during an evacuation but to meet them at pre-designated reception centers to which the children would be transported by school buses.

Plant Description. Nearly 75 percent of the communication materials contained a description of how a nuclear plant produces electricity. These descriptions were often accompanied by schematic drawings of the various reactor and power production systems.

Summary. About two-thirds of the materials contained a summary of emergency notification, sheltering, and evacuation procedures. In some cases the summary was included on the same page as the evacuation map so that essential emergency information could be removed from the publication, apparently for quicker access.

Planning Rationale. About one-third of the calendars and two-thirds of the booklets contained a brief section, separate from the introduction, in which the utility explained why emergency planning was necessary and what govermental groups were involved. In some cases this rationale was added to the end of other sections.

Glossary. Slightly more than one-third of the booklets and one-half of the calendars contained a glossary of nuclear terms. Terms defined included "control rods," "emergency core cooling system," "fuel rods," "uranium," and various radiation terms such as "rem" and "millirem."

Other Information. All of the booklets and calendars contained telephone numbers that EPZ residents could call to obtain further information about emergency planning, and nine provided special rumor "hotline" telephone numbers that residents could use during an emergency. Some of the brochures and calendars discussed steps that farmers should take to protect livestock and crops during an emergency, although in some cases readers were referred to other publications available from the utility and/or local emergency management officials. Two calendars also discussed the value of electricity to society.

VISUAL PRESENTATION

Graphic design—the combination of typography, color, paper, layout, photographs, and artwork—is a particularly important component of emergency communication materials. "Graphic design is one of the more important factors affecting comprehensibility," notes FEMA in its guide to preparing emergency public information materials. "Effective graphic design reduces the level of effort for the reader, motivating interest and making a clear impression . . . Most adult readers are flooded with printed materials. This makes good graphic design all the more important if emergency preparedness documents are to compete for reader attention."[96]

With the emergence of calendars as important communication tools, graphic design takes on a new significance as a factor in effective emergency communication. If EPZ residents are to keep calendars and the emergency information they contain within easy access on a wall or desk, they must be designed so that they are attractive. The problem for the graphic designer, of course, is that the effort to please the eye may overwhelm the importance of the information contained within. Calendars have traditionally been a *visual* rather than a *textual* medium of communication, so photographs take on added significance as framing devices when important information is included. Table 6 compares several visual elements of the booklets and calendars examined for this study.

It is apparent from the table that calendars rely much more heavily on visual elements than do booklets. The page size of calendars is more than 50 percent larger than booklets. Four of five calendars had photographs on the cover, compared to 43 percent of the booklets, and all of the calendars contained at least one photograph; nearly one-half of the booklets did not. Indeed, calendars on average contained nearly eight times the photographs as booklets and were much more likely to use color photography. When color photographs were included in both

Table 6
Visual Elements in Calendars and Booklets

Element	Calendar	Booklet
Avg. Page Size[1]	103.4	67.3
No. Using Photos	16.0	12.0
No. Using Cover Photos	13.0	10.0
Total Photographs Used	234.0	43.0
Avg. Photos/Material	14.6	1.9
No. Using Full-Color Photos	14.0	4.0
Total Color Photos Used	137.0	33.0
Avg. Color Photos/Material	9.8	8.3
Avg. Color Photo Size[1]	80.5	39.4
No Using Artwork	13.0	16.0
Total Artwork Used	81.0	80.0
Avg. Artwork/Material	6.2	5.0
No. Using Symbols	5.0	10.0
Evacuation Map Size[1]	62.5	45.9

[1] Square inches.

calendars and booklets, the calendar photographs were, on average, twice as large as those in the booklets. Average color photograph size for calendars was 80.5 square inches, compared to 39.4 square inches for booklets.

When comparisons are made between other visual elements, such as artwork and charts, booklets compared more equally with calendars. Eighty-one percent of the calendars and 70 percent of the booklets used artwork to complement points in the text, and calendars averaged slightly more drawings per material than did booklets. Booklets contained twice as many symbols as calendars (e.g., a wheelchair for special needs, car for evacuation, etc.) to identify important sections of text.

One apparent advantage of the calendar format is that the larger page size permits utilities that use calendars to publish larger evacuation maps. When the ten-mile EPZ was measured on the maps printed in the booklets and calendars, calendar maps were 36 percent larger than booklet maps. Some booklet designers solved the problem by printing maps across two pages, on fold-out paper, or by inserting large printed maps into "pockets" designed into the booklet cover. Evacuation maps are perhaps the most *important* visual feature of nuclear emergency communication materials because they detail both evacuation planning zones and approved evacuation routes to shelters and reception areas. Twenty-one of the thirty-nine materials examined contained maps that divided the ten-mile EPZ into zones to permit partial evacuation. Six maps had EPZs divided by township or county; twelve maps did not divide the

EPZ due to low population density, geographical considerations, or limited highway access out of the area. Under the premise of zonal evacuation, a radiological release into the atmosphere from a nuclear plant would most likely affect only part of the EPZ (the part downwind from the plant). Emergency officials would therefore order an evacuation of only that portion of the EPZ directly affected by the release. Announcements to the public would designate the area to be evacuated by zone number or some other designation; residents living in other EPZ "zones" would be asked to remain in their homes until the emergency passed. Thus it is important for EPZ residents to be able to clearly identify and remember their zone designation from the evacuation maps so that they do not needlessly evacuate and clog roadways for those who must get out.

As noted earlier, the heavy emphasis placed on visual attractiveness for calendars presents the graphic designer with a dilemma that is obliquely acknowledged in the FEMA guide to preparing emergency public information materials. The guide notes that by making a document "attractive and useful" so that it is "placed in plain sight, like a kitchen calendar," EPZ residents will be encouraged to keep the instructions handy. But a few sentences later, the guide admonishes designers to use photographs and artwork in such a way that they "highlight the subject matter that requires most attention."[97] The problem for utility communication specialists is to select photographs and other visual elements that are both visually attractive and that complement the text, in effect, that draw readers to the text and help communicate the importance of the emergency information it contains.

In an effort to see how the photographic selection process has been carried out in nuclear plant emergency information materials, I coded all photographs by theme in the thirty-nine calendars and booklets obtained for this study. Photographs were classified into categories on the basis of the images depicted. The results of the photographic analysis are shown in Table 7.

Photographs were classified "nuclear" if they contained images of nuclear plant equipment or individuals working in a nuclear environment, such as a plant control room. Photographs that depicted elements of emergency safety, such as sirens, police directing traffic, or first aid equipment, were classified "safety/evacuation." Photographs were classified "rural/agricultural" if they depicted crops, agricultural/pastoral landscapes, forest/mountain scenes, people in agricultural settings, or buildings such as barns that are part of an agricultural/rural environment. Photographs in which a body of water was the focal point, such as a river, pond, lake, or ocean scene, were classified as "water." Any photograph in which an animal was the focal point was classified "animal," as were photographs of animals and people together. Scenes of

Table 7
Photographs Classified by Themes

Theme	Calendars	Booklets	Total	Percentage
Rural/Agricultural	51	1	53	19
Nuclear	17	23	40	14
Animals	34	0	34	12
Water	32	1	33	12
People Scenes	21	1	21	8
Historic Landmarks	22	0	22	8
Safety/Evacuation	9	9	18	6
Flowers	12	0	12	4
Portraits	7	2	9	3
City Scenes	7	1	8	3
Sunrise/Sunset	6	1	7	3
Churches	5	1	6	2
Seasonal Symbolic	5	0	5	2
Houses	4	0	4	1
Industrial	2	1	3	1
Electricity	0	2	2	1
Totals	234	43	277	99[1]

[1] Does not equal 100 percent due to rounding.

Table 8
Photographs Classified by Nuclear and Non-nuclear Themes (in percentages)

Material	Calendars (N = 234)	Booklets (N = 43)	Total (N = 277)
Nuclear	11.1	74.4	20.9
Non-Nuclear	88.9	25.6	79.1

people working or playing together, exclusive of agricultural settings, were classified "people scenes." If a photograph was made of a city scene, such as a busy street corner where people were subordinated to other elements of the photograph, or if there were no people visible in a city photograph, it was classified a "city scene." Industrial scenes involving non-nuclear industrial equipment were classified "industrial." Photographs were placed in the "historic landmark" category if they were so identified by caption. Classifications of photographs into "flowers," "houses," "churches," "sunrise/sunset," and "head shots" are self-evident.

In general, nuclear emergency communication materials use a variety of photographic themes, yet as Table 7 shows, *most of these visual themes do not complement a text devoted to issues involving emergency notification, sheltering, evacuation, and radiation protection.* Only one-fifth of all photographs analyzed could be classified as fitting in either the "nuclear" or "safety/evacuation" themes. The lack of photographs that tie into nuclear emergency issues becomes even more evident when the "nuclear" and "safety evacuation" themes are combined into one category labeled "nuclear" and all other photographs are classified "non-nuclear," as shown in Table 8.

From this comparison we can see that calendar designers are much more inclined to select photographs depicting non-nuclear themes than are those who design emergency booklets. This does not suggest that calendar designers and their employers make a conscious effort to subvert or minimize the seriousness of the communication process by selecting photographs that avoid nuclear themes. However, it is apparent that when nuclear utilities communicate emergency information through calendars, the medium of communication dictates selection of photographs that are aesthetically pleasing. Whereas creative industrial photographers can soften the appearance of mechanical equipment, few would disagree that photographs of reactors, cooling towers, and containment buildings are less pleasing to the eye than pictures of horses grazing in fields, winter farm scenes, and people having fun on the Fourth of July.

The problem, of course, is the subtle message that such photographs convey to EPZ residents. By loading calendars with benign images to keep the communication medium within reach, graphic designers may be de-emphasizing the seriousness of the messages. At a minimum, calendars give nuclear utilities the license to "naturalize" nuclear power by subtly associating photographs of nature and animals with nuclear images. (In some cases a less than subtle connection is made, as in one photograph showing two horses playing under a cooling tower.) In effect, calendars legitimize the nuclear publicists' historic image of the "machine in the meadow" by associating "things nuclear" with sunsets and sunrises, green fields teeming with crops, and the timeless rush of water—images that evoke a sense of the natural continuation of the world as we know it. Indeed, the very act of using a calendar to mark off or measure the future implies that *there will be a future*, free from disruption, and that nuclear energy has a place in that future.

Although the majority of images in the calendars and booklets are non-nuclear, some photographs do depict both "nuclear" and "evacuation/safety" themes. They accounted for only 6 percent of the photographs examined, but all of the "evacuation/safety" photographs complemented the text by depicting either safety equipment, such as sirens, radios, ambulances, and first aid kits, or played an instructional role by showing people closing windows, listening intently to a radio for emergency instructions, or obeying police at a roadblock.

However, many of the photographs classified as "nuclear" maintained the tradition of the industry either to minimize or to naturalize images of power plants. In the materials examined, twenty-four of the forty-three photographs classified as "nuclear" were either full views or partial views of the plant buildings and cooling towers. Twelve of the twenty-four building/cooling tower photographs were taken from the air, minimizing the size of the buildings and towers; four of the remaining twelve ground-level photographs were framed so that the plant was photographed near water, a traditional technique for making plants blend into the environment (one photograph showed a power boat zipping past the plant). Two ground-level photographs framed plant buildings between the legs of electric transmission towers, making a visual connection between nuclear energy and electricity, and two other ground-level photographs were shot at dusk, so that the contrast between the sky and the lighted plant outline caused the building to take on an almost ethereal image (in one of these photographs, a quarter-moon rises over the plant). Only two photographs showed the inside of containment buildings, and only one of these showed the nuclear reactor. Seven photographs showed the inside of plant control rooms, all containing operators either monitoring or manipulating instruments in a manner that suggested control. The remaining photographs were either of buildings not readily identifiable as nuclear plant buildings (plant information

Table 9
Drawings Classified by Themes (in percentages)

Theme	Calendars (N = 81)	Booklets (N = 80)	Totals (N = 161)
Support Text	54.3	48.8	51.6
Non-Safety/Nuclear	17.3	12.5	14.9
Schematic	7.4	15.0	11.2
Radiation Charts	3.7	12.5	8.1
General Radiation	8.6	5.0	6.8
General Nuclear	8.6	6.3	7.5
Totals[1]	99.9	100.1	100.1

[1]Does not equal 100 percent due to rounding.

centers) or of people performing maintenance operations on plant equipment.

The nuclear industry, as noted earlier, has traditionally used drawings and cartoons to educate and promote nuclear power, and in its emergency communication materials the industry uses artwork as another tool for education. As shown in Table 9, there were 161 drawings split almost equally between the thirty-nine calendars and booklets examined for this study. In contrast to the photographs, of which barely 21 percent dealt with nuclear images, more than one-half of the drawings supported the emergency information contained within the text, and another one-third complemented information about radiation or nuclear power. Drawings were used to symbolize emergency warning devices such as sirens and radios, the need to pay attention to emergency broadcast messages, and highlighted sheltering and evacuation information. General radiation drawings illustrated sources and types of radiation. Radiation charts were either pie or bar charts depicting the contribution of various radiation sources to background radiation. General nuclear drawings were most commonly of plant buildings, accompanied by a key that identified features of the plant layout. Schematic drawings illustrated the nuclear generation process, showing how the reactor heated water to produce steam and drive electrical generating turbines, and visually demonstrated that nuclear plants differed only from conventional electrical generating plants by fuel type.

The twenty-four drawings that did not relate to safety or nuclear information were primarily contained in two communication materials. In one booklet, the utility chose to use drawings of area scenes rather than photographs, whereas another utility placed drawings of animals at the bottom of calendar pages.

It should not be surprising that nuclear utilities are more likely to use drawings rather than photographs to support text about potential emergencies. By using drawings to illustrate sheltering and evacuation, utilities do not have to photograph "real" people taking steps to protect their health and safety. A drawing of a family gathered together around a radio, or loading suitcases in a car in preparation to leave home, is more detached from reality than is a photograph. And, of course, by using a drawing, the utility sends the subtle message that nothing has occurred that could be photographed—no evacuation has taken place, hence none likely will ever take place. Drawings and charts illustrating various points about radiation sources and relative levels of exposure also tend to distance the viewer from the realities of exposure. Rather than photograph workers in protective clothing using Geiger counters, utilities depict radiation either with abstract charts or through drawings that illustrate natural radiation sources such as the sun and brick buildings.

TEXTUAL THEMES

This analysis shows that nuclear utilities have continued their historic tendency to associate nuclear power with positive images that do not complement the critical information contained within nuclear emergency communication materials. Although the positive, aesthetically pleasing photographs selected for these materials may be more a product of relying on calendars as a communication medium than of deliberately trying to "naturalize" nuclear power, the result is the same. Important information about surviving a radiological emergency is framed by images that visually construct a world separate from nuclear power plants, radiation, and even technology. Even when images are chosen that do relate to nuclear power and safety issues, most have been composed to minimize the connection between nuclear power and public safety.

The visual impact of these communication materials raises serious questions about the effectiveness of calendars as a medium for communicating important information about nuclear plant emergencies, but equal concerns have been raised about the textual content of both booklets and calendars. In his 1986 analysis of forty booklets, brochures, and calendars, Philip Rutledge concluded that the materials "tend to present information about plant design, low level radiation, and nuclear energy 'issues' in such a way that an emergent thesis becomes apparent that the risk posed by the nuclear plant is low. Thus, the additional information, rather than reinforcing the critical information, obscures it. Second, by playing down the risk posed by the plants, the booklets may negatively influence receptivity to the critical information."[98]

At the heart of Rutledge's study is a content analysis in which he coded text paragraphs by information themes. He found that 65 percent of the forty-one booklets examined devoted less than one-half of their text to essential information about notification and protective actions, and the remainder provided information on radiation, plant design or operation, and nuclear energy issues that was "superfluous and compromise the efficacy of the [education] program in fulfilling its required function."[99] Of more relevance to this study was Rutledge's finding that many of the topics discussed in the booklets contained what he termed "reassurances" that presented "nuclear energy to the reader in a favorable light" and worked to "reinforce an emergent thesis that the nearby nuclear plant does not pose a significant risk to the public."[100] He found that reassurances were most common in discussions of nuclear issues, radiation, and plant design:

Thus, a typical public education booklet might reassure the reader that an accident isn't likely to happen (ever), the plant is well designed and operated, the nuclear industry has an excellent safety record, the emergency plans are the best they can be, radiation is not harmful (at least during periods of normal plant operation), and that even if an emergency were to happen there would be plenty of time to escape.[101]

What Rutledge calls "reassurances" seem to be a manifestation of the nuclear industry's historic strategy to "naturalize" nuclear power in the public mind through rhetoric associated with the nuclear ethic that (1) makes nuclear power production appear to be no different than any other industrial process, particularly the production of electricity from other sources, (2) equates radiation as another industrial risk with no greater consequences, and (3) stresses the "control" that scientists and engineers have over the "good atoms" that produce nuclear energy. In an effort to confirm this thesis, I analyzed the text of thirty-nine booklets and calendars for specific statements that presented nuclear energy favorably. The results are shown in Table 10. The unit of analysis was the text paragraph, and each paragraph was classified as to whether it contained a reassurance statement(s).

Knowing the nuclear industry's historic concern with public fear of radiation and such issues, it is not surprising that 42 percent of all reassurance statements were found in sections of the materials dealing with radiation information. Sections detailing how nuclear plants produce electricity accounted for nearly 26 percent of the reassurance statements; sections on the need for emergency planning contained about 10 percent of the total. Sections on emergency notification, sheltering, and evacuation contained only about 4 percent of the reassurances.

Reassurance statements averaged about eleven per booklet and about eight per calendar analyzed. Part of this disparity may be explained by

Table 10
Number of Reassurance Paragraphs Ranked by Section

Section	Calendar	Booklet	Total
Radiation	59	99	153
Plant Description	33	63	96
Need for Plans	1	37	38
Introduction	12	18	30
Notification/Sheltering/Evacuation	6	10	16
Summary	1	2	3
Total	129	245	374
Avg./Mat.	8.06	10.65	9.60

the fact that the booklets had more textual material than did calendars. For example, a paragraph count of the radiation sections showed that booklets averaged about one more paragraph than did calendars. Reassurance statements in both the booklets and the calendars tended to follow historic rhetorical themes of the nuclear power industry. A sampling demonstrates how these statements conform to the industry's strategy to "naturalize" nuclear power and rhetorically proclaim control over the atom.

One of the nuclear industry's traditional methodologies has been to stress the theme that nuclear power is similar to other industries and particularly to conventional electric generating plants. In the emergency communication materials examined, this theme was presented in several ways. For example, two reassurance statements emphasized that many industries besides the nuclear industry do emergency planning:

Nuclear power plants are not unique in having emergency plans. Oil, chemical and transportation industries require such plans as well. Nuclear emergency plans are more detailed than others because the federal regulations are more demanding.

No energy source can be free of all risks even though such steps have been taken to make it safe. That is why special safety plans like these have been made. They can help people who live near the plant to be safe if an emergency were ever to happen.

Many statements reassured EPZ residents that although nuclear plants may use a different fuel source than coal or oil-fired electric generating plants, all other equipment and processes are essentially the same:

A nuclear power reactor in short, is very similar to a furnace in a fossil-fuel plant. Instead of producing steam by burning coal, it is done with fuel rods heated by nuclear fission. Everything used in the design of conventional boilers applies here also.

A nuclear energy plant is much like a power plant that burns coal or oil. At the Perry Plant, heat comes from uranium instead of coal or oil.

Some statements sought to compare the environmental impacts of nuclear power plants favorably with those of other generating sources: "When any fuel is used to make energy, some waste products result. Coal power plants have smoke, slag and ashes as waste. Nuclear power plants collect wastes right in the fuel pellets, rather than releasing them to the environment. These waste products could be hazardous and must be kept sealed away from our environment."

Much of the industry's effort to "naturalize" nuclear power has centered on radiation. As noted earlier, the industry has historically sought to show that nuclear plants do not measurably add to the "natural" background and man-made radiation that is already present in the environment, and as one reassurance statement points out, other energy production technologies produce radiation also: "Coal-fired electric power plants emit measurable amounts of radioactivity, due to the presence of radioactive materials in coal. Geothermal power plants emit radioactivity, too, due to the natural presence of radon gas in steam from the earth. Nuclear power plants also emit low-level radioactivity to the environment." Many statements sought to reduce public fear about radiation by pointing out that it was a part of the "natural" world:

There is nothing new or mysterious about radiation.

Radiation is all around us in the world. It is in the air, in food and in water. It is in our homes and in our bodies. This is background radiation. Man-made radiation is used by doctors and dentists in the form of X-rays and gamma rays.

It [radiation] is a very natural part of our daily world. It has been since the world began. Most of the natural radiation we receive is from the sun. Very small amounts of radiation are also present in the food we eat. It is also in the air we breathe and the water we drink. It is even in the materials we build with.

An operating nuclear power plant produces radiation that is basically no different from nature's radiation.

Some reassurances also stressed that the contribution of nuclear power to radiation in the environment was similar to that of more familiar radiation sources:

In addition to background radiation, there is also man-made radiation. It comes from such things as medical and dental X-rays, color televisions, smoke detectors and some watches with dials that glow in the dark. Very small amounts of radiation come from nuclear power plants.

Within a decade after X-rays came into use, it became apparent that they could be either beneficial or harmful depending on their use and control and that protective measures were necessary. This applies to other kinds of radiation as well, including that produced in the nuclear power industry.

As shown here and stressed throughout this book, the nuclear power industry from its infancy has emphasized that the magic of the "good" atoms has always been under the control of scientists, the modern alchemists, and by proxy the engineers and technicians who design and build nuclear power plants. A number of statements in the emergency communication materials demonstrate that the industry has the knowledge necessary to control the atom and that scientists, engineers, and trained technicians have designed and are operating the plants to keep them under control:

Rancho Seco was designed with safety as the most important consideration. Engineers and scientists contributing to the project used "Safety in Depth" as their criterion. Multiple barriers and redundant systems were used extensively to provide protection for the employees as well as for the public. This means that if for some reason one essential system fails, there is a second, or back-up, safety system ready to take over.

Medical scientists have been studying radiation and its effects on human health for more than 80 years. The National Academy of Sciences has stated, " . . . it is fair to say that we have more scientific evidence on the hazards of ionizing radiation than most, if not all, other environmental agents that affect the general public."

The plant operators must meet stringent licensing requirements of the Nuclear Regulatory Commission. What's more, they receive refresher training throughout the year to assure that they remain prepared to cope with any equipment failures or malfunctions which may occur.

Chances are that an emergency involving public actions would never develop, but specially-trained personnel are ready for action—just in case.

You cannot see or smell radiation, but it can be detected, accurately and easily, with the aid of instruments designed for that purpose. Highly trained technicians using these instruments are continually checking radiation in and around Cooper Station. Should a nuclear incident occur, they will check all areas that might be affected.

Scientists have been studying radiation for nearly a century, and all evidence of harmful health effects is based on exposures that are hundreds of times higher than the level that we receive from nature. The scientific and medical communities have worked to keep the average exposure to medical and dental X-rays to that same level and to keep other man-made exposures, like consumer products and nuclear power plants, to small fractions of the total exposure.

The nuclear industry's major metaphor for "control" has become "safety," and many of the reassurance statements reassured EPZ residents that "their" plant was designed and operated with safety as the number one consideration:

Operation of the reactor is controlled by rods which contain a neutron-absorbing substance. These control rods absorb neutrons much as a blotter soaks up ink.

A serious emergency at the Brunswick plant is not likely for two reasons. First, it was planned and built with many safety systems. Second, both CP&L and government agencies watch as it operates.

When a nuclear energy plant makes electricity, its fuel becomes more radioactive. But the plant is built to protect the public. The fuel is kept in special metal tubes. The tubes are kept in a steel reactor. Around this are thick walls of concrete and steel.

Safety comes first in all nuclear plants. At the first sign of trouble, the nuclear reactor is turned off. The plant has many automatic safety devices. If one does not work, another will take its place. Even if several do not work, others will protect the plant and local residents. Nuclear power plants are designed with safety in mind.

Nuclear utilities also emphasize their control of the technology by pointing out the industry's safety record, even to the extent of using well-known nuclear plant accidents as positive rather than negative examples:

With more than 90 nuclear powered commercial electric plants operating around the country, there has never been an accident that has exposed a member of the public even to the level of a year's natural radiation. At Three Mile Island in 1979, the containment building was able to prevent a major release of radiation, as it is intended to do, even during a complicated accident.

Nuclear power stations are designed and built to prevent radioactivity from reaching the environment, both during normal operation and in the event of an accident. These intensive efforts by the industry have worked in the more than 20 years of nuclear power production in this country. Not a single death or serious injury from radiation has ever been recorded among the public. The likelihood of such an occurrence in the future is extremely small.

Nuclear power stations have been producing electricity in the United States for more than 20 years. During this time no member of the public has been killed or seriously injured as a result of commercial generation of nuclear power.

Because of fundamental differences between Maine Yankee and Chernobyl, it is extremely unlikely that an accident like the one at Chernobyl could happen here. The Chernobyl accident involved unstable reactor design and inadequate containment. These situations are prevented by regulation, procedure and design at Maine Yankee.

And despite more than thirty years of intensive public education programs to separate the "good" controlled atoms from the "bad" uncontrolled atoms, emergency communication specialists still feel compelled to emphasize the differences between reactors and bombs:

A nuclear plant cannot explode like an atomic bomb. The kind of uranium used for fuel makes a nuclear explosion physically impossible.

Many safety systems and the building design at the Sequoyah Nuclear Plant are intended to protect you and the plant workers. Keep in mind that a nuclear reactor cannot explode like an atomic bomb.

Could a nuclear plant blow up? A nuclear plant is *not* like a bomb. It *cannot* explode.

There are other, isolated examples within the emergency communication materials that tap into well-worn themes of the industry. For example, one utility uses its emergency communication booklet to tout nuclear power as a deterrent to increased usage of foreign oil: "By using nuclear fuel, the Nine Mile Point One and Two and FitzPatrick plants make unnecessary the burning of more than 15 million barrels of imported oil each year. By substituting nuclear energy for imported oil, the three plants save consumers hundreds of millions of dollars a year in electric rates." But perhaps the most prevailing theme that comes through the materials is a sense of denial that accidents can even happen. When reading these booklets and calendars, one is struck by the effort to minimize and downplay the risk of a serious nuclear power plant accident by encouraging EPZ residents to put their trust in those who operate and regulate the plants:

It's unlikely that anything serious will ever happen at the Farley Nuclear Plant. There are many safety features in the plant to prevent accidents. Alabama Power and government agencies constantly check the plant's operation.

This booklet contains important information. You will need this if there is an emergency at the Perry Plant. That should not happen, but you need to be prepared.

Nuclear power plant operators are required to have emergency plans to handle any incident, no matter how unlikely their chances of happening are.

Nuclear power plants are much less likely to produce fatal accidents than many things we do every day.

If an emergency occurred at Cooper Station, it is unlikely that everyone in the 10–mile radius would be affected.

The law requires emergency plans for every nuclear plant. These plants have been making electricity for almost 30 years. In all that time, no member of the public has been hurt as a result of an accident at a U.S. nuclear power plant. But it is best to be prepared.

The federal government has set protective action guidelines for radiation exposure to the public from nuclear plant accidents.

The Brunswick Steam Electric Plant near Southport has produced power since 1975. Carolina Power & Light built the plant to run safely. Like all nuclear plants, the Brunswick plant is run under strict safety rules. These have been set and are watched by the Nuclear Regulatory Commission (NRC). This is the office which has been set up to be sure nuclear plants are safe.

It should be apparent that nuclear emergency communication materials are a mixed bag of warnings and reassurances, benign images and life-saving information. Calendars, in an effort to become something that people will keep handy, are loaded with attractive photographs that have nothing to do with emergency communication and, indeed, present a view of the world that confirms its normalcy rather than its dangers. Booklets rely more on rhetoric that reassures EPZ residents that accidents are unlikely and that nuclear plants are under the control of scientists, engineers, technicians, and government officials. It seems that the central message of nuclear emergency communication has become, to parrot a line from a popular song. "Don't worry about a thing, 'cause every little thing's gonna be allright!"

I am convinced and have demonstrated that this subversion of nuclear risk communication is the direct result of the influence of the historic promotional strategy of the nuclear power industry. That strategy created a public relations campaign that emphasized control of the atom by scientists and engineers and "naturalized" commercial nuclear power within American culture—a strategy whose elements are only too apparent in the images and rhetoric of the emergency communication materials examined for this study. Indeed, the "culture" of nuclear power promotion—its nuclear ethic—has become the "culture" of nuclear risk communication. Obviously, the most important question is what has been the impact of that "culture" on the knowledge and attitudes of people who live within the shadow of the nation's nuclear power plants? Do they know how to survive a radiological emergency, or have they been lulled into a false sense of security by booklets and calendars reassuring them that nuclear accidents will never happen. Chapter 4 provides some answers to these and other questions surrounding the impact of nuclear risk communication on those who read it—and whose lives may one day depend on it.

NOTES

1. *The New York Times*, 20 November 1956, 1.

2. Spencer Weart, *Nuclear Fear: A History of Images* (Cambridge: Harvard University Press, 1988), 170.

3. Charles Robbins, "Uses of Atomic Energy," in *Public Relations for the Atomic Industry: Proceedings of a Meeting for Members, March 19 and 20, 1956, Plaza Hotel, New York, N.Y., by the Atomic Industrial Forum, Inc.*, ed. Oliver Townsend and James Green (New York: Atomic Industrial Forum, 1956), 1; hereafter referred to as *Public Relations for the Atomic Industry*.

4. *Time*, 31 March 1947, 49.

5. Lebaron R. Foster, "Public Thinking on the Peacetime Atom," in *Public Relations for the Atomic Industry*, 81.

6. Ibid., 83.

7. Dr. Frank K. Pittman, "AEC Safety Requirements," in *Public Relations for the Atomic Industry*, 95.

8. Ibid., 101.

9. The most serious accident to this point in the U.S. civilian nuclear power program had occurred in November 1955 when a small experimental breeder reactor (EBR-I) suffered a core meltdown. No one was injured and no radioactivity was released into the environment. See Richard E. Webb, *The Accident Hazards of Nuclear Power Plants* (Amherst: University of Massachusetts Press, 1976), 187–189.

10. Harold A. Beaudoin, "Locating a Reactor in a Populated Area," in *Public Relations for the Atomic Industry*, 105.

11. Ibid., 106.

12. Ibid., 107.

13. Ibid. See also "Producing a Three-Minute Spectacular," *GE Review* 59 (September 1956): 52–59. Then actor Ronald Reagan was host of the "GE Television Theatre."

14. Beaudoin, 107–108. The distribution figure for *Inside the Atom* was provided the author by E. J. Clark, manager of Educational Communications Pro-

grams for the General Electric Company, Fairfield, Connecticut, in a letter dated June 28, 1989.

15. Ibid., 103, 104.

16. Ibid., 107.

17. Ibid., 108.

18. Weart, 108–109.

19. Ibid., 110. See also Stephen Hilgartner, Richard C. Bell, and Rory O'Connor, *Nukespeak*. (San Francisco: Sierra Club Books, 1982), 73–74.

20. Atomic Energy Commission, *Sixteenth Semiannual Report* (Washington, D.C.: GPO, 1954), 52–53. See also Peter Pringle and James Spigelman, *The Nuclear Barons* (New York: Holt, Rinehart, and Winston, 1981), 245.

21. William A. Stenzel, "Developing Consumer Acceptance of Radioactivity," in *Public Relations for the Atomic Industry*, 111.

22. Ibid., 113.

23. Charles D. Matthews, "What Communities Want to Know," in *Public Relations for the Atomic Industry*, 60.

24. Oliver Townsend, "Opening Statement," in *Public Relations for the Atomic Industry*, 2.

25. Stuart Hall, "Encoding/Decoding," chap. in *Culture, Media, Language: Working Papers in Cultural Studies, 1972–79*, eds. Stuart Hall et al. (London: Hutchinson, 1980), 132.

26. Atomic Energy Commission, *Twentieth Semiannual Report* (Washington, D.C.: GPO, 1956), 67.

27. Ibid., 67–68.

28. Atomic Energy Commission, *Twenty-Fourth Semiannual Report* (Washington, D.C.: GPO, 1958), 113.

29. Ibid.

30. Atomic Energy Commission, *Twenty-First Semiannual Report* (Washington, D.C.: GPO, 1957), 64.

31. Atomic Energy Commission, *Twenty-Second Semiannual Report* (Washington, D.C.: GPO, 1957), 82.

32. Atomic Industrial Forum, *Annual Report* (New York: AIF, 1983), 23.

33. Robert Charpie, "Power Reactors," *Public Relations for the Atomic Industry*, 15.

34. David E. Nye, *Image Worlds: Corporate Identities at General Electric 1890–1930* (Cambridge: MIT Press, 1985), 27.

35. "Atoms At Work," General Electric Company special supplement to *Senior Scholastic* 67 (20 October 1955): 1–8.

36. *GE Review*, May 1954, 4.

37. John Hogerton, ed., *Atoms for Peace*, prepared for the U.S. Atomic Energy Commission by Arthur D. Little, Inc. (Cambridge, Mass., 1958), 1.

38. *GE Review*, July 1957, 30–31.

39. For example, see *GE Review*, March 1957, 28.

40. Nye, 119.

41. *Harper's* October 1956, 13.

42. Nye, 68.

43. Weart, 361.

44. Hogerton, *Atoms for Peace*, front and back cover.

45. John Hogerton, *Background Information on Atomic Power Safety* (New York: Atomic Industrial Forum, 1964).

46. Weart, 361. For one of numerous examples of "fishing under the cooling towers" photographs, see Atomic Industrial Forum, *Annual Report* (New York: AIF, 1986), 22.

47. Edward H. Sewell, Jr., and Roy L. Moore, "Cartoon Embellishments in Informative Presentations," *Education Communication and Technology Journal* 28, no. 1 (Spring 1980): 39–46, and Philip Rubens, "The Cartoon and Ethics: Their Role in Technical Information," *IEEE Transactions on Professional Communication* PC–30, no. 3 (September 1987): 200.

48. General Electric Company, Educational Relations, *Inside the Atom* (Schenectady, N.Y., 1955).

49. Ibid., 1–3.

50. Ibid., 15.

51. Edward Booth-Clibborn and Daniele Baroni, *The Language of Graphics* (New York: Harry W. Abrams, 1980), 55.

52. *Inside the Atom*, 16.

53. Ibid., 14.

54. U.S. Atomic Energy Commission, *Radiation Safety Primer*, 2d ed. rev. (Washington, D.C.: GPO, 1955), n.p.

55. Atomic Industrial Forum, *Harry Gibbs Finds Out About: The What and Why of Atomic Power* (New York: AIF, 1966).

56. The success of that advertising campaign is documented in U.S. Committee on Energy Awareness, *Electric Advertising* (Washington, D.C.: U.S. Committee on Energy Awareness, 1980).

57. U.S. Atomic Energy Commission, *Twelfth Semiannual Report* (Washington, D.C.: GPO, 1952), 45.

58. A. Costandina Titus, "Back to Ground Zero: Old Footage Through New Lenses," *Journal of Popular Film and Television* 11, no. 1 (Spring 1983): 2–11.

59. Ibid., 6.

60. *A Is for Atom*, 16mm, 16 min., 1964, John Sutherland Productions, Inc., and General Electric Company.

61. Weart, 404.

62. Leonard Maltin, *The Disney Films* (New York: Crown, 1973), 294.

63. *Our Friend the Atom*, 16mm, 48 minutes, 1957, Walt Disney Company. See also Heinz Haber, *Our Friend the ATOM* (New York: Simon and Schuster, 1956).

64. Atomic Industrial Forum, *Annual Report* (New York: AIF, 1981), 27–28.

65. Ralph Lapp and George Russ, *Radiation Risks for Nuclear Workers* (Washington, D.C.: Atomic Industrial Forum, 1979), n.p.

66. Hogerton, *Atoms for Peace*, 2.

67. Atomic Industrial Forum, *Annual Report* (New York: AIF, 1982), 24.

68. U.S. Atomic Energy Commission, *27 Questions and Answers about Radiation and Radiation Protection* (Washington, D.C.: GPO, 1951) and *18 Questions and Answers about Radiation* (Washington, D.C.: GPO, 1960).

69. *18 Questions and Answers about Radiation*, 2.

70. Ibid., 3.

71. Weart, 360.

72. *18 Questions and Answers about Radiation*, 6–17.

73. Hogerton, *Background Information on Atomic Power Safety*, 18–24.

74. Ibid., 28–29.

75. Ibid., 9.

76. Ibid., 11.

77. *Harry Gibbs Finds Out About: The What and Why of Atomic Power*, 5.

78. Ibid., 11.

79. Ibid., 14.

80. John F. Hogerton, *Notes on Nuclear Power*, 2d ed. (New York: Atomic Industrial Forum, Inc., 1970), 5.

81. Hogerton, *Background Information on Atomic Power Safety*, 17.

82. Ibid., 18.

83. Hogerton, *Notes on Nuclear Power*, 4.

84. *Harry Gibbs Finds Out About: The What and Why of Atomic Power*, 19.

85. *Nuclear News*, mid-February 1976, 102.

86. *Harry Gibbs Finds Out About: The What and Why of Atomic Power*, 16, 19.

87. Atomic Industrial Forum, *How Nuclear Plants Work* (Washington, D.C.: AIF, 1976), n.p.

88. Atomic Industrial Forum, *Why Nuclear Energy* (Washington, D.C.: AIF, 1976), 3, 4, 14.

89. An example of the use of patriotic themes to promote nuclear power can be found in U.S. Council for Energy Awareness, *Nuclear Electricity and Energy Independence* (Washington, D.C.: U.S. Council for Energy Awareness, n.d.).

90. U.S. Council for Energy Awareness, "Reactor Information Report," Energy Data press release, June 23, 1989, Washington, D.C.

91. NUREG–0654, 11.

92. Ibid., 49.

93. See Appendix B at note 3.

94. See Chapter 1 at note 61.

95. *A Guide to Preparing Emergency Public Information Materials*, FEMA, REP–11, 20.

96. Ibid., 16.

97. Ibid., 14.

98. Philip L. Rutledge, "An Assessment of the Public Education Program for Nuclear Power Emergencies," Master's thesis, University of North Carolina, Greensboro, preface.

99. Ibid., 91.

100. Ibid., 77, 91.

101. Ibid., 74–80.

Chapter Four

"How Do You Keep Them Down on the Farm after the Sirens Blow?" The Failure of Nuclear Risk Communication

The irony of the nation's nuclear risk communication program is that the federal agencies charged with regulating it have made little effort to assess whether individuals living around nuclear power plants understand the risk communication materials they receive or know the actions they must take in a radiological emergency. As noted earlier, the Federal Emergency Management Agency (FEMA) conducts limited surveys that determine only if some Emergency Planning Zone (EPZ) residents have received the risk communication materials, but the agency does not attempt to measure comprehension. Moreover, 43 percent of the utilities surveyed for this study indicated that they make no effort to determine residents' knowledge of emergency information procedures. Of the utilities that do make such an assessment, only about one-third do so annually.

In his 1986 study of the McGuire Nuclear Station in North Carolina, Rutledge found that although 77 percent of the EPZ residents surveyed by telephone recognized that sirens were the principal emergency notification method for an emergency, less than one-half knew that their next step after hearing the sirens was to turn on the radio or television set for instructions. Forty-four percent indicated that they either did not know what they would do if the sirens sounded or that they would evacuate the area immediately.[1] As noted in Chapter 1, the tendency of individuals to evacuate spontaneously in a nuclear plant emergency without first receiving instructions has severe implications for emergency plans predicated on evacuating only a *portion* of the EPZ depending upon the nature of the radiation release from the nuclear plant. In some situations, it may be safer for people to remain inside their homes until the emergency

Table 11
Characteristics of Nuclear Plants Selected for Survey

Plant	State	EPZ	Media	R[1]	I[2]
Palo Verde	AZ	1,672	Calendar	8	13
Summer	SC	10,000	Calendar	7	1
Clinton	ILL	13,500	Booklet	19	0
Susquehanna	PA	70,000	Booklet	7	0

[1]Reassurance statements. [2]Non-nuclear images.

passes. Wholesale evacuation also has the potential of clogging roads, hence preventing those in serious risk of radiation exposure from leaving the area. Thus utility public education efforts are aimed at cautioning people to *listen first to instructions and then take the appropriate action*. Rutledge's findings, albeit limited to one EPZ, give some indication that this fundamental objective is not being achieved.

It is the premise of this book that by allowing nuclear utilities to frame their risk communication messages with rhetoric and images that downplay or mask the seriousness of nuclear plant emergencies, federal regulatory agencies have contributed to the apparent inability or unwillingness of EPZ residents to respond properly. As noted, many nuclear risk communication materials are dominated by rhetoric and images that have roots in the long promotional history of nuclear power development in the United States, and some materials frame the information with aesthetically pleasing images that may de-emphasize the seriousness of the emergency messages. Yet, all materials reassure the reader that nuclear plant accidents are highly unlikely. The next phase of this analysis attempts to determine the level of EPZ residents' knowledge about what to do in a nuclear plant emergency at four nuclear plants that produce risk communication materials of varying content and design. Table 11 summarizes the characteristics of the EPZs and the communication materials selected for this analysis.

The four EPZs are located in different regions, ranging from a rural area in Arizona to a heavily populated area in Pennsylvania. Residents of two EPZs, Palo Verde (Arizona) and V.C. Summer (South Carolina), receive calendars that vary widely as to the number of non-nuclear images but contain a similar number of reassurance statements. Residents of the Clinton (Illinois) and Susquehanna (Pennsylvania) EPZs receive booklets that do not contain non-nuclear images but vary widely in the number of reassurance statements. Thus these EPZs are dispersed geographically across the United States, represent both urban and rural environments, and receive varying risk communication treatments.

One concern in the selection process for this study was that the operating history of the plants might have an impact on EPZ residents' knowledge of emergency communication procedures. For example, residents living near a plant that had experienced a highly publicized radiological event might be more knowledgeable about emergency procedures than people living near a plant that had operated without incident. To determine plant operating history, a copy of *Nuclear Power Safety: 1979–1989* was obtained from the Critical Mass Energy Project in Washington, D.C.[2] The report compiles Licensee Event Reports (LERs) that utilities are required to file with the NRC whenever breakdowns of nuclear plant systems or procedures occur. Thus the LERs are an effective way to determine if the plants in question have had an unusual operating history that might have generated concern on the part of residents living nearby. According to the Critical Mass report, an average of thirty-five LERs were filed with the NRC per U.S. reactor for the period 1984–1988. The Clinton plant, with thirty-nine LERs, was the only one of the four plants that averaged more LERs than the national average during this period, but this number was not considered a significant factor that would affect the study.[3]

Of more concern to the study, however, was a widely publicized $250,000 NRC fine of the Palo Verde plant in December 1988 for a variety of infractions, including allowing a worker to receive excessive exposure to radiation; several violations of regulations related to sealing off and posting areas of high radiation within the plant; the inadvertent shutdown of a part of a reactor's air-conditioning system; and the failure of a radiation oversight committee to fulfill its responsibilities.[4] Despite having experienced this incident, the Palo Verde plant was retained in the study for geographic reasons. Of the seven nuclear plants located in the western United States, three are in California and have received extensive publicity for many years due to a variety of nuclear protests and referenda on the continued development of nuclear power. The Fort St. Vrain reactor in Colorado, the only high-temperature, gas-cooled reactor in the nation, was retired from service on August 31, 1989. The lone commercial reactor in Washington is operated by the Washington State Public Power Supply System, which has received considerable national publicity because of its shaky financial circumstances, whereas the Portland (Oregon) General Electric Company, which operates the Trojan reactor, did not respond to the May 1989 survey until it was too late to be included in this phase. Only by leaving the Palo Verde plant within the study could geographic diversity be assured.

To test EPZ residents' knowledge of emergency communication procedures, a mail survey of 500 residents living near each plant was conducted in July of 1989. A random sample of the names and addresses of 500 heads of households was drawn from each EPZ using ZIP codes.[5] Since ZIP code boundaries do not correspond to the roughly circular

EPZs, the sample included people who lived outside the EPZ and thus permitted comparisons between EPZ residents who receive risk communication materials and non-EPZ residents who do not.

The mail survey instrument consisted of a letter to each head of household explaining the nature of the study and an enclosed, stamped postcard on which the respondents could check off answers to three questions.[6] Respondents were asked to estimate their distance from the nuclear plant so that the analysis could differentiate between individuals receiving the principal utility communication material and those living outside the EPZ who did not receive the material. Although it was not possible in this study to test the reliability of the respondents' estimates of distance, a study of residents living around the Shoreham Nuclear Plant on Long Island, New York, found that perceived distance from the plant correlated strongly with actual distance ($r = +.90$).[7] A second question described a situation in which the nuclear plant sirens had sounded and the respondent knew that the sirens were not being tested. Respondents were asked to choose what their *first* action would be in such a situation from among several possible courses of action. They were also allowed to indicate that none of the actions listed would be their first choice. The third question was designed to test attitudes of those living near the plants about plant safety practices. This question was included to see if the actions that people said they would take in an emergency were related to their attitudes about nuclear power, and whether attitudes were related to the distance that people lived from a nuclear plant and/or the risk communication material received.

As noted above, each of the EPZs selected for this analysis received either a booklet or calendar containing various combinations of rhetorical messages and visual images. Summarized below is a brief description of each of the surveyed plants and the risk communication materials that each provides to EPZ residents.

PALO VERDE

The Palo Verde Nuclear Generating Station, the largest commercial nuclear plant complex in the United States, is located about forty-five miles west of Phoenix, near the town of Wintersburg in the Arizona desert. It is the only nuclear plant either operating or under construction in Arizona.[8] The plant is owned by the Arizona Nuclear Power Project, a consortium of utility companies consisting of Arizona Public Service Company, Salt River Project, El Paso Electric Company, Public Service Company of New Mexico, Southern California Edison Company, Southern California Public Power Agency, and Los Angeles Department of Water and Power. Arizona Public Service Company is the largest shareholder with 29.1 percent and is the plant's project manager.[9]

Palo Verde consists of three Combustion Engineering nuclear reactors, each with a generating capacity of 1,270 megawatts. The first reactor began commercial operation in January 1986, followed by Unit 2 in September and Unit 3 in January 1988. Electricity produced by the plant is shared by the participating utilities. Arizona Public Service Company's share goes into the company's electric generating and transmission system that serves about 1.5 million people in eleven of Arizona's fifteen counties, some 45 percent of the state's population.[10]

According to a representative of the plant's emergency planning department who responded to the May 1989 survey, 1,672 people live in the circular ten-mile EPZ surrounding Palo Verde. The plant uses a variety of communication materials to provide information to residents and transients, including brochures, telephone book inserts, letters, newsletters, and posters, but relies primarily on calendars to communicate emergency information. The plant takes primary responsibility for seeing that the calendars are distributed by mail to the public living nearby and updates the information annually. Palo Verde annually determines whether EPZ residents understand the information in the calendars and conducts the assessment from surveys of residents and through letters and informal comments. State and local officials do not actively participate in the writing/editing, photography, and graphic design of the calendars, and although FEMA has reviewed the calendars, the utility says that FEMA has not made suggestions to improve either the content or design.

The 1989 Palo Verde calendar is a striking document that employs large color photographs throughout. The calendar pages, or panels, are 132.25 square inches (11.5 × 11.5), the second largest page size examined in this study. The calendar is designed so that the cover unfolds vertically into four panels. The cover panel is a color photograph of what the text describes as one of Arizona's "secret crops"—wheat. The second "outside" panel is a photograph of the plant taken at night with the cooling pond in the foreground and the lighted plant in the background. The two "inside" panels contain the evacuation map and emergency information about notification, sheltering, evacuation, locations of reception and care centers, provisions for the disabled, and emergency telephone numbers. Following the fold-out panels, the second page contains information on radiation, a glossary of nuclear terms, and the names of various government emergency response agencies.

With the exception of the last two panels, which contain information on how Palo Verde generates electricity and a description of various plant buildings, the remaining panels are designed in typical calendar format. The calendar unfolds vertically so that it can be hung on a wall with a large color photograph at the top and the days of each month at the bottom. The panels for each month contain a short sentence advising residents to turn on their radios or televisions when the plant's emergency sirens sound. There is also a sentence at the bottom of each month's panel telling readers whom they should call for assistance during an emergency.

Including the cover, there are sixteen color photographs in the 1989 calendar, about one more than the average for calendars analyzed in this study. Thirteen of the photographs depict non-nuclear themes; seven reproduce rural, desert, or agricultural scenes; two contain children; and there are single photographs of animals and flowers. The remaining two non-nuclear photographs are seasonally symbolic—one illustrates Independence Day through a scene in which an American flag is draped over a rustic porch railing; the other is of a holiday Christmas wreath. In addition to the photograph of the plant at night near water, there are two other plant photographs; one is a full view of all plant buildings, photographed from the air, and the other is a long-range photograph of part of the plant shot at ground level with desert mountains in the background. A schematic diagram showing how Palo Verde produces electricity and a drawing of the various plant buildings are also included.

The text contained within the 1989 Palo Verde calendar has eight reassurance statements about nuclear power, the average for calendars examined for this study. Two of the statements characterize emergencies associated with two levels of emergency classifications as "minor problems." Two statements are contained in a "Dear Neighbors" introduction section in which the text reassures readers that accidents are "unlikely" at Palo Verde due to the "safeguards and safety systems" built into the plant. The remaining reassurance statements are contained within a section on radiation that begins by pointing out that radiation "is a very natural part of our environment." The text notes that "public safety officials take great care to make sure the public is not exposed to any unnecessary radiation" after first pointing out that "no long-term effects have been found for acute (instantaneous) radiation doses smaller than 10,000 millirem." The section compares the small radiation exposure received from living near a nuclear plant with the larger exposures from dental X-rays, coast-to-coast airplane flights, and watching color television. The section concludes with the reassurance that "there are no identifiable health effects" from low levels of radiation exposure and that the health effects of receiving "350 millirems of radiation over the course of a year has been estimated to have roughly the same risk to life as smoking 3 to 7 cigarettes."

Thus the Palo Verde 1989 calendar is typical of most nuclear plant calendars in that it frames emergency information primarily with large, striking photographs of non-nuclear images. The selection of photographs, and particularly the cover photograph of wheat, creates an image of a world surrounding Palo Verde that has been virtually unchanged, and perhaps even improved, by the plant's presence in the environment. By composing photographs of the plant buildings with water, at night, and in a setting in which the plant is framed by desert and mountains, the calendar designer has further naturalized the plant into its surrounding environment.

V.C. SUMMER

The V.C. Summer Nuclear Station is located on the Broad River about thirty miles northwest of Columbia, South Carolina. It is a joint project of South Carolina Electric & Gas Company and the South Carolina Public Service Authority, and is one of seven nuclear power plants now being operated in the state. The other six are owned by Carolina Power & Light and Duke Power Company. South Carolina Electric & Gas operates V.C. Summer and receives two-thirds of the plant's electrical output with the remainder going to the South Carolina Public Service Authority.[11]

The V.C. Summer plant consists of one Westinghouse nuclear reactor with a generating capacity of 885 megawatts. The reactor went into commercial operation in January 1984. Electricity from V.C. Summer goes into the South Carolina Electric & Gas transmission system that serves twenty-four counties in central, southern, and southwestern South Carolina. The utility provides electricity to 417,800 retail customers and wholesale electricity to two electric cooperatives, three municipalities, one public power authority, and one investor-owned utility.[12]

According to a representative of the utility who filled out the May 1989 survey, approximately 10,000 people live in the ten-mile EPZ around V.C. Summer. The utility uses calendars, quarterly newsletters, and signs to communicate emergency information to EPZ residents and transients, but, like Palo Verde, relies on calendars as the primary communication tool for reaching residents. South Carolina Electric & Gas takes primary responsibility for seeing that the calendars are updated and mailed annually to residents. State and local governmental officials do not actively contribute to the writing/editing, photography, and graphic design of the calendars beyond routine reviews. The utility reports that FEMA has reviewed the calendars and made suggestions for both the format and organization of the information and the graphic design. The utility does not assess whether EPZ residents understand the information contained within the calendars.

The 1989 V.C. Summer emergency calendar is as simple graphically as the Palo Verde calendar is complex. The calendar contains only one photograph and the panel size is 93.5 square inches (8.5 × 11), several inches less than average for calendars analyzed in this study. The front cover unfolds into six panels and is designed so that it can be hung vertically on a wall with the color photograph at the top and the days of the month pages at the bottom. Four of the panels contain the evacuation map, a "To Our Neighbors" letter of introduction, descriptions of evacuation routes and shelter locations, and notification, sheltering and evacuation instructions. The remaining panel contains a headline reading "To Our Neighbors from V.C. Summer Nuclear Station" and is designed to be addressed for mailing to EPZ residents. This panel, which functions as the calendar's outside cover, identifies the contents as "Emergency Information" and asks the recipient to "Please read and keep this important information." Panels containing the days of the month are reproduced without emergency text; and the last two panels contain text and a schematic drawing describing the plant's operation, a glossary of nuclear terms, information about radiation, and a listing of the various classes of nuclear plant emergencies.

The lone photograph in the 1989 V.C. Summer calendar is a full-color photo of Canada geese on the ground with an electric transmission tower in the background. The caption to the photograph notes that "Canada Geese are a familiar sight in the area around V.C. Summer Nuclear Station" and that the utility, along with the South Carolina Wildlife and Marine Resources Department, began a Canada goose restoration program in 1979 that has turned the area around the plant into the "year-round home to a substantial breeding population of the birds." Thus the photograph and caption convey an image of the nuclear plant peacefully coexisting with the natural environment.

The text of the 1989 calendar contains seven reassurance statements, about one statement less than the average for calendars analyzed in this study. In its introductory section, the text points out that it is "unlikely that an emergency at V.C. Summer Station" will make it necessary for EPZ residents to leave their homes. In the section describing how the plant produces electricity, two paragraphs point out how V.C. Summer differs from conventional electric plants only in the fuel used to produce power. One of the classes of emergency notification is described as consisting of "minor events." The remaining three reassurance statements are contained within the radiation section where radiation is described as a "natural part of our environment" and comparisons are made between the small amount of radiation given off by an operating nuclear plant and the amount of radiation received from a coast-to-coast airplane flight, X-rays, and "natural background" radiation in South Carolina.

Thus, although the V.C. Summer calendar uses one non-nuclear photograph, the design permits use of the calendar format without framing nuclear risk communication messages with numerous non-nuclear images. This makes V.C. Summer an interesting contrast to the Palo Verde calendar and other nuclear plant emergency calendars.

CLINTON

The Clinton Power Station is located in central Illinois about thirty miles west of Champaign. Illinois Power Company owns 86 percent of the plant with the remainder shared between Soyland Power Cooperative and Western Illinois Power Cooperative. Clinton is one of thirteen commercial nuclear reactors operating in the state of Illinois; the other plants are operated by the Commonwealth Edison Company of Chicago. The Clinton reactor was manufactured by General Electric and has a rated generation capacity of 933 megawatts. Illinois Power operates the plant, which began commercial electric power production in November 1987. Electricity from the plant goes into Illinois Power's transmission system that directly serves 1,415,000 people in southern, central, and northern Illinois. The company also sells wholesale power to one city, two electric utilities, and the Illinois Municipal Electric Agency, which represents ten cities.[13]

According to a utility representative who filled out the May 1989 questionnaire, there are 13,500 people who live within the ten-mile EPZ surrounding the Clinton plant. The utility relies on a newsletter and a booklet to communicate emergency information to EPZ residents and transients. The booklet is mailed annually to residents by Illinois Power, and state and local governmental officials do not get actively involved in the writing/editing, photography, and graphic design. Illinois Power reports that FEMA has reviewed the content and design of the booklet but made no suggestions for improvements. Illinois Power does not assess whether EPZ residents understand the contents.

The 1989 Clinton emergency information booklet consists of fourteen pages that are bound together with staples. Page size is 93.5 square inches (8.5 × 11), about 40 percent larger than the average page size of the booklets included in this study. There is a color photograph on the cover, and the inside pages include an evacuation map and one schematic drawing showing how the plant produces electricity. Small black-and-white drawings identify various sections of the text; for example, a drawing of a siren is placed at the top of the page containing information on notification, a drawing of a stick figure inside a house on the page with sheltering information, a drawing of stick figures running to an automobile to symbolize evacuation, etc.

The booklet cover is dominated by a full-color photograph of the Clinton plant. The photograph is shot at ground level with Lake Clinton, from which the plant draws its cooling water, in the foreground and the buildings in the background. A power boat is shown crossing the lake in front of the plant, obviously traveling at high speed due to a distinctive "rooster tail" spray of water coming from the back of the boat. Headlines on the cover identify the booklet's contents as "Emergency Information" and request the reader to "Keep This Booklet in a Safe Place."

The 1989 Clinton emergency booklet contains a total of nineteen reassurance statements in support of nuclear power, almost twice the average for booklets analyzed in this study. The booklet begins with "A Message to Our Neighbors and Friends" from Illinois Power Chairman and President Wendell J. Kelley in which EPZ residents are reassured that the "Nuclear power plant experience in the United States indicates that it is unlikely we will ever have a serious accident." Elsewhere throughout the text, readers are told that emergencies are "unlikely" and that chances of an emergency are "slim."

The text devotes considerable attention to reassuring the reader that the plant's emergency planning process is designed to work swiftly and efficiently. "If a serious problem occurred at Clinton, government officials would be notified immediately" and the emergency plan "would immediately go into effect. All authorities would be kept up-to-date on plant conditions." The plan is "tested at regular periods" to make sure that it works; and officials in these tests, or exercises, "respond as if in a real emergency."

The Clinton booklet also contains a number of reassurance statements dealing with radiation. The text describes radiation as being "in the air we breathe, the food we eat, the water we drink, the homes we live in, and the earth we walk on. Even our bodies are mildly radioactive." Radiation has the potential to harm people, but "Decades of experience have shown that the use of radioactive materials in medicine and industry as well as in producing electricity has greatly benefited our society." The text states that "there is no measurable effect" from low levels of radiation and that "the benefit [from nuclear power] greatly outweighs the risk." Radiation from living near a nuclear plant is compared with that received from a coast-to-coast airplane flight, and the reader is assured that "In most cases, there would be no excessive radiation released to the environment [from a nuclear plant], even in the case of a serious accident."

The concluding sections of the booklet focus on how nuclear power is produced. After several paragraphs that explain that the uranium fuel source makes nuclear power plants different from other electric generating plants, the reader is assured that "Because nuclear power plants use a very diluted form of uranium, the reactor could never explode like an atomic bomb." The various levels of plant safety systems and equipment are also described. "The combination of fuel rods, reactor pressure vessel, and containment building provides three safety barriers to contain the radiation produced when the uranium atoms are split. It is very unlikely that these three safety barriers would all fail."

The Clinton 1989 booklet is a classic example of the use of reassurance statements to characterize nuclear plant risk. With the exception of the cover photograph, which naturalizes the plant into its environment, the booklet relies on text to minimize the risk of a severe radiological emergency and to reassure EPZ residents that "experts" are in control.

SUSQUEHANNA

The Susquehanna Steam Electric Station is located in eastern Pennsylvania on the Susquehanna River about twenty miles southwest of Wilkes-Barre. Ninety percent of the plant is owned by Pennsylvania Power & Light Company and the remainder is owned by Allegheny Electric Cooperative, Inc. The plant is operated by Pennsylvania Power & Light and consists of two General Electric reactors, each with a generating capacity of 1,050 megawatts. Unit 1 began commercial generation of electricity in June of 1983 and Unit 2 in February of 1985. Pennsylvania Power & Light's share of the electricity produced by the Susquehanna plant goes into an electric transmission system that serves 2,500,000 people in twenty-nine counties of central-eastern Pennsylvania.[14] In addition to the Susquehanna reactors, there are ten commercial nuclear reactors in Pennsylvania owned by a variety of utilities, including Duquesne Light Company, GPU Nuclear Corporation, and Philadelphia Electric Company. Eight of the reactors are operating, one (Three Mile Island 2) is permanently shut down, and one is under construction.[15]

According to the May 1989 survey returned by Pennsylvania Power & Light, the Susquehanna plant has an EPZ population of approximately 70,000 people, the largest of the four plants included in this portion of the study. The utility relies on calendars, broadcast and print advertisements, booklets, and newsletters to communicate emergency information to residents and transients, but primarily relies on a booklet for EPZ residents. The booklet is updated and mailed annually and the utility indicates that state and local officials provide about 10 percent of the writing and editing effort. According to Pennsylvania Power & Light, FEMA has reviewed the content and design of the booklet and has made suggestions for improving the format and organization of the information but not the booklet's graphic design. The utility does not assess whether EPZ residents understand the booklet's contents.

The booklet analyzed for this study was issued in November 1988 and is considerably smaller than the Clinton booklet, consisting of ten pages (including the front and back covers) stapled across the top that unfold vertically. Booklet page size is 56.25 square inches (6.25 × 9), slightly smaller than the average page size for booklets analyzed in this study and about two-thirds the size of the Clinton booklet. An aerial photograph tinted in green of the Susquehanna plant and its cooling towers dominates the cover, which identifies the contents as "Important Emergency Information" across the top. The cover also lists the names of municipalities around the plant for which the booklet has been produced.

Other visual elements within the booklet are a schematic drawing showing how the plant produces electricity and a pie chart illustrating various sources of natural and man-made radiation. This particular pie chart, or a slightly modified version, was used in thirteen of the thirty-nine calendars and booklets obtained for this study and illustrates the relatively small contribution that the nuclear industry makes to an individual's yearly radiation dose.

The Pennsylvania Power & Light booklet contained seven reassurance statements, well below average for the booklets and calendars examined in this study. Three of the statements describe how Susquehanna produces electricity, and four are located in the section on radiation. Two paragraphs detailing how Susquehanna works describe how, "as in other generating plants," fuel is burned at Susquehanna in a "furnace"; only the furnace is a "Boiling Water Reactor." In another paragraph, the reader is reassured that the "cloud" seen rising from the plant's two large cooling towers was "harmless water vapor" and not radioactivity.

The radiation section of the text describes the various sources of "natural" radiation and compares radiation from power plants to that produced by "medical and dental procedures and X-rays," "television sets," and "microwave ovens." The text points out that Susquehanna contributed "less than 1 millirem annually" to the average background radiation of about seventy-five millirems in the area around the plant and that Susquehanna has both in-plant radiation monitors and environmental monitoring stations located outside the plant boundary to detect and measure radiation.

The Susquehanna emergency booklet provides a contrast to the Clinton booklet in terms of the number of reassurance statements, and its visual impact is simple and subdued. Of the four communication materials examined for this study, the Susquehanna booklet is the least striking both visually and rhetorically.

ANALYSIS OF SURVEY DATA

The postcard suvey was mailed on July 17, 1989, to 2,000 heads of households living around the four plants, and 568 usable responses were received by August 17, for an overall response rate of 30.6 percent. As shown in Table 12, the response rate ranged from a low of 22 percent

Table 12
Survey Response Analyzed by Plant Location

Plant	Mailed	Delivered	Returns[1]	Percentage Returned
Palo Verde (AZ)	500	431	95	22.0
Summer (SC)	500	461	110	23.9
Clinton (ILL)	500	484	189	39.0
Susquehanna (PA)	500	481	174	36.2
Totals:	2000	1857	568	30.6

[1]Twenty-eight post cards were returned that could not be used because respondents either failed to answer all of the questions or gave multiple answers to question 2. These non-useable returns are not included.

Table 13
First Actions Selected by All Respondents upon Hearing Warning Sirens

Action	Responses	Percentage
Turn on radio-TV	262	46.1
Evacuate	108	19.0
Contact family members	105	18.5
Telephone for information	46	8.1
None of these	33	5.8
Collect belongings/pets	14	2.5
Totals:	568	100.0

from residents around the Palo Verde plant in Arizona to a high of 39 percent from the Clinton (Illinois) plant. Due to limited resources, it was not possible to increase the response rate through follow-up mailings or other techniques. However, it is possible to draw some tentative conclusions from the survey findings concerning choices that nuclear plant residents say they would make in an emergency.

The survey postcard form asked respondents to assume that the plant's emergency sirens had sounded and that the sirens were not being tested. Respondents were asked to select what their *first* action would be from a group of six possible actions, including not selecting any of the proposed actions. Table 13 reproduces the results for *all* respondents.

As the table shows, nearly 46 percent of all respondents chose the recommended response of turning on the radio or television to receive instructions from emergency officials; 54 percent chose another course of action. Nineteen percent said they would immediately evacuate; more than 18 percent indicated they would first attempt to make contact with family members who were not at the respondent's location. Eight percent said they would first use the telephone to obtain more information about the emergency from neighbors, police, or nuclear plant officials;

Table 14
First Actions of EPZ and Non-EPZ Residents upon Hearing Warning Sirens
(in percentages)

Action	EPZ (N = 244)	Non-EPZ (N = 324)
Turn on radio-TV	33.6	55.6
Contact family members	23.8	14.5
Evacuate	22.1	16.7
Telephone for information	9.4	7.1
None of these	6.6	5.2
Gather belongings, pets	4.5	0.9

NOTE: EPZ and non-EPZ residents differed significantly:
chi-square = 31.77, df = 5, p < .001.

nearly 3 percent said they would collect valuable belongings, pets, and items of sentimental value. Almost 6 percent indicated that they would not take any of the listed actions first.

Because these results involved *all* respondents, it could be assumed that a higher percentage of residents living within the plant EPZs would choose the correct action of turning on the radio or television for instructions because they receive risk communication materials from the plants recommending them to take this action. However, when the responses were analyzed by EPZ and non-EPZ residents, EPZ residents were *significantly less likely* to choose the correct first response than were non-EPZ residents, as Table 14 indicates.

Less than *34 percent* of the EPZ residents said that their first action would be to turn on the radio and television, whereas nearly *56 percent* of respondents living outside the EPZ indicated that they would first turn on either a radio or television to receive instructions. This finding is consistent with Rutledge's 1986 survey of EPZ residents living around the McGuire Nuclear Station in which 41 percent responded to an open-ended question by stating that they would turn on the radio or TV upon hearing the warning sirens at the plant. Rutledge also found that many EPZ residents expressed concerns for their families, although he did not quantify these responses. The results from this survey show a similar pattern, as 24 percent of the respondents said they would attempt to contact family members who were not at the respondent's location as their first action in an emergency. In all, *two-thirds* of EPZ residents said they would take another action before listening for emergency instructions.[16]

However, the apparent willingness of a majority of non-EPZ residents first to obtain information about a radiological emergency via the broad-

Table 15
Comparison of Attitudes of All Respondents toward Safety Practices at Selected Plants

Attitude	Responses	Percentage
Safe enough	212	37.3
More strict	256	45.1
No opinion	100	17.6
Totals:	568	100.0

cast media is not surprising when one considers that the homes of non-EPZ residents are located outside the areas that would be in immediate danger in a radiological emergency. More than 65 percent of the non-EPZ residents in this study indicated that they lived between eleven and twenty miles from the plants. Because a radiological release would take longer to reach residents living outside the EPZ, the first reaction of these respondents to gather more information about the emergency through the broadcast media seems both logical and reasonable. Likewise, many EPZ residents apparently feel that their close proximity to the plant requires them to take immediate action to protect themselves and their families without pausing to listen to radio and television instructions. *For whatever reasons, it is evident from this finding that the most basic risk communication message of nuclear utilities to EPZ residents—to stop and listen before taking action—is not being well received.*

In an effort to measure attitudes toward nuclear power, respondents were also asked if the safety practices of "their" plant were safe enough or whether stricter practices should be put into effect. When results of the analysis were analyzed for *all* respondents (Table 15), about 37 percent thought their plant was safe enough, whereas 45 percent thought stricter safety practices should be put into effect. Nearly 18 percent had no opinion.

These findings generally conform to a body of survey research collected over the past decade indicating that people would like to see stricter safety practices at nuclear power plants, although the differences between those with opinions are not as pronounced as in other surveys. This may be a factor of the phrasing of the question and timing of the survey. For example, a 1980 national Gallup poll asked respondents if they felt that nuclear power plants operating today were safe enough with the present safety regulations, or did they feel that their operations should be cut back until more strict regulations could be put into effect? Fifty-five percent thought the plants should be cut back, 30 percent found them safe enough, and 15 percent had no opinion. When the same question was asked shortly after the Chernobyl accident in 1986, 66

Table 16
Attitudes of EPZ and Non-EPZ Residents toward Safety Practices at Selected Plants (in percentages)

Attitude	EPZ (N = 244)	Non-EPZ (N = 324)
Safe enough	38.1	36.7
More strict	48.0	42.9
No opinion	13.9	20.4

percent of the respondents said the plants should be cut back, 25 percent said they were safe enough, and 9 percent had no opinion.[17]

In an effort to see if persons living close to nuclear plants differ in their attitudes toward nuclear power from those living farther away, the survey data were broken down between EPZ and non-EPZ residents, as shown in Table 16. Although the differences were not statistically significant, these findings suggest that people living within ten miles of the four nuclear plants were more concerned about the safety of "their" plant than were non-EPZ residents, whereas the number of people with no opinion about the issue increased as distance from the plant increased. This latter finding may reflect a sense of optimism about the impact of an accident on the part of residents who do not live within the emergency planning zone. As Sandman et al. have pointed out from their study of public perceptions of radon risk, people who do not expect a risk to affect them personally are apt to react apathetically toward that risk, an observation that has been confirmed by follow-up studies after the Three Mile Island accident. In one study conducted four months after the accident, residents around the plant were asked whether they had considered moving out of the area. As the distance the respondents lived from Three Mile Island increased, the percentage of those who indicated they had thought about moving dropped very quickly.[18]

When attitudes about safety were compared with the actions respondents said they would take in an emergency (Table 17), it was found that both EPZ and non-EPZ residents who believed the plant safe were significantly more inclined to take an appropriate first response than people who did not believe it to be safe.

These findings seem to suggest that people who believe the nuclear plants near where they live are safe are more inclined to listen first for emergency instructions given over the broadcast media in a radiological emergency than are people who have safety concerns. The differences were statistically significant and suggest that the appropriate response by residents to a nuclear plant emergency may be influenced by *their perception of the plant's safety practices*. Thus the attitudes people have

Table 17
**Comparison of First Response to Sirens with Attitudes about Nuclear Plant
Safety (in percentages)**

Attitude	EPZ		Non-EPZ	
	Radio-TV (N = 82)	Other (N = 162)	Radio-TV (N = 180)	Other (N = 144)
Safe Enough	48.8	32.7	42.2	29.9
More Strict	41.5	51.2	35.0	52.8
No Opinion	9.8	16.0	22.8	17.4

Note: Both EPZ and non-EPZ residents who believed the plants were safe enough and
who chose radio-TV differed significantly from residents making other choices: EPZ
residents, chi square = 6.31, df = 2, p <.05; non-EPZ residents, chi square = 10.37,
df = 2, p <.01.

Table 18
Location of Heads of Households Responding to the Survey (in percentages)

Plant	Inside EPZ (N = 244)	Outside EPZ (N = 324)
Palo Verde (AZ)	2.9	27.2
Summer (SC)	7.8	28.1
Clinton (ILL)	56.1	16.0
Susquehanna (PA)	33.2	28.7

toward "their" nuclear plant in advance of an emergency may help
determine choices they make when responding to an emergency.

When comparing responses at individual plants, it was not possible
to compare knowledge of emergency actions and attitudes of Palo Verde
EPZ residents with those of the other three plants because of the limited
number of cases. As Table 12 shows, sixty-nine Palo Verde surveys were
returned by the U.S. Post Office as undeliverable, almost twice the
number of returns for any of the other plants. In addition, the ZIP code
boundaries around the Palo Verde plant are much larger than those
around the other plants, with the outer edges of some of the boundaries
being as much as forty-miles away from the plant. The small number
of EPZ respondents may be the result of random sampling from these
large ZIP code boundaries and also because the area immediately around
the plant contains no sizeable population centers.

Table 18 breaks down the sample by EPZ and non-EPZ respondents
and illustrates that the majority of the Palo Verde respondents are located
outside the plant's EPZ. Because the samples were drawn randomly
from the ZIP codes surrounding each of the plants, it was decided to

Table 19
Comparisons of First Actions Taken by EPZ Residents at Three Nuclear Plants (in percentages)

Action	Summer (N = 19)	Clinton (N = 137)	Susquehanna (N = 81)
Turn on radio-TV	36.8	29.9	40.7
Other actions	63.2	70.1	59.3

Note: EPZ residents choosing to turn on the radio or television differed significantly from EPZ residents making other choices for Clinton and Susquehanna: Clinton, chi-square = 12.39, df = 1, p <.001; Susquehanna, chi-square = 8.95, df = 1, p <.01.

Table 20
Attitudes toward Safety Practices at Three Nuclear Plants

Attitude	Summer (N = 19)	Clinton (N = 137)	Susquehanna (N = 81)
Safe enough	31.6	33.6	45.7
More strict	31.6	56.2	39.5
Don't know	36.8	10.2	14.8

include the Palo Verde data in the combined statistical analysis of results, although the small number of respondents located within the Palo Verde EPZ precluded any meaningful comparisons between Palo Verde and the other three plants. Comparisons, however, could be made between V.C. Summer, Clinton, and Susquehanna.

Table 19 compares the first actions that EPZ residents at the three plants said they would take in the event of an emergency; Table 20 compares their attitudes toward safety practices at the plants—attitudes that were more negative than positive. As the table illustrates, *70 percent* of the EPZ respondents at Clinton, *more than 63 percent* of those at V.C. Summer, and *more than 59 percent* at Susquehanna indicated that they would choose an *inappropriate first action* upon hearing the emergency warning sirens. The differences between EPZ residents choosing to turn on the radio-television or make other choices at Clinton and Susquehanna were statistically significant. Attitudes toward safety practices at the three plants were most negative at Clinton and least negative at Susquehanna, whereas a large percentage of respondents said they had no opinion about safety practices at the V.C. Summer plant.

Although sweeping conclusions about the effectiveness of nuclear emergency communication programs cannot be drawn from these data, it is apparent that *none of the plants surveyed has been successful* in convincing even a *majority* of EPZ residents to turn to the broadcast media for instructions as their first action in a radiological emergency. Even at

Susquehanna, where nearly 46 percent of the respondents felt that the plant was being operated safely, only about 41 percent said they would first turn on the radio or television in an emergency.

DISCUSSION

Above all, this survey indicates that nuclear risk communication materials are *not* meeting their major objective under current federal regulations: convincing EPZ residents to turn to the broadcast media for information about what to do in a radiological emergency. Although EPZ residents are instructed in the risk communication materials to turn on the radio or television *first*, and not to evacuate or tie up telephone lines, nearly 66 percent of the EPZ residents sampled for this study at four nuclear power plants said that their first action in an emergency would be contrary to this directive. Indeed, EPZ residents were *significantly more inclined* to select an inappropriate first response to an emergency than were people living outside the ten-mile zone.

Under certain circumstances, those contrary actions could be extremely harmful to public health and safety. For example, 22 percent of the EPZ respondents said they would immediately evacuate to a safe location without knowing whether or not they were at risk. Such an action could unnecessarily clog roadways and prevent others who were at risk from leaving the area. Likewise, the characteristics of some radiological emergencies might make it safer for people to remain *inside* their homes rather than outside in the open air. Evidence suggests that some of the Soviet citizens living around the Chernobyl plant were spared many of the harmful effects of the radiation releases from the accident by staying inside concrete apartment buildings rather than evacuating the area immediately.[19] Persons evacuating the area at the first sound of the emergency sirens might be unnecessarily exposing themselves to airborne radiation.

Nearly 24 percent of the EPZ residents who responded to the survey said that upon hearing the emergency sirens, they would attempt to make contact with other family members who were not at home. Respondents were not asked to specify how they would make contact, but it could be assumed that most would begin with the telephone and that some would attempt to reach the dislocated person or persons by automobile or other means, adding to highway congestion. Another 9 percent said that their first action would be to use the telephone to obtain more information about the emergency. These contrary actions also have the potential to create a dangerous situation in a severe radiological emergency by tying up telephone lines needed by officials to direct emergency operations.

What, then, are the ramifications of these findings for nuclear risk communication beyond the obvious indication that EPZ residents are either not reading or not following the advice contained within the booklets and calendars distributed by these nuclear utilities? The survey indicates that the *attitudes* of EPZ residents toward the nuclear plant near which they live may have an impact on their actions during an emergency. It appears from this study that people who believe "their" nuclear plant is being operated safely are more inclined to take the correct first action of turning on the radio or television in an emergency than are people who have reservations about plant safety practices. But the data also suggest that these *attitudes are not being formed by the reassurances and images contained within utility risk communication materials.*

For example, nearly 46 percent of the EPZ residents living around the Susquehanna plant indicated that they believed the plant's safety practices were adequate, the highest percentage for any of the plants.[20] Yet, 59 percent of those residents said they would choose a first response *other* than turning on the radio or television in an emergency. The Susquehanna risk communication brochure has the *fewest* number of nuclear reassurance statements and images of the plants included in the study, yet EPZ residents living around Susquehanna still choose to take an inappropriate response in numbers comparable to the other plants. This suggests that EPZ residents are either not reading the risk communication materials or do not believe what they read. In either case, it would seem that the reassurance statements and images contained within nuclear risk communication materials are not influencing either the attitudes of EPZ residents toward the plants or their behavior in a radiological emergency.

Although this study did not attempt to ascertain what factors may be influencing the attitudes of EPZ and non-EPZ residents toward nuclear power, several respondents wrote unsolicited comments on their survey postcards that reflected their concerns. A few were fatalistic. "If there is a radiation leak in the plant that escapes to the outside, you are dead," wrote one V.C. Summer resident who would not check any of the actions. Several comments seemed to equate mechanical breakdowns at the nuclear plants with safety problems. "Plant is a joke. Down more than up," wrote one Clinton resident who checked "Needs Stricter Practices" on the survey. Another Clinton resident said he/she would not take any of the listed actions first because the plant "is always breaking down . . . we would be leaving town all the time."

Other comments reflected a sense of distrust about information coming from the plants. "I do not think they would even warn anybody," wrote a Palo Verde resident, and another Palo Verde resident commented that the plant "should be closed down; has poor management and poor construction." Next to the question about safety practices, a Susquehanna resident wrote "Who really knows? Can only judge from what we are told," whereas a Clinton resident who believed the plant needed stricter safety practices asked a series of questions: "How do you know? Who do you trust? Kerr-Megee [sic] or 3 [sic] Mile Island? Could we have another?"[21] One V.C. Summer resident called for "more dope (drug) tests" and a Clinton resident commented that the plant "is *definitely* not safe enough—it's down more than up. I worked there and know what went on. Thanks for asking." Another Clinton resident simply wrote "Scarey" [sic] at the bottom of the postcard.

It would appear from this survey that both EPZ and non-EPZ residents have formed attitudes and opinions about nuclear power safety that most likely will not be overcome by sweeping reassurance statements and non-nuclear images contained within the nuclear risk communication materials being distributed today. It is beyond the purview of this study to suggest ways in which nuclear utilities can overcome these attitudes and the impact they may have on behavior during a radiological emergency. However, the most important questions remain: can utilities successfully communicate appropriate emergency information to EPZ residents so they can survive a radiological emergency, and what role should federal, state, and local governments share in the nuclear risk communication process that could make the difference between the life and death of their citizenry?

These questions are addressed in the final chapter.

NOTES

1. Rutledge, Philip I., "An Assessment of the Public Education Program for Nuclear Power Plant Emergencies," Master's thesis, University of North Carolina, Greensboro, 1986.

2. Kenneth Boley, *Nuclear Power Safety*: 1979–1989 (Washington, D.C.: Critical Mass Energy Project, 1989).

3. Ibid., 4, 24–26.

4. *The New York Times*, 4 December 1988, 36. See also U.S. Nuclear Regulatory Commission, Office of Governmental and Public Affairs, "NRC Staff Proposes $200,000 Fine and $50,000 Fine Against Arizona Nuclear Power Project," press release, 2 December 1988.

5. The author hired Zeller & Letica, Inc., 15 East 26th St., New York City, to prepare the sample from its computerized data base of ZIP code mailing lists. Zeller & Letica provides mailing lists to marketers and others and guarantees a 95 percent accuracy rate. ZIP Codes were selected by using the *Zip code Atlas & Market Planner* (New York: Rand McNally, 1988).

6. Research has indicated that a postcard survey can appreciably improve response rate in mail surveys among certain groups though the size of the postcard limits the number of questions that can be asked. See Robert C. Kochersberger, "Post-Card Questionnaires May Boost Response Rate," *Journalism Quarterly* 64, no. 4 (Winter 1987): 861–863.

7. James H. Johnson, Jr., and Donald J. Zeigler, "Distinguishing Human

Responses to Radiological Emergencies," *Economic Quarterly* 59, no. 4 (October 1983): 386–402.

8. U.S. Council for Energy Awareness, *Electricity from Nuclear Energy* (Washington, D.C.: USCEA, 1989), 12.

9. *Moody's Public Utility Manual* (New York: Moody's Investors Services, 1988), 2:4573.

10. Ibid.

11. Ibid., 2:3283. See also *Electricity from Nuclear Energy*, 19.

12. Ibid.

13. Ibid., 1:1931–1933. See also *Electricity from Nuclear Energy*, 14–15.

14. Ibid., 2:3072.

15. *Electricity from Nuclear Energy*, 18–19.

16. The finding that people living near a nuclear power plant are unlikely to follow official instructions in an emergency is also consistent with a 1982 study by James H. Johnson, Jr., and Donald J. Zeigler of 2,595 households living around the Shoreham Nuclear Power Plant in Long Island, New York. That study, which asked residents to indicate what their response would be to three different scenarios, indicated that 27 percent of the population of Suffolk and Nassau counties would follow emergency instructions during an emergency, whereas between 25 and 50 percent of the households would be likely to evacuate, depending upon the scenarios. However, it should be noted that at the time of the study the plant was not yet completed and had been strongly opposed by residents since the start of construction in 1969. See Johnson and Zeigler, 386–402.

17. George Gallup, Jr., *The Gallup Poll: Public Opinion 1986* (Wilmington, Del.: Scholarly Resources, 1987), 141. See also Stanley M. Nealey, Barbara D. Melber, and William L. Rankin, *Public Opinion and Nuclear Energy* (Lexington, Mass.: D.C. Heath, 1983).

18. Peter M. Sandman, Neil D. Weinstein, and M. L. Klotz, "Public Response to the Risk from Geological Radon," *Journal of Communication* 37, no. 3 (Summer 1987): 100. See also Nealey et al., 24–25.

19. *National Geographic*, May 1987, 640. See also Christopher Flavin, *Reassessing Nuclear Power: The Fallout From Chernobyl*, Worldwatch Paper No. 75 (Washington, D.C.: Worldwatch Institute, 1987), 12.

20. An industry publication recently praised Susquehanna's operating performance and its public information programs designed to maintain good relations with the communities surrounding the plant. See J. R. Wargo, "Good Neighbors," *Nuclear Industry* (second quarter 1989), 34–41.

21. The Kerr-McGee Nuclear Corporation operated a plutonium conversion plant near Cresent, Oklahoma, until it was closed and dismantled in the late 1970s. The company received considerable notoriety when one of its employees, Karen Silkwood, was killed in 1974 when her car ran off the highway at night while she was traveling to a meeting with a *New York Times*' reporter to discuss irregularities at the plant. Silkwood became a martyr to the American anti-nuclear power movement and the circumstances surrounding her death were the subject of several books and a major motion picture. See Richard Rashke, *The Killing of Karen Silkwood* (Boston: Houghton Mifflin, 1981).

Chapter Five

The Need for "Authentic" Nuclear Risk Communication

Americans appear to have settled into an uneasy peace with commercial nuclear power. The 1979 accident at Three Mile Island has faded into a distant, though still uncomfortable memory; and although the Chernobyl accident in 1986 revived public misgivings about nuclear power, differences between Soviet and American nuclear technology reassured many that a Chernobyl-type disaster could not happen at a U.S. reactor. In fact, there is some limited evidence to suggest that Chernobyl had a minimal impact on public perception of nuclear power risk.[1]

Although there have been no new orders for reactors in the United States since 1978, during the first three months of 1989, nuclear power produced more than 18 percent of the country's total electricity supply, and plants ordered before 1978 are still being completed and brought into operation.[2] And although safety considerations and economics have severely curtailed nuclear power development in the United States, there is an indication that the industry may be on the brink of a rebirth. The effect of fossil fuels on global warming, predictions that national demand for electricity has finally caught up with supply, and new developments in the design of safer reactors have all breathed a bit of life into the moribund industry.

This is not to suggest that nuclear power in the United States will ever return to the halcyon days of the 1960s and early 1970s; nonetheless, Americans do seem to be learning to live, albeit uneasily, with nuclear power plants. At a time when headlines focus on the shutdown of a plant in California due to economic concerns and the problems of operating completed plants in New York and New Hampshire because of resistance from state governments uneasy about emergency preparedness, more than 100 nuclear reactors are producing electricity in thirty-four states with little notice from the average American. And although there have been isolated protests at nuclear plants and news stories about malfunctions and safety violations, more than three million Americans apparently are willing to allow a proven "risky" technology to operate in their backyards and go about their business each day within the shadow of nuclear power plants.

Thus, whereas Americans as a group may not "trust" nuclear power and a substantial percentage do not want a nuclear plant built near them,[3] several million people apparently are willing to live in close proximity to the technology. Moreover, research indicates that many of these "nuclear neighbors" do not consider moving once a plant has been built in their neighborhoods.[4] The apparent willingness of so many people to coexist with a dangerous technology provides scholars with a number of "living laboratories" around nuclear power plants in which to study the impact of communication on people's awareness of and behavior toward risk. Such a resource may prove extremely valuable as regulatory agencies and other groups seek to learn more about how best to meet their responsibilities for protecting human life and property by providing the public with information on ways either to avoid risk or to mitigate its effects.

The nation's nuclear risk communication program has a decade of experience, making it one of the country's most sustained programs to communicate information about technological risk. However, despite a substantial effort to provide people living around nuclear plants with a variety of risk information, evidence suggests that nuclear public education programs are not communicating the *critical* safety information that would be needed in a radiological emergency. In Chapter 4 I show that *two-thirds* of a sample of residents living within ten miles of four nuclear power plants indicated that in a plant emergency they would take a first action *contrary to the recommended response* of turning on a radio or television for instructions. This finding follows a 1986 assessment of a North Carolina nuclear plant in which 59 percent of a sample of EPZ residents indicated they would not take the recommended action first.[5] Instead of waiting for official instructions in a nuclear plant emergency, a *majority* of EPZ residents are more likely to try to contact family members not at home, telephone for more information, or simply leave the area. Yet, as noted, most emergency plans around nuclear power plants are predicated on people turning to the broadcast media for instructions on whether they should take shelter indoors or, in extreme emergencies, evacuate.

Throughout this study I have resisted the temptation to create "scare" scenarios of what might happen to people living around a nuclear plant that experiences a major radiological emergency necessitating evacuation within the EPZ. At a minimum, based on this study, as well as analysis of the Three Mile Island accident and studies of evacuation behavior in natural and other technological disasters, we would expect a considerable portion of the population to immediately leave the area via automobile or other means of transportation, after first attempting to make contact with missing family members. Under some circumstances, immediate evacuation may be the most appropriate behavior for these residents. Under other conditions, as Chernobyl demonstrated, remaining inside the home or an office building may be the safest response. Most likely, in a severe nuclear plant accident situation, some people would be told by officials to leave and others would be instructed to stay, clearing the highways for those most at risk. The key problem for those managing the emergency is to convince people to follow instructions so that those most at risk will have a chance to survive the accident. But how? Before answering this question, we must re-examine the deep roots of distrust that, as this study shows, have permeated our cultural consciousness about nuclear power.

The finding that people disregard what officials ask them to do in a nuclear plant emergency confirms the disparity that exists between technical and lay perceptions of nuclear risk, a disparity that has grown out of the cultural heritage of the nation's nuclear power program and its effect on nuclear risk communication. For decades, people were told by "experts" in government and industry that accidents at nuclear power plants were extremely unlikely. However, accidents did happen, and investigations revealed that the experts had been overconfident or simply wrong in their analysis of what could and could not happen at a nuclear power plant. As Otway points out, the public responded to this perceived failure of expertise by steadily increasing its participation in technological decision making, either intervening in the decision-making process or simply preventing the implementation of decisions made by others.[6] Over the years, as the experts attempted to reassert their expertise and the public observed continuing technological failures such as the Chernobyl disaster, the gap between technical and lay perceptions of what is risky about nuclear power and what is not has enlarged to the point that it is doubtful that the relationship will ever be the same again.

If we are serious about creating an environment in which critical nuclear risk messages can be heard and understood as essential and authentic information that can save lives, we must start by removing the elements of the historical promotional heritage of nuclear power from modern risk communication programs—a heritage that represents the extremes of the expert-public debate over the nature of nuclear power risk. As already demonstrated, that heritage includes more than three decades of nuclear power promotion by the industry, the federal government, and the scientific community. By and large, as Chapter 3 indicates, nuclear risk communication programs are a product of nuclear plant owner/operators with only minimal attention from the federal government and virtually none from state and local governments. In effect, an industry that has *actively promoted* the idea that commercial nuclear power is safe for more than thirty years has been handed by default the task of providing information that *raises questions* about the very safety of the industry itself. This places the industry in an impossible dilemma, and as noted in Chapter 3, nuclear utilities have resolved that dilemma by framing risk messages with promotional rhetoric and images that downplay the possibility of an accident and mask the seriousness of the emergency information being communicated to people living near the plants.

My analysis of risk communication at four nuclear plants suggests that residents either do not read or do not trust the messages they are receiving from the utilities operating the plants. Instead, their response to a nuclear plant emergency seems to be predicated on the attitudes they have formed about the plant. People who believe that a nuclear plant is being operated safely appear more inclined to take an appropriate first response in an emergency than people who do not believe the plant is operated safely. However, the findings also suggest that promotional messages and images contained within risk communication materials *have no effect* on the choice of first action by residents, except possibly *a negative effect*.

These findings point to what Otway and Wynne have described as the "credibility-authenticity paradox" of risk communication, which draws a distinction between credible information and authentic communication. They identify credible information as material "presented in discreet and carefully designed packages," as distinguished from "authentic communication," which involves trusting relationships in which "mutual trust and respect are nurtured."[7] Further, Otway and Wynne argue that, although it might appear that a presentation of authentic information "would entail open recognition of the unavoidable uncertainties and difficulties of managing technological risks," and hence be considered a hindrance to credibility, in actuality the development and maintenance of credibility depends less on the *packaging of information* than on the *quality of the relationships* between risk communicators and those receiving the communication. Otway and Wynne point out that by putting the emphasis on authentic rather than merely credible communication, the public will be less likely to become complacent with technology management and be more diligent about maintaining high levels of safety.[8] The question for nuclear power, of course, is whether *more* public concern for safe plants is a desired goal for those managing the technology and the risk communication.

Can authentic, open, two-way communication take place between a nuclear utility and the "neighbors" surrounding its plant so that the objectives of nuclear risk communication programs will be achieved? The evidence is not encouraging, even in the best of circumstances. The Susquehanna plant in Pennsylvania operates fifteen public-information programs, supports a committee of thirty community leaders who advise the plant management on residents' concerns, and gives tours that allow the public to see every aspect of the plant. One official is quoted in an industry trade publication as saying that Susquehanna "put[s] out more news material on this plant than goes out on any other plant in the country."[9] Yet, my study found that although 46 percent of the EPZ residents living around Susquehanna thought the plant's safety practices were safe enough, only 41 percent said they would take the first response recommended by officials in a radiological emergency. This was the highest percentage for the plants surveyed, but it is still a woefully inadequate response that illustrates that even when a nuclear utility makes a sincere effort to improve its credibility with the public, the gap between instruction and public response may be too wide to bridge.

Let me emphasize here that I do not believe that utility communication specialists deliberately try to mislead the public about the dangers of nuclear power. Nonetheless, such specialists are participants in an organizational culture that has put heavy faith in the ability of scientists, engineers, and technicians to control the power locked inside the atom—a culture founded, as we have seen, on an ethic that equates national progress and, indeed, national survival with the successful development of commercial nuclear power. It is therefore not surprising that messages produced by these specialists about risk have become diluted with rhetoric and images that support the cultural milieu in which they work.

Likewise, the people who live around commercial nuclear power plants are products of a larger national culture that has seen atomic energy evolve from a savior of humankind into a destructive force evoking images of terrible death and devastation. Since the beginning of the twentieth century, Americans have been bombarded by a myriad of conflicting atomic images. Those images associated with the promise of nuclear power—unlimited electric power, "cures" for cancer and other diseases, new ways of growing crops—now clash with sinister pictures of missile silos, the mushroom clouds over Hiroshima and Nagasaki, and the smoky radioactive cloud rising from the top of the Chernobyl reactor building. Is it any wonder that the public's reaction to a nuclear plant emergency differs so greatly from what is expected by the utility culture?

If people's actions in a nuclear emergency are predicated on their attitudes toward nuclear power and those attitudes are *not* influenced by the rhetoric and images contained within nuclear risk communication materials, why do utilities persist in communicating messages that have so little effect on behavior? One answer may be found in the long path that atomic scientists, American governmental officials, and the nuclear industry have taken to reach the present state of nuclear risk communication. Evidence in Chapters 2 and 3 demonstrates that public education about nuclear power has been a significant element of the nuclear industry's public relations strategy since the early 1950s, despite the fact that researchers have found a very weak relationship between education and behavior. The industry, however, has persisted in a public relations program that equates *understanding* of nuclear power with *acceptance* of nuclear power, and that thread of the industry's strategy has found its way into modern nuclear risk communication materials. Unfortunately, the promotional rhetoric and images that have marked these education programs also have found their way into the risk communication effort, reducing the authenticity of its message and masking the critical safety information contained within its materials.

Many of the promotional themes that frame modern nuclear risk communication messages have evolved from the industry's effort to "naturalize" nuclear power by making nuclear plants appear to blend into America's technological culture. Since the 1950s, industry executives have recognized that the economics of power production dictated the locating of larger reactors near population centers and that people would be more willing to accept a nuclear power plant in their communities if they could be convinced that nuclear power production was no different from any other industrial process. This strategy was successfully carried out throughout the late 1950s and 1960s, but when safety concerns about nuclear power began to emerge in the 1970s, capped by Three Mile Island in 1979, a strategy based on naturalization was inadequate to sway negative public attitudes. Nuclear power was no longer just another industry and radiation was not simply another industrial hazard. Unfortunately, as shown in Chapter 3, much of the superfluous rhetoric in emergency calendars and booklets distributed by nuclear utilities continues the charade of trying to make nuclear power blend into the technological landscape. With Three Mile Island and Chernobyl now a part of the technological legacy of nuclear power, this is obviously a strategy whose time has long since passed.

A second contributing factor to the apparent failure of nuclear risk communication is the industry's historic reluctance to raise issues it considers "negatives" about nuclear power for fear that these issues will somehow "delegitimize" the industry as a contributing force toward achieving societal goals of safety and security. Industry executives can read polls and no doubt fully recognize that the public today distrusts nuclear power. However, the industry still has billions of dollars invested in plants and equipment, with hopes for further development of nuclear power through safer reactor designs and increasing public concerns over the impact of fossil fuels on the environment. A risk communication effort that strips away reassurance statements and benign images to focus solely on nuclear risks may become more authentic and thereby more functional, but it might also destroy what little confidence remains in the public mind about an industry that "cannot be allowed to fail" because the consequences of that failure are too great.

Yet the industry, for all practical purposes, has faltered in the United States. There have been no new reactors ordered since 1978, and it is doubtful that even the most ardent advocate of commercial nuclear power will argue that authentic risk communication is going to "kill" the industry's hopes for a comeback. Safer reactors, solutions to the problems of waste disposal, and better economics may help revive nuclear power, but not a continuation of the false premise that accidents won't happen. For too long, that premise has governed the nuclear risk communication process—and its falsity is becoming more and more apparent as nuclear plants in this country continue to age.

Why have federal regulatory agencies failed so far to insist on a nononsense approach to nuclear risk communication? As argued in Chapter 1, risk communication programs symbolically serve to confirm with the public that regulatory organizations support societal norms of safety and security. Regulatory agencies may be concerned that an intensive effort to force nuclear utilities to remove promotional rhetoric and images from their public education materials and concentrate solely on the risks of nuclear power operations may be considered an admission that the regulators cannot guarantee with certainty that the industry will operate safely. Rosener and Russell point out that state and local governments also steer clear of nuclear risk communication programs because of the expense involved and/or because they fear being dragged into the nuclear debate. My survey of state and local involvement in utility risk communication programs confirms this tendency—only sixteen of the forty-six nuclear utilities responding indicated that state and local governments contributed 25 percent or more of the writing effort required to produce utility risk communication materials. As a result, most nuclear utilities are virutally left on their own in the production of risk communication materials.

There are some concerned with risk management, however, who believe that open, authentic communication about risk can happen between the public and various federal, state, and local agencies responsible for protecting public safety in a radiological emergency. Paulette L. Stenzel argues that by becoming more active in the development of meaningful public risk communication programs, government agencies can help themselves better manage the public debate about "acceptable" risks:

By conveying risk information to the public in a systematic, meaningful manner, administrative agencies could assist people in learning to recognize and confront uncertainties. This would promote at least two general benefits to society. First, the public would begin to realize that there is no such thing as absolute safety in life and would learn to tolerate risk. Second, the public would learn to distinguish those risks which warrant investment of limited social resources from those which they must simply tolerate.[10]

Stenzel proposes the creation of a national "Risk Assessment Communication Policy Act" (RACPA) patterned somewhat along the lines of legislation that has been introduced on several occasions by Congressman Don Ritter of Pennsylvania. Ritter is primarily concerned that science and the federal government work together to develop a "consistent scientific methodology to identify and evaluate risk" so that government can pursue a rational plan to "address the worst risks first."[11] He has also made provisions in his legislation for a study to make recommendations for increasing public awareness and understanding of risk and regulatory decisions related to risks.[12]

Stenzel would carry Ritter's proposal a step further by requiring that all federal regulatory agencies that are required by law to engage in risk assessment to convey those assessments to the public "in a consistent, meaningful manner."[13] She would have Congress create a non-partisan advisory board made up of a diverse body of laypeople, scientists, scholars, and federal officials to develop guidelines for describing risks. Congress would establish "educational" requirements within the RACPA that describes "how, where, and when risk assessments must be disseminated to the public" and would include methods for funding the programs. Stenzel believes that:

If agencies share risk information with the public in a consistent, straight-forward manner, the public will become more knowledgeable about risk. The use of consistent sets of assumptions and the comparison of new risk assessments of familiar, everyday risks will help each individual build a body of knowledge about risk. More information will reduce the public's misperceptions about risks.[14]

She argues that one of the benefits from her proposal will be to open up the lines of communication between lay public and administrative agencies charged with regulating risk—in other words, the development of "authentic" communication:

The public must perceive administrative agencies as straight-forward and honest. Studies by risk perception experts demonstrate that people must trust the disseminator of information before they will accept that information. By establishing consistent, open communication by agencies in the area of risk assessment, the RACPA will assist agencies in improving their public image. In turn, the public will accept and support administrative decisions more readily. Such acceptance and support will lead to reduced public furor in response to regulatory decisions, fewer lawsuits, and more efficient overall operation of the administrative agency.[15]

Stenzel's proposal to make risk communication more open and consistent is one approach to helping the public and administrative regulatory agencies grapple with the problems of risk communication. However, an administrative mechanism is already in place that could be used to improve risk communication around the nation's nuclear power plants. The Federal Emergency Management Agency (FEMA), as part of its oversight of off-site emergency plans at nuclear power plants, maintains close contact with utility risk communication programs through contractor review of materials distributed by nuclear utilities to EPZ residents. The review program has reached most nuclear utilities; forty-three of the forty-six nuclear utilities responding to my survey reported that their communication materials had been analyzed by FEMA.

However, as described in Chapter 1, FEMA unfortunately does not attempt to determine whether EPZ residents *understand* the information contained within these materials and reviews the materials solely to improve readability and graphic design. Why is FEMA's overseeing function so limited? One reason is that in 1981 the agency was *prohibited* by the Office of Management and Budget (OMB) from conducting annual surveys of EPZ residents nationwide to determine how much the public knew about radiological emergency procedures. This decision was strongly criticized by the General Accounting Office in a 1987 report, which also noted that an OMB official was "surprised" that FEMA had not revised its survey and resubmitted it for approval.[16] Instead, FEMA attempts only to assess whether EPZ residents have *received* the emergency communication materials by including a question about receipt as part of a telephone survey to determine the adequacy of coverage of the plant's emergency siren system.

Moreover, as of the summer of 1989, FEMA had no plans to request that OMB remove its restriction on EPZ surveys to determine residents' knowledge of emergency procedures, according to Bill McAda of the agency's Office of External Affairs:

At the present time, FEMA does not intend to request that OMB modify the current survey format in order to determine EPZ residents' knowledge of emergency procedures. Each year since 1981 FEMA has been required to receive approval from OMB to continue the [siren coverage] surveys. OMB was very specific in outlining the information FEMA would be allowed to gather in the surveys and we have no reason to believe that OMB has changed its mind in the interim.[17]

McAda noted that turning on the Emergency Broadcast System (EBS) for emergency instructions is emphasized in the emergency materials distributed by utilities, but that "the decision to act on those instructions rests with the individual." Although McAda said he had no data to contradict the finding that most EPZ residents would not turn on the radio or television, "it is extremely difficult to accept the idea that a person, upon hearing an alert signal, would not turn on the EBS for official information and guidance."[18]

The decision not to assess EPZ residents' knowledge of emergency procedures is unfortunate because FEMA is in a unique position to significantly improve the public's ability to cope with nuclear plant accidents. Armed with the administrative responsibility for overseeing nuclear risk communication and at least not directly involved in the long history of government promotion of nuclear power, FEMA seems to be the appropriate federal agency to improve the authenticity of the nation's nuclear risk communication. That process should begin with a broad-based study of nuclear utility risk communication efforts that would address the following questions, among others:

1. Who should be responsible for nuclear risk communication?
2. What role should citizens living near the plants play in the development of nuclear risk communication programs?
3. What information should be included in nuclear risk communication programs and who should make the final choices as to what is included and omitted?
4. What should be the criteria for evaluating the success of a nuclear risk communication program?

Such a study could begin with surveys of EPZ residents, not only to determine the level of their knowledge of emergency preparedness information, but also to explore the complex relationship between their attitudes toward nuclear power and their receptiveness to nuclear risk communication. Otway and Wynne have argued that the current risk communication paradigm "rests on unexamined and unarticulated assumptions about who is communicating what, to whom, and in what context."[19] By focusing *less* on the "nuts and bolts" of the communication process—readability and comprehension of information, retention of materials, etc.—and *more* on the historic attitudes and relationships of people to nuclear power, such studies would shed considerable light on why current nuclear risk communication programs apparently fail so dismally. As Plough and Krimsky have emphasized, studies of risk communication cannot be divorced from their cultural milieu.[20]

An effective technique for further involving the public in the development of authentic risk communication has been suggested by William

H. Desvousges and V. Kerry Smith. They propose using focus groups of citizens to supplement other methods for gathering data on how people respond to risk. Desvousges and Smith believe that by listening to the "consumers" of risk messages, risk communicators can make their messages more effective:

Too often, risk communicators are more concerned with educating the public, rather than first listening to them and then developing communication policies. Focus groups allow the consumers of risk messages or communication programs to provide critiques and feedback to their designers. Using feedback from focus groups, researchers can gain qualitative insights on how people perceive risk, as well as evaluations of the perceptual or cognitive effects of the risk information format. Such feedback is crucial to communicating risk more effectively.[21]

By talking to EPZ residents in small groups, FEMA would learn much more about how the people most affected by nuclear power plants feel about living near a risky technology, the language they use to discuss that risk, and their attitudes toward those who operate the technology. "Focus groups improve the quality of information ultimately acquired in surveys," note Desvousges and Smith. "[Focus groups] suggest hypotheses for testing with those data; and, equally important, provide a wealth of insights (and anecdotes) that can vividly illustrate the findings from the quantitative results."[22]

Perhaps the most promising approach for developing meaningful public involvement in nuclear risk communication is presently underway as a state initiative in California. On September 30, 1988, the California Radiation Protection Act of 1988 was signed into law.[23] Developed to improve the state's capability to respond to a nuclear emergency, the act created a Citizens Advisory Committee on Emergency Planning charged with the task of providing public input into nuclear risk communication and other aspects of the emergency planning process.

The California Radiation Protection Act resulted from a series of recommendations made by a Task Force on California Nuclear Emergency Response created by the state senate in 1986 as a result of the Chernobyl accident. The state senate instructed the task force to "formulate a report on the State of California's present medical and emergency response capacity in the event of a major nuclear facility accident, including recommendations as to how the state might improve this capacity and limit damage from, or limit exposure to, radiation in the event of such an accident."[24]

The task force report to the senate, completed in April 1988, listed thirty-one specific recommendations on how the state could improve its capability to respond to a nuclear emergency. Included was a recognition that nuclear public education materials distributed by the state's utilities "lack credibility in the eyes of many residents within the EPZs," and a recommendation for more public involvement in the emergency planning process to increase public confidence in the plan and to give the planners more credibility with the public.[25]

The report was particularly concerned that the focus of nuclear risk communication materials be altered to point out to EPZ residents the *negative* results of *not following the recommended protective action* of turning on the radio and television for instructions in a nuclear plant emergency. The report recommended that risk materials specifically address why residents, upon hearing the emergency sirens, should *not* immediately evacuate the area, call local authorities for more information, or pick up their children at school.[26]

The report recommended establishing a citizens' advisory committee as an "independent ongoing forum" for citizens to have input into nuclear emergency planning. The committee was created under the act passed by the legislature in September 1988 and charged with the following specific responsibilities:

• Determining whether emergency information materials convey information and recommendations that the public will be inclined to follow in an emergency.
• Obtaining public comment on the adequacy of nuclear plant emergency response plans.
• Determining whether citizens should be allowed to observe the annual emergency preparedness exercises conducted by the nuclear utilities and state and local emergency officials.
• Assessing the validity of assumptions in nuclear emergency response plans that are related to public response. For example, the committee is specifically instructed to investigate whether it is a valid assumption that parents will not pick up their children from school during an emergency.
• Determining whether efforts should be made to provide nuclear emergency information materials to non-English-speaking populations within the EPZs.
• Determining whether "special response personnel," such as bus drivers and teachers, need additional information.
• Providing an annual report to the appropriate legislative committees with specific recommendations on how emergency plans can be improved. The first report is due in 1990.[27]

The act creates a nine-person committee appointed by the governor, the senate, and the speaker of the assembly. The act requires that three members of the committee be residents of the EPZs of the state's three nuclear plants. It further requires that the committee include a nuclear utility employee, a health physicist, a physician familiar with radiological procedures, a local governmental official who works in emergency planning, a member of an environmental organization, and a licensed psychologist or psychiatrist in human behavior. Funding for the committee's activities will be provided under existing California law that requires the state's nuclear utilities to reimburse state and local agencies for emergency planning costs.[28]

Whether the California Citizens Advisory Committee on Nuclear Emergency Planning will become a model for increasing public participation in nuclear risk communication throughout the nation remains to be seen. As noted earlier, states have been reluctant to participate in the risk communication process; and under the California statute, there is no obligation on the part of California utilities to implement the committee's recommendations, although the utilities may recognize that there are obvious public relations advantages in cooperating.

Could FEMA play a role in the establishment of local citizens' advisory committees for nuclear plant risk communication? As noted in Chapter 1, through a cooperative relationship with the NRC, FEMA judges the adequacy of off-site emergency planning through periodic evaluations of emergency preparedness exercises at the plants. FEMA reports its findings to the NRC, which can then decide whether the planning is adequate to allow the plant to continue operating. Although there is no federal statute requiring state and local governments to prepare emergency plans, most have cooperated in the planning effort, particularly because many states and some local governments have developed financial arrangements with the utilities to cover planning costs.[29]

Under this process, local citizens' advisory committees could be established to assess utility risk communication programs and make recommendations to FEMA as part of its periodic assessment of off-site emergency planning. Through its relationship with the NRC licensing process, FEMA could put "teeth" into the committees' recommendations and encourage state and local governments to take a more active role in the preparation of nuclear risk communication materials. Local committees could be convened to review utility risk communication programs at the time FEMA conducts its assessment of off-site emergency planning, make recommendations for improvements, and then be disbanded until the next periodic assessment.

As noted earlier, FEMA presently conducts its review of nuclear risk communication materials through a contractor but does not assess public reaction to the information. Local advisory committees composed of members of the public who reside in the EPZ—as well as experts in the assessment, management, and communication of risk, psychologists, environmental planners, and representatives of the affected utility—could help bridge the gap between the industry's view of nuclear plant risk and that of objective experts and members of the public living near the plants. A public participation approach to risk communication may be a more acceptable alternative to the utility industry because most nuclear utilities have had some experience with public participation, particularly in conjunction with the NRC licensing process. And by becoming more active in the evaluation of nuclear risk communication programs, FEMA could become a clearinghouse for evaluating successful nuclear risk communication strategies and pass those strategies along to other local committees and nuclear utilities.

An alternative approach for improving nuclear risk communication would involve shifting the risk communication function away from the nuclear utilities entirely to organizations that are in a better position historically to establish "authentic" communication with EPZ residents, such as state and/or local governmental bodies or even FEMA itself. Nuclear risk communication materials now list the names and telephone numbers of responsible state and local emergency agencies, but only a handful of nuclear utilities indicate that state or local officials contribute more than a review to the content of these materials. However, it is clear to the EPZ resident receiving these materials that the *utility* is the source of the information.

Whereas the latter recommendation might ultimately be more effective as a mechanism for improving the climate for authentic communication between emergency officials and the public, the former may be more practical. The American nuclear industry, with billions of dollars invested in plants and equipment and hundreds of thousands of employees, is a powerful political force in the United States. The industry's political clout may be one explanation for OMB's refusal to allow FEMA to obtain more information about what knowledge EPZ residents have concerning emergency procedures and for FEMA's reluctance to challenge that decision. Furthermore, giving state and local governments more responsibility for emergency planning may be anathema to an industry already concerned about the refusal of state governments to cooperate in developing emergency plans as a mechanism for delaying or halting nuclear power plant licensing. Finally, FEMA historically has opposed a broader federal role in nuclear emergency planning, contending that state and local governments are in the best position to determine the specific emergency planning requirements around "their" nuclear plants.[30]

Whatever the long-term plan for the improvement of nuclear risk communication, we must begin acknowledging that there are considerable gaps in our knowledge concerning how people respond to nuclear plant risk, gaps that must be studied and understood before nuclear risk communication programs will succeed in preparing people for radiological emergencies. As Baruch Fishhoff points out, "It is both unfair to the public and corrosive for the social fabric to criticize laypeople for failing to respond wisely to risk situations for which they are not adequately equipped to make the appropriate response."[31] By analyzing its cultural context, we have seen how modern nuclear risk communication, rather than fulfilling its functional role as a realistic appraisal of nuclear power risk, became a memorial to the hopes of the nuclear industry for commercial development of atomic energy. The future of nuclear power may be uncertain, but the nuclear industry must realize that it can no longer afford to perpetuate the promotional history of the nuclear ethic. For the safety of those who live near our nation's nuclear plants, can we afford to allow nuclear risk communication to do otherwise?

After all, accidents can, and do, happen.

NOTES

1. Timothy L. McDaniels, "Chernobyl's Effect on the Perceived Risks of Nuclear Power: A Small Sample Test," *Risk Analysis* 8, no. 3 (September 1988): 457–461.

2. U.S. Council for Energy Awareness, "Reactor Information Report," Energy Data press release, Washington, D.C., 23 June 1989.

3. According to a 1986 Gallup poll, 73 percent of a national sample said they would not want a nuclear power plant built within five miles of their communities. See George Gallup, Jr., *The Gallup Poll: Public Opinion 1986* (Wilmington, Del.: Scholarly Resources, 1987).

4. Stanley M. Nealey, Barbara D. Melber, and William L. Rankin, *Public Opinion and Nuclear Energy* (Lexington, Mass.: D.C. Heath, 1983).

5. Philip L. Rutledge, "An Assessment of the Public Education Program for Nuclear Power Plant Emergencies," Master's thesis, University of North Carolina, Greensboro, 1986.

6. Harry Otway, "Experts, Risk Communication, and Democracy," *Risk Analysis* 7, no. 2 (June 1987): 126.

7. Harry Otway and Brian Wynne, "Risk Communication: Paradigm and Paradox," *Risk Analysis* 9, no. 2 (June 1989): 144.

8. Ibid.

9. J. R. Wargo, "Good Neighbors," *Nuclear Industry* (2nd quarter 1989): 34–41.

10. Paulette L. Stenzel, "The Need for a National Risk Assessment Communication Policy," *Harvard Environmental Law Review* II, no. 2 (1987): 389.

11. Cong. Don Ritter, "The Need for Risk Assessment Legislation," *Risk Analysis* 8, no. 2 (June 1988): 169.

12. Ritter last proposed legislation on September 30, 1988 (H.R.5435), but hearings were not held on the bill. According to his staff, the legislation will be reintroduced in 1990. Jean Perih, legislative assistant to Ritter, Washington, D.C., telephone conversations with the author, August, December 1989.

13. Stenzel, 395.

14. Ibid., 402.

15. Ibid., 404.

16. *Nuclear Regulation: Public Knowledge of Radiological Emergency Procedures*, 5.

17. Bill McAda, Office of Public and Intergovernmental Affairs, Federal Emergency Management Agency, Washington, D.C., LS to the author, n.d. (postmarked 29 August 1989), author's files.

18. Ibid.

19. Otway and Wynne, "Risk Communication," 141.

20. Alonzo Plough and Sheldon Krimsky, "The Emergence of Risk Communication Studies, Social and Political Context," *Science Technology & Human Values* 12, no. 5 (1987): 6.

21. William H. Desvousges and V. Kerry Smith, "Focus Groups and Risk Communication: The 'Science' of Listening to Data," *Risk Analysis* 8, no. 4 (December 1988): 479.

22. Ibid., 484.

23. California, Senate Bill No. 2591, Chapter 1607, approved by the governor of California 30 September 1988.

24. Dan Flynn, ed., *Final Report of the Senate Task Force on California Nuclear Emergency Response* (Sacramento: Joint Publications of the State of California, 1988), 1.

25. Ibid., 33.

26. Ibid., 29–30.

27. California, Senate Bill No. 2591.

28. Ibid.

29. *Further Actions Needed To Improve Emergency Preparedness Around Nuclear Powerplants*, 14–16.

30. Ibid.

31. Baruch Fischhoff, "Managing Risk Perceptions," *Issues in Science and Technology* 2, no. 1 (Fall 1985): 94.

Appendix: Utilities Returning Questionnaires

Alabama

Alabama Power Co.

Arizona

Arizona Public Service Co.

Arkansas

Arkansas Power and Light Co.

California

Pacific Gas and Electric Co.
Sacramento Mun. Utility District
Southern California Edison Co.

Colorado

Public Service Co. of Colorado

Connecticut

Northeast Utilities

Florida

Florida Power Corporation
Florida Power and Light Co.

Illinois

Commonwealth Edison Co.
Illinois Power Co.

Kansas

Kansas Gas and Electric Co.

Louisiana

Gulf States Utilities Co.
Louisiana Power and Light Co.

Maine

Yankee Atomic Electric Co.

Maryland

Baltimore Gas and Electric Co.

Massachusetts

Boston Edison Company
Yankee Atomic Electric Co.

Michigan

Consumers Power Co.
Detroit Edison Co.
Indiana Michigan Power Co.

Minnesota

Northern States Power Co.

Mississippi

System Energy Resources, Inc.

Missouri

Union Electric Co.

Nebraska

Nebraska Public Power District
Omaha Public Power District

New Jersey

GPU Nuclear Corporation
Public Service Electric and Gas

New York

Consolidated Edison Co.
New York Power Authority
Niagara Mohawk Power Corporation
Rochester Gas and Electric Corp.

North Carolina

Carolina Power and Light Co.[1]

Ohio

Cleveland Electric Illuminating Co.
Toledo Edison Co.

Oregon

Portland General Electric Co.

Pennsylvania

Duquesne Light Co.

GPU Nuclear Corporation
Pennsylvania Power and Light Co.

South Carolina

South Carolina Electric & Gas Co.

Tennessee

Tennessee Valley Authority[2]

Texas

Houston Lighting and Power Co.

Virginia

Virginia Electric Power

Washington

Washington Public Power Supply Systems

Wisconsin[3]

Wisconsin Electric Power Co.
Wisconsin Public Service Corp.

[1]Also operates reactors in South Carolina.
[2]Also operates reactors in Alabama.
[3]The Wisconsin utilities operate plants that are five miles apart and share a combined EPZ. Because the utilities use the same brochure to communicate with EPZ residents, they have been treated as one utility operating two plants in the survey.

Bibliography

PRIMARY SOURCES

A Is for Atom. John Sutherland Productions, Inc., and General Electric Company. 16 mm., 16 min., 1964.

Atomic Industrial Forum, Inc. *Annual Report*. New York: AIF, 1954–1986.

———. *The Forum Memo to Members*, May 1954, 3.

———. *The Forum Memo to Members*, August 1958, 39–40.

———. *The Forum Memo to Members*, September 1960, 47–48.

———. *Harry Gibbs Finds Out About: The What and Why of Atomic Power*. New York: Atomic Industrial Forum, 1966.

———. How Nuclear Plants Work. Washington, D.C.: Atomic Industrial Forum, Inc., 1976.

———. Why Nuclear Energy. Washington, D.C.: Atomic Industrial Forum, Inc., 1976.

"Atomic Power in Ten Years?" *Time*, 27 May 1940, 46–47.

"Atoms at Work." General Electric Company special supplement. *Senior Scholastic* 67 (20 October 1955): 1–8.

GE Review, May 1954; March, July 1957.

Harper's, October 1956.

Hogerton, John. *Background Information on Atomic Power Safety*. New York: Atomic Industrial Forum, Inc., 1964.

———. *Notes on Nuclear Power*, 2d ed. New York: Atomic Industrial Forum, Inc., 1970.

———, ed. *Atoms for Peace*. Cambridge: Arthur D. Little, 1958.

Inside the Atom. Schenectady, N.Y.: General Electric Co., 1955.

Langer, R. M. "Fast New World." *Collier's*, 6 July 1940, 18.

Lapp, Ralph, and George Russ. *Radiation Risks for Nuclear Workers*. Washington, D.C.: Atomic Industrial Forum, 1979.

Matthews, Charles D. "What Communities Want to Know." In *Public Relations for the Atomic Industry*, eds. Oliver Townsend and James Green, 59–63.

Nuclear News, mid-February, 1976.

O'Neill, John J. "Enter Atomic Power." *Harper's*, June 1940, 1.

Our Friend the Atom. 16 mm., 48 min., 1957. Walt Disney Company.

Perih, Jean. Legislative assistant to Cong. Don Ritter, Washington, D.C. Telephone conversations with the author, August, December 1989.

Pittman, Frank K. "AEC Safety Requirements." In *Public Relations for the Atomic Industry*, eds. Oliver Townsend and James Green, 94–102.

"Putting the Atom to Work." *Popular Mechanics*, May 1938: 690.

Robbins, Charles. "Uses of Atomic Energy." In *Public Relations for the Atomic Industry*, eds. Oliver Townsend and James Green, 1.

Russell, Christine. "Risk vs. Reality: How the Public Perceives Health Hazards." *The Washington Post*, 14 June 1988 (Health).

Stenzel, William A. "Developing Consumer Acceptance of Radioactivity." In *Public Relations for the Atomic Industry*, eds. Oliver Townsend and James Green, 110–117.

Townsend, Oliver. "Opening Statement." In *Public Relations for the Atomic Industry*, eds. Oliver Townsend and James Green, 2–3.

Townsend, Oliver, and James Green, ed. *Public Relations for the Atomic Industry: Proceedings of a Meeting for Members, March 19 and 20, 1956, Plaza Hotel, New York, N.Y., by the Atomic Industrial Forum, Inc.* New York: Atomic Industrial Forum, Inc., 1956.

U.S. Atomic Energy Commission. *27 Questions and Answers About Radiation and Radiation Protection*. Washington, D.C.: GPO, 1951.

———. *Twelfth Semiannual Report*. Washington, D.C.: GPO, 1952.

———. *Sixteenth Semiannual Report*. Washington, D.C.: GPO, 1954.

———. *Radiation Safety Primer*. 2d ed. rev. Washington, D.C.: GPO, 1955.

———. *Seventeenth Semiannual Report*. Washington, D.C.: GPO, 1955.

———. *Eighteenth Semiannual Report*. Washington, D.C.: GPO, 1955.

———. *Nineteenth Semiannual Report*. Washington, D.C.: GPO, 1956.

———. *Twentieth Semiannual Report*. Washington, D.C.: GPO, 1956.

———. *Twenty-First Semiannual Report*. Washington, D.C.: GPO, 1957.

———. *Twenty-Second Semiannual Report*. Washington, D.C.: GPO, 1957.

———. *Twenty-Fourth Semiannual Report*. Washington, D.C.: GPO, 1958.

———. *18 Questions and Answers About Radiation*. Washington, D.C.: GPO, 1960.

U.S. Council for Energy Awareness. *Nuclear Electricity and Energy Independence*. Washington, D.C.: U.S. Council for Energy Awareness, n.d.

"A Wand Wave, A New Era." *Life*, 20 September 1954, 141.

SECONDARY SOURCES

Adato, Michelle, James MacKenzie, Robert Pollard, and Ellyn Weiss. *Safety Second: The NRC and America's Nuclear Power Plants*. Bloomington: Indiana University Press, 1987.

Adler, Robert S., and R. David Pittle. "Cajolery or Command: Are Education Campaigns an Adequate Substitute for Regulation?" *Yale Journal on Regulation*, 1, no. 2 (1984): 159–193.

Allardice, Corbin, and Edward R. Trapnell. *The Atomic Energy Commission*. New York: Praeger Publishers, 1974.

Anders, Roger M., ed. *Forging the Atomic Shield: Excerpts from the Office Diary of Gordon E. Dean*. Chapel Hill: University of North Carolina Press, 1987.

"The Atom and Industry." *Newsweek*, 27 November 1950, 72.

Atomic Industrial Forum, Inc. Public Affairs and Information Program. *Report to Subscribers 1980–1981*. Washington, D.C.: AIF, 1981.

Babbie, Earl. *The Practice of Social Research*, 3rd ed. Belmont, Calif.: Wadsworth Publishing, 1983.

Barthes, Roland. *Image-Music-Text*, trans. Stephen Heath. New York: Hill and Wang, 1977.

Becton, Julius W., Jr., Federal Emergency Management Agency, signed letter, to The Honorable Jack Brooks, Chairman, House Committee on Government Operations, 11 August 1987. Author's files.

Blavers, Andrew, and David Pepper, eds. *Nuclear Power in Crisis: Politics and Planning for the Nuclear State*. New York: Nichols Publishing, 1987.

Boley, Kenneth. *Nuclear Power Safety: 1979–1989*. Washington, D.C.: Critical Mass Energy Project, 1989.

Booth-Clibborn, Edward, and Daniele Baroni. *The Language of Graphics*. New York: Harry W. Abrams, 1980.

Bupp, Irvin C. and Jean-Claude Derian. *Light Water: How the Nuclear Dream Dissolved*. New York: Basic Books, 1978.

———. *The Failed Promise of Nuclear Power: The Story of Light Water*. New York: Basic Books, 1981.

Campbell, John L. *Collapse of an Industry: Nuclear Power and the Contradictions of U.S. Policy*. Ithaca, N.Y.: Cornell University Press, 1988.

Christensen, Larry, and Carlton E. Ruch. "Assessment of Brochures & Radio & Television Presentations on Hurricane Awareness." *Mass Emergencies* 3 (1978): 209–216.

Clark, E. J., General Electric Company, signed letter to author, 28 June 1989. Author's files.

Compton, Karl Taylor. "The Battle of the Alchemists." *The Technology Review* 35 (1933): 165.

Conn, W. David, and Nickolaus R. Feimer, "Communicating with the Public on Environmental Risk: Integrating Research and Policy." *The Environmental Professional* 7, no. 1 (1985): 39–47.

Cutlip, Scott M., Allen H. Center, and Glen M. Broom. *Effective Public Relations*, 6th ed. Englewood Cliffs, N.J.: Prentice-Hall, 1985.

Cutter, Susan. "Emergency Preparedness and Planning for Nuclear Power Plant Accidents." *Applied Geography* 4 (1984): 235–245.

Cutter, Susan, and Kent Barnes. "Evacuation Behavior and Three Mile Island." *Disasters* 6 (1982): 116–124.

Davis, Howard, and Paul Walton, eds. *Language, Image, Media*. New York: St. Martin's Press, 1983.

Dawson, Frank G. *Nuclear Power: Development and Management of a Technology*. Seattle: University of Washington Press, 1976.

De Boer, Connie, and Iuke Catsburg. "The Impact of Nuclear Accidents on

Attitudes Toward Nuclear Energy." *Public Opinion Quarterly* 52 (Summer 1988): 254–261.

Desvousges, William H., and V. Kerry Smith. "Focus Groups and Risk Communication: The 'Science' of Listening to Data." *Risk Analysis* 8 (December 1988): 479–484.

Douglas, Mary, and Aaron Wildavsky. *Risk and Culture: An Essay on the Selection of Technical and Environmental Dangers.* Berkeley: University of California Press, 1982.

Dynes, Russell R., Arthur H. Purcell, Dennis E. Wenger, Philip S. Stern, Robert A. Stallings, and Quinten T. Johnson. *Staff Report to the President: Commission on the Accident at Three Mile Island: Report of the Emergency Preparedness and Response Task Force.* Washington, D.C.: GPO, 1979.

Easlea, Brian. *Fathering the Unthinkable: Masculinity, Scientists and the Nuclear Arms Race.* London: Pluto Press, 1983.

Electronic Advertising. Washington, D.C.: Committee for Energy Awareness, 1980.

Eliade, Mircea. *The Forge and the Crucible: Origins and Structures of Alchemy,* trans. Stephen Corrin. New York: Harper & Row, 1962.

Faltermayer, Edmond. "Taking Fear Out of Nuclear Power." *Fortune,* 1 August 1988, 105.

Fessenden-Raden, June, Janet M. Fitchen, and Jennifer S. Heath. "Providing Risk Information in Communities: Factors Influencing What Is Heard and Accepted." *Science, Technology, & Human Values* 12, nos. 3–4 (Summer/Fall 1987): 94–101.

Fischhoff, Baruch. "Managing Risk Perceptions." *Issues in Science and Technology* 2 (Fall 1985): 83–96.

Fischhoff, Baruch, Sarah Lichtenstein, Paul Slovic, Stephen L. Derby, and Ralph L. Keeney. *Acceptable Risk.* Cambridge: Cambridge University Press, 1981.

Flavin, Christopher. *Reassessing Nuclear Power: The Fallout From Chernobyl.* Washington, D.C.: Worldwatch Institute, 1987.

Flynn, Dan, ed. *Final Report of the Senate Task Force on California Nuclear Emergency Response.* Sacramento: Joint Publications of the State of California, 1988.

Ford, Daniel. *The Cult of the Atom: The Secret Papers of the Atomic Energy Commission.* New York: Simon and Schuster, 1982.

———. *Meltdown.* New York: Simon and Schuster, 1986.

Gallup, George H. *The Gallup Poll.* New York: Random House, 1972.

Gallup, George, Jr. *The Gallup Poll: Public Opinion 1986.* Wilmington, Del.: Scholarly Resources, Inc., 1987.

Goodchild, Peter. *J. Robert Oppenheimer: "Shatterer of Worlds."* London: BBC, 1980.

Green, Harold P., and Alan Rosenthal. *Government of the Atom: The Integration of Powers.* New York: Atherton Press, 1963.

Haber, Heinz. *Our Friend the ATOM.* New York: Simon and Schuster, 1956.

Hafstad, Lawrence R. "Reactor Program of the Atomic Energy Commission: Outlook for Industrial Participation." *Vital Speeches of the Day,* 1 February 1951, 249–253.

Hall, Stuart, Dorothy Hobson, Andrew Lowe, and Paul Willis, eds. *Culture, Media, Language: Working Papers in Cultural Studies, 1972–79.* London: Hutchinson, 1980.

Hertsgaard, Mark. *Nuclear Inc.: The Men and Money Behind Nuclear Energy*. New York: Pantheon Books, 1983.

Hewlett, Richard G., and Francis Duncan. *Atomic Shield, 1947/1952*. Vol. II. *A History of the United States Atomic Energy Commission*. University Park: The Pennsylvania State University Press, 1969.

———. *Nuclear Navy 1946–52*. Chicago: University of Chicago Press, 1974.

Hewlett, Richard G., and Oscar E. Anderson, Jr. *The New World, 1939/1946*. Vol. I. *A History of the United States Atomic Energy Commission*. University Park: The Pennsylvania State University Press, 1962.

Hiltgartner, Stephen, Richard C. Bell, and Rory O'Connor. *Nukespeak*. San Francisco: Sierra Club Books, 1982.

Hohenemser, Christoph, Roger Kasperson, and Robert Kates. "The Distrust of Nuclear Power." *Science* 196 (1 April 1977): 25–34.

Houts, Peter S., Paul D. Cleary, and Teh-Wei Hu. *The Three Mile Island Crisis: Psychological, Social, and Economic Impacts on the Surrounding Population*. University Park: Pennsylvania State University Press, 1988.

Institute for Nuclear Power Operations. *Emergency Information Planning Observations—Experiences in Crisis Communications: Industry Lessons Learned*. Atlanta: Institute for Nuclear Power Operations, 1983.

Jacobs, Mark. "Closing the Generating Gap." *Public Relations Journal*, May 1987, 19.

Jamieson, G. H. *Communication and Persuasion*. London: Croom Helm, 1985.

Johnson, F. Reed, and Ralph A. Luken. "Radon Risk Information and Voluntary Protection: Evidence from a Natural Experiment." *Risk Analysis* 7, no. 1 (March 1987): 97–107.

Johnson, James H., Jr. "A Model of Evacuation-Decision Making in a Nuclear Reactor Emergency." *The Geographical Review* 75 (October 1985): 405–418.

Johnson, James H., Jr., and Donald J. Zeigler. "Distinguishing Human Responses to Radiological Emergencies." *Economic Geography* 59, no. 4 (October 1983): 386–402.

Joskow, Paul L., and Roger G. Noll. "Regulation in Theory and Practice: An Overview." In *Studies in Public Regulation*, ed. Gary Fromm, 1–65. Cambridge: MIT Press, 1981.

Kasper, Raphael G. "Perceptions of Risk and Their Effects on Decision Making." In *Societal Risk Assessment: How Safe is Safe Enough*, ed. Richard C. Schwing and Walter A. Albers, Jr., 71–80. New York: Plenum Press, 1980.

Kasperson, Roger E., Gerald Berk, David Pijewka, Alan B. Sharaf, and James Wood. "Public Opposition to Nuclear Energy: Retrospect and Prospect." *Science, Technology, & Human Values* 5 (Spring 1980): 11–23.

Keating, William Thomas. *Politics, Technology and the Environment: Technology Assessment and Nuclear Energy*. New York: Arno Press, 1974.

Kochersberger, Robert C. "Post-Card Questionnaires May Boost Response Rate." *Journalism Quarterly* 64 (Winter 1987): 861–863.

Kunetka, James W. *Oppenheimer: The Years of Risk*. Englewood Cliffs, N.J.: Prentice-Hall, 1982.

La Porte, Todd R. "On the Design and Management of Nearly Error-Free Organizational Control Systems." In *Accident at Three Mile Island: The Human*

Dimension, ed. David L. Sills, C. P. Wolf, and Vivien B. Shelanski, 185–200. Boulder, Colo.: Westview Press, 1982.

La Porte, Todd R., and Paula M. Consolini. "Theoretical and Operational Challenges of 'High Reliability Organizations': Air Traffic Control and Aircraft Carriers." Paper prepared for the 1988 Annual Meeting of the American Political Science Association, Washington, D.C., September 1–4, 1988.

Lilienthal, David E. *Change, Hope, and the Bomb*. Princeton: Princeton University Press, 1963.

———. *The Atomic Energy Years 1945–1950*. Vol. II. *The Journals of David E. Lilienthal*. New York: Harper & Row, 1964.

———. *Atomic Energy: A New Start*. New York: Harper & Row, 1980.

———. "Free the Atom." *Collier's*, 17 June 1950, 13.

———. "Toward the Industrial Atomic Future." *Collier's*, 15 July 1950, 14.

McAda, Bill, Office of Public & Intergovernmental Affairs, Federal Emergency Management Agency, signed letter to author, n.d. (postmarked 29 August 1989), author's files.

McDaniels, Timothy L. "Chernobyl's Effect on the Perceived Risks of Nuclear Power: A Small Sample Test." *Risk Analysis* 8 (September 1988): 457–461.

McGraw-Hill Encyclopedia of Science & Technology, 5th ed., S.v. "Heavy Water."

Maleson, Diane Carter. "The Historical Roots of the Legal System's Response to Nuclear Power." *Southern California Law Review* 55 (1982): 597–640.

Maltin, Leonard. *The Disney Films*. New York: Crown, 1973.

Metzger, H. Peter. *The Atomic Establishment*. New York: Simon and Schuster, 1972.

Meyer, John W., and Brian Rowan. "Institutionalized Organizations: Formal Structure as Myth and Ceremony." *American Journal of Sociology* 83, no. 2 (September 1977): 340–363.

Meyer, John W., W. Richard Scott, and Terrence E. Deal. "Explaining the Structure of Educational Organizations." In *Organization and Human Services*, ed. Herman D. Stein, 151–179. Philadelphia: Temple University Press, 1981.

Mileti, Dennis S. *Natural Hazard Warning Systems in the United States: A Research Assessment*. Denver: Institute of Behavioral Science, University of Colorado, 1975.

Moody's Public Utility Manual. Vols. I and II. New York: Moody's Investors Services, 1988.

Morgan, Gareth. *Images of Organizations*. Beverly Hills: Sage Publications, 1986.

Morone, Joseph G., and Edward J. Woodhouse. *The Demise of Nuclear Energy? Lessons for Democratic Control of Technology*. New Haven: Yale University Press, 1989.

Mushkatel, Alvin H., and Louis F. Weschler. "Emergency Management and the Intergovernmental System." *Public Administration Review* 45 (January 1985): 49–56.

Myers, Richard. "The Gathering Storm." *Nuclear Industry*, second quarter 1989, 6–7.

National Geographic, May 1987, 640.

Nealey, Stanley M., Barbara D. Melber, and William L. Rankin. *Public Opinion and Nuclear Energy*. Lexington, Mass.: D. C. Heath, 1983.

Nelkin, Dorothy, ed. *Controversy: Politics of Technical Decisions.* Beverly Hills: Sage Publications, 1979.

The New York Times. 31 January 1933; 8 January, 27 February 1946; 20 November 1956; 17 January 1975; 20, 30 November, 4 December 1988; 16 July 1989.

Noll, Roger G., ed. *Regulatory Policy and the Social Sciences.* Berkeley: University of California Press, 1985.

Nye, David E. *Image Worlds: Corporate Identities at General Electric 1890–1930.* Cambridge: MIT Press, 1985.

Okrent, David. *Nuclear Reactor Safety: On the History of the Regulatory Process.* Madison: University of Wisconsin Press, 1981.

Otway, Harry. "Experts, Risk Communication, and Democracy." *Risk Analysis* 7 (June 1987): 125–129.

Otway, Harry, and Kerry Thomas. "Reflections on Risk Perception and Policy. *Risk Analysis* 2 (1982): 69–82.

Otway, Harry, and Brian Wynne. "Risk Communication: Paradigm and Paradox." *Risk Analysis* 9 (June 1989): 141–145.

Perrow, Charles. *Normal Accidents: Living with High-Risk Technologies.* New York: Basic Books, 1984.

———. "The President's Commission and the Normal Accident." In *Accident at Three Mile Island: The Human Dimension,* ed. David L. Sills, C. P. Wolf, and Vivien B. Shelakski, 173–184. Boulder, Colo.: Westview Press, 1982.

Perry, Ronald W. "Population Evacuation in Volcanic Eruptions, Floods, and Nuclear Power Plant Accidents: Some Elementary Comparisons." *Journal of Community Psychology* 11 (January 1983): 36–47.

Perry, Ronald W., Michael K. Lindell, and Marjorie R. Greene. *Evacuation Planning in Emergency Management.* Lexington, Mass.: D. C. Heath, 1981.

Perry, Ronald W., and Joanne M. Nigg. "Emergency Management Strategies for Communicating Hazard Information." *Public Administration Review* 45 (January 1985): 72–76.

Pfau, Richard. *No Sacrifice Too Great: The Life of Lewis L. Strauss.* Charlottesville: University Press of Virginia, 1984.

Plough, Alonzo, and Sheldon Krimsky. "The Emergence of Risk Communication Studies: Social and Political Context." *Science, Technology, & Human Values,* 12, nos. 3–4 (Summer/Fall 1987): 4–10.

Polmar, Norman, and Thomas B. Allen. *Rickover.* New York: Simon and Schuster, 1982.

Pringle, Peter, and James Spigelman. *The Nuclear Barons.* New York: Holt, Rinehart and Winston, 1981.

"Producing a Three-Minute Spectacular." *GE Review* 59 (September 1956): 52–59.

Rabi, I. I., Robert Serber, Victor F. Weisskopf, Abraham Pais, and Glenn T. Seaborg. *Oppenheimer.* New York: Charles Scribner's Sons, 1969.

Raphael, Beverly. *When Disaster Strikes: How Individuals and Communities Cope with Disaster.* New York: Basic Books, 1986.

Rashke, Richard. *The Killing of Karen Silkwood.* Boston: Houghton Mifflin, 1981.

Read, John. *Through Alchemy to Chemistry: A Procession of Ideas & Personalities.* London: Bell and Sons, 1957.

Ritter, Don. "The Need for Risk Assessment Legislation." *Risk Analysis* 8 (1988): 169–170.

Rogers, Everett M. *Diffusion of Innovations*. New York: Free Press, 1961.

Rogovin, Mitchell, and George T. Frampton, Jr. *Three Mile Island: A Report to the Commissioners and to the Public*. Vol. I. Washington, D.C.: GPO, 1980.

Rolph, Elizabeth S. *Nuclear Power and the Public Safety: A Study in Regulation*. Lexington, Mass.: Lexington Books, 1979.

Rosener, Judy B., and Sallie C. Russell, "Cows, Sirens, Iodine, and Public Education about the Risks of Nuclear Power Plants." *Science, Technology, & Human Values* 12 (Summer/Fall 1987): 111–115.

Rubens, Philip. "The Cartoon and Ethics: Their Role in Technical Information." *IEEE Transactions on Professional Communication* PC–30 (September 1987): 196–201.

Rubin, David M. "How the News Media Reported on Three Mile Island and Chernobyl." *Journal of Communication* 37 (1987): 42–57.

Russell, Christine. "Risk vs. Reality: How the Public Perceives Health Hazards." *The Washington Post*, 14 June 1988, pp. 14–18 (Health).

Rutherford, Ernest. *The Newer Alchemy*. New York: Macmillan, 1937.

Rutledge, Philip L. "An Assessment of the Public Education Program for Nuclear Power Plant Emergencies." Master's thesis, University of North Carolina, Greensboro, 1986.

Salove, Richard E. "From Alchemy to Atomic War: Frederick Soddy's 'Technology Assessment' of Atomic Energy, 1900–1915." *Science, Technology, & Human Values* 14 (Spring 1989): 163–194.

Sandman, Peter M., Neil D. Weinstein, and M. L. Klotz. "Public Response to the Risk from Geological Radon." *Journal of Communication* 37, no. 3 (Summer 1987): 93–108.

Schurr, Sam H., and Jacob Marschak. *Economic Aspects of Atomic Power*. Princeton, N.J.: Princeton University Press, 1950.

Schwing, Richard C., and Walter A. Albers, Jr. *Societal Risk Assessment: How Safe is Safe Enough?* New York: Plenum Press, 1980.

Selznick, Philip. *TVA and the Grass Roots: A Study of Politics and Organization*. Berkeley: University of California Press, 1949; repr., California Library Reprint Series Edition, 1980.

———. "Foundations of the Theory of Organizations." *American Sociological Review* 18, no. 1 (February 1948): 25–35.

Sewell, Edward H., Jr., and Roy L. Moore. "Cartoon Embellishments in Informative Presentations." *Education Communication and Technology Journal* 28 (Spring 1980): 39–46.

Sills, David L., C. P. Wolf, and Vivien B. Shelanski, eds. *Accident at Three Mile Island: The Human Dimension*. Boulder, Colo.: Westview Press, 1982.

Simon, Herbert A. *Administrative Behavior*. New York: Macmillan, 1947.

Sims, John H., and Duane D. Baumann. "Educational Programs and Human Response to Natural Hazards." *Environment and Behavior* 15, no. 2 (March 1983): 165–189.

Slovic, Paul. "Informing and Educating the Public About Risk." *Risk Analysis* 6, no. 4 (1986): 403–415.

Slovic, Paul, Baruch Fischhoff, and Sarah Lichtenstein. "Facts and Fears: Understanding Perceived Risk." In *Societal Risk Assessment: How Safe is Safe Enough?* eds. Richard C. Schwing and Walter A. Albers, Jr., New York: Plenum Press, 1980, 183–189.

———. "Regulation of Risk: A Psychological Perspective." In *Regulatory Policy and the Social Sciences*, ed. Roger Noll, 241–278. Berkeley: University of California Press, 1985.

Smith, Alice Kimball. *A Peril and a Hope: The Scientists' Movement in America: 1945–47*. Cambridge: M.I.T. Press, 1965.

Smith, Alice Kimball, and Charles Weiner, eds. *Robert Oppenheimer: Letters and Recollections*. Cambridge: Harvard University Press, 1980.

Soddy, Frederick. *The Interpretation of Radium*, 3d ed. London: Murray, 1912.

Sorensen, John, Jon Soderstrom, Emily Copenhaver, Sam Carnes, and Robert Bolin. *Impacts of Hazardous Technology: The Psycho-Social Effects of Restarting TMI–1*. Albany: State University of New York Press, 1987.

Stein, Herman D., ed. *Organization and Human Services*. Philadelphia: Temple University Press, 1981.

Stenzel, Paulette L. "The Need for a National Risk Assessment Communication Policy." *Harvard Environmental Law Review* 11 (1987): 381–413.

Sylves, Richard T. *The Nuclear Oracles: A Political History of the General Advisory Committee of the Atomic Energy Commission*. Ames: Iowa State University Press, 1987.

———. "Nuclear Power Plants and Emergency Planning: An Intergovernmental Nightmare." *Public Administration Review* 44, no. 5 (September/October 1984): 393–401.

Taylor, F. Sherwood. *The Alchemists*. New York: Henry Schuman, 1949; repr., New York: Arno Press, 1974.

Time, 31 March 1947.

Titus, A. Costandina. "Back to Ground Zero: Old Footage Through New Lenses." *Journal of Popular Film and Television* 11 (Spring 1983): 2–11.

Tomain, Joseph P. *Nuclear Power Transformation*. Bloomington: Indiana University Press, 1987.

Tozzi, Jim J., Deputy Administrator, Office of Information and Regulatory Affairs, Office of Management and Budget, signed letter to Louis O. Giuffrida, Director, Federal Emergency Management Agency, 13 July 1981, author's files.

Union of Concerned Scientists. *The Risks of Nuclear Power Reactors: A Review of the NRC Reactor Safety Study WASH–1400* (NUREG–75/014). Cambridge, Mass.: Union of Concerned Scientists, 1977.

U.S. Committee on Energy Awareness. *Electronic Advertising*. Washington, D.C.: U.S. Committee on Energy Awareness, 1980.

U.S. Congress. House. Subcommittee of the Committee on Government Operations. *Emergency Planning Around U.S. Nuclear Powerplants: Nuclear Regulatory Commission Oversight*. 96th Cong., 1st Sess., 7, 10, 14 May 1979.

———. Joint Committee on Atomic Energy. *Atomic Development and Private Enterprise: Hearings Before the Joint Committee on Atomic Energy*. 81st Cong., 1st Sess., 26 May 1949.

———. Joint Committee on Atomic Energy. *Atomic Power and Private Enterprise*. 82d Cong., 2d Sess., December 1952.

————. Joint Committee on Atomic Energy. *Atomic Power Development and Private Enterprise.* 83d Cong., 1st Sess., 24, 25, 29 June; 1, 6, 9, 13, 15, 16, 20, 22, 23, 27, 31 July 1953.

————. Senate. Special Committee on Atomic Energy. *Hearings Before the Special Committee on Atomic Energy on S. 1717: A Bill for the Development and Control of Atomic Energy.* 79th Cong., 2nd Sess., 7–8, 11, 13–14, 18–19, 27 February 1946, pts. 3 and 4.

————. Senate Section. Joint Committee on Atomic Energy. *Hearing Before the Senate Section of the Joint Committee on Atomic Energy on Confirmation of the Atomic Energy Commission and the General Manager.* 80th Cong., 1st Sess., 27–28, 30–31 January; 3–8, 10–12, 17–22, 24–26 February; and 3–4 March, 1947.

U.S. Council for Energy Awareness. *Electricity from Nuclear Energy.* Washington, D.C.: U.S. Council for Energy Awareness, 1989.

————. "Reactor Information Report." Energy Data press release. Washington, D.C., 23 June 1989.

U.S. Federal Emergency Management Agency. *Criteria for Preparation and Evaluation of Radiological Emergency Response Plans and Preparedness in Support of Nuclear Power Plants.* NUREG–0654, FEMA-REP–1, Rev. 1. Washington, D.C.: GPO, 1980.

————. *Guide for the Evaluation of Alert and Notification Systems for Nuclear Power Plants.* FEMA-REP–10. Washington, D.C.: Federal Emergency Management Agency, 1985.

————. *A Guide to Preparing Emergency Public Information Materials.* Washington, D.C.: Federal Emergency Management Agency, 1985.

U.S. General Accounting Office. *Further Actions Needed to Improve Emergency Preparedness Around Nuclear Powerplants.* Washington, D.C.: U.S. General Accounting Office, 1984.

————. *Nuclear Regulation: Public Knowledge of Radiological Emergency Procedures.* Washington, D.C.: U.S. General Accounting Office, 1987.

U.S. Nuclear Regulatory Commission. *Reactor Safety Study: An Assessment of Accident Risks in U.S. Commercial Nuclear Power Plants.* Washington, D.C.: U.S. Nuclear Regulatory Commission, 1975.

————. *Report to Congress on Status of Emergency Response Planning for Nuclear Power Plants.* Washington, D.C.: U.S. Nuclear Regulatory Commission, 1981.

————. Office of Governmental and Public Affairs. "NRC Staff Proposes $200,000 Fine and $50,000 Fine Against Arizona Nuclear Power Project." Press release, 2 December 1988.

U.S. President's Commission on the Accident at Three Mile Island. *The Need for Change: The Legacy of TMI.* Washington, D.C.: U.S. GPO, 1979.

————. *Report of the Emergency Preparedness and Response Task Force.* Washington, D.C.: U.S. GPO, 1979.

————. *Report of the Office of Chief Counsel on Emergency Preparedness.* Washington, D.C.: U.S. GPO, 1979.

————. *Report of the Public's Right to Information Task Force.* Washington, D.C.: U.S. GPO, 1979.

Wald, Matthew L. "The Nuclear Industry Tries Again." *The New York Times*, 26 November 1989, 1(F).

The Wall Street Journal, 8 August 1988, 23.

Wargo, J. R. "Good Neighbors." *Nuclear Industry*, Second quarter 1989, 34–41.

The Washington Post, 15 May, 20 November 1988; 14 November 1989.

"Watching the Watchdogs: How the OMB Helps Shape Federal Regulations." *Newsweek*, 20 February 1989, 34.

Weart, Spencer R. *Nuclear Fear: A History of Images*. Cambridge: Harvard University Press, 1988.

Webb, Richard E. *The Accident Hazards of Nuclear Power Plants*. Amherst: University of Massachusetts Press, 1976.

Weber, Robert Philip. *Basic Content Analysis*. Sage University Paper series on Quantitative Applications in the Social Sciences, series no. 07–049. Beverly Hills: Sage Publications, 1985.

Wood, William C. *Nuclear Safety: Risks and Regulation*. Washington, D.C.: American Enterprise Institute, 1983.

Wright, James D., and Peter H. Rossi, eds. *Social Science & Natural Hazards*. Cambridge: Abt Books, 1979.

Zeigler, Donald J., Stanley D. Brunn, and James H. Johnson, Jr. "Evacuation From a Nuclear Technological Disaster." *The Geographical Review*, 71, no. 1 (January 1981): 1–16.

Zeigler, Donald J., James H. Johnson, Jr., and Stanley D. Brunn. *Technological Hazards*. Washington, D.C.: Association of American Geographers, 1983.

Zimmerman, Rae. "A Process Framework for Risk Communication." *Science, Technology & Human Values*, 12, nos. 3–4 (1987): 131–137.

ZIP Code Atlas & Market Planner. New York: Rand McNally, 1968.

Index

About the Author

LOUIS GWIN is an associate professor of communication studies in the Department of Communication Studies at Virginia Polytechnic Institute and State University in Blacksburg. From 1973 to 1983 he worked in the Information Office of the Tennessee Valley Authority, including the last three years as assistant director of information for media relations, where he was involved in communicating information about the agency's nuclear power program to the public and the news media.